D0846129

CLOSELY GUARDED

JOHN STARNES

Closely Guarded:
A Life in Canadian Security
and Intelligence

UNIVERSITY OF TORONTO PRESS
Toronto Buffalo London

© University of Toronto Press Incorporated 1998
Toronto Buffalo London

Printed in Canada

ISBN 0-8020-0975-1 (cloth)

Printed on acid-free paper

Canadian Cataloguing in Publication Data

Starnes, John
Closely guarded: a life in Canadian security and intelligence

Includes index.
ISBN 0-8020-0975-1

1. Starnes, John.   2. Royal Canadian Mounted Police. Security Service –
Biography.*   3. Canada. Dept. of External Affairs – Officials and employees
– Biography.   4. Intelligence officers – Canada – Biography.   I. Title.

FC601.S72A3 1998   327.12′092   C98-930587-2
F1034.3S72A3 1998

University of Toronto Press acknowledges
the financial assistance to its publishing program of
the Canada Council for the Arts and
the Ontario Arts Council.

To my friends
and to my grandchildren,
Matthew Lauriston Starnes and
Wendy Margaret McCrea Starnes

Contents

Preface

I decided to start my memoir at the beginning of the Second World War, because Canada was at that time propelled into intelligence and security activities as a result of its decision to ally itself with the coalition of nations at war with Germany and other Axis powers and because it also happened to coincide with my own introduction to the frustrating, seductive, and unusual world of security and the very different business of gathering intelligence. From the outbreak of hostilities, the prime minister, members of cabinet, and numerous officials became deeply involved in these top-secret activities, and they and their successors continued their involvement throughout the decades following the war's end. The precise nature of these activities remained a closely guarded state secret until only very recently. This is my story of my small part in those unfolding events.

It had never occurred to me to write about my own life. I was therefore both surprised and pleased to receive a letter, dated 6 December 1995, from Robert Ferguson, associate editor at University of Toronto Press, asking me to consider publishing my memoirs. About six or seven years ago I'd had a similar suggestion from the editor-in-chief of a well-known publishing house in Toronto, and had turned it down.

My first reaction to Ferguson's suggestion was to decline the offer. After discussing the matter with him and with my wife, Helen, and our sons, Colin and Patrick, I was persuaded to think of ways I might be able to write only about certain events and periods of my life, concentrating on a common thread of my career: security and intelligence as functions of government.

While the skills of the diarist are not those of the autobiographer, to my mind Charles Ritchie's diaries are a perfect autobiography. In the

preface to *The Siren Years* (1974) Ritchie wrote, 'A diary is not an artis-
tic creation. It has – or should have – a breath of immediacy but at the
expense of form and style. Life is not transmuted into art.' In my opinion his diaries convey a sense of immediacy, but not at the expense of
form and style. They are lively, beautifully written, amusing, evocative,
and informative, never boring or irrelevant. I wish I had his skills. More
important, I wish he were still alive!

What follows is my attempt to recall the events that led to my
becoming involved in intelligence and security work and certain
aspects of foreign affairs, first as a member of the Canadian armed
forces and subsequently in the Department of External Affairs and in
the Royal Canadian Mounted Police (RCMP). I have tried to give the
flavour of those times, especially for such dramatic events as the Six
Day War in Egypt in 1967.

I have drawn from a number of sources, but in the earlier periods
principally on the three hundred and fifty letters I wrote to Helen from
England between 1942 and 1945. Surprisingly, the majority of these
wartime letters survived. The earlier ones were subject to vetting by the
British and Canadian censors, but most of those written from mid-
1944 to mid-1945 went by diplomatic pouch; since the latter were not
subject to censorship, I was able to write more frankly.

No correspondence exists for times when Helen and I were together,
such as in Ottawa, New York, Cairo, or Paris. For these periods I have
had to rely on memory and such other documentation as exists. For
example, for the Egyptian phase of my career (1966–7) I was able to
obtain the text of the classified telegrams I sent to Ottawa from Cairo,
all released to me under Canada's federal Access to Information Act,
1989, and now made public. Much material, particularly that related to
security and intelligence, was hard to locate or impossible to obtain.
For example, information concerning communications intelligence
(COMINT) and communications security (COMSEC) was always
treated with extraordinary secrecy.

Fortunately I was able to draw on valuable data concerning communications intelligence released under the Access to Information
Act, in particular, the excellent three-volume history of the Communications Branch of the National Research Council (CBNRC), prepared
in 1987 by Kevin O'Neill, its former and distinguished director. Without O'Neill's well-researched and well-documented study I would not
have been able to recount so much of what went on during the years

when, as director of Communications Security, I had responsibility for the policy aspects of Canada's signals intelligence activities. Even with their numerous excisions, the various documents I was able to obtain were invaluable in my attempts to recall dates, events, and people.

Some decisions, particularly in security and intelligence, never were committed to paper. This is particularly true of External Affairs, National Defence, the Privy Council Office, the former Security Service of the RCMP, and other, less run-of-the-mill intelligence-gathering agencies, such as the Joint Intelligence Bureau (JIB) and the CBNRC. Modern researchers who assume that they have the whole story sometimes can be quite mistaken in their assumption.

For example, when I headed Defence Liaison Division (2) in External Affairs in the late 1950s, Ralph Harry, head of the new Australian Secret Intelligence Service, paid an official visit to Ottawa. We had first met in New York in the late 1940s at meetings of the United Nations General Assembly, when we were members of our respective delegations. During our conversation in Ottawa he raised the desirability of Canada's having its own secret intelligence service. The Australians, he said, would welcome that kind of a Canadian presence in Southeast Asia. I reluctantly agreed to raise the matter with Norman Robertson, deputy minister at External Affairs. When I did speak to Robertson, he gave one of his huge sighs and looked at me rather reproachfully but said nothing. He had decided to refuse the proposal, but so far as I know, it never was recorded – not by him and certainly not by me.

Indeed, such suggestions for a Canadian secret intelligence service are not unlike proposals put forward more recently. I have views on the subject, some of which have been published. It is a matter that deserves serious discussion, and I attempt below to deal with it.

I would like to thank a number of people for their generous help and constructive criticisms. My wife, Helen, helped my work at every stage and encouraged me throughout, as did our sons, Colin and Patrick. I also would like to acknowledge the valuable assistance given me by, among others, Owen Davey, John Fraser, Alex Inglis, John Lawrence, Bernard McNaught of Peach Microsystems, Peter Marwitz, Ken Merklinger, Richard Mongeau, John Parry, Geoffrey Pearson, Jack Pickersgill, Basil Robinson, Bill ('Suds') Sutherland, Don Wall, and Wesley Wark.

Contrary to what I expected, I found that I enjoyed writing the book. As I got into the work, however, I began to realize that time had become an unforgiving enemy, ready to take advantage of any sign of weakness of the flesh or spirit, procrastination, or sheer laziness.

St Andrews, New Brunswick

Part One:
Intelligence Officer
1939–1945

1

Joining Up

It was the beginning of the Second World War. I spent the first week-end of September 1939 with my wife-to-be, Helen Robinson, and her parents at their cottage in St Andrews, New Brunswick. The next week I had to get back to my job in Montreal (a proofreader with the Montreal *Gazette*). I recall driving back with my wife's cousin, Allan Magee. We were close friends, having been together at Bishop's University. On the long journey we talked about the things that young men talk about – sex, booze, and the future. In particular, we talked about 'joining up.' Allan said that he would try to join the Royal Canadian Regiment, in which his father had served with distinction during the First World War. I said that I thought I would try the Royal Canadian Air Force (RCAF).

It was a strange time for those of us who had just graduated from university or were continuing their studies. None of us had very clear ideas about what we wanted to do, except for the few who had already planned careers in medicine, law, or some such demanding vocation. In 1938 I had made application to join the Department of External Affairs, receiving a brief acknowledgment signed by Marjorie McKenzie, who was later a valued colleague. I had formed a latent interest in foreign affairs, sparked in part by my attendance at some of the League of Nations meetings in Geneva in the mid-1930s.

Among my friends very few had chosen careers in the armed forces. At Trinity College School in Port Hope, Ontario, I was a member of the cadet corps (it was compulsory) but elected not to join the officer's training corps at university, since, among other things, it might have conflicted with football and hockey.

I think that my parents were surprised when I announced that I intended to join up, since I had not evinced any particular interest in things military. Having little interest in such matters was typical of many of those in my age group. Many of us were rather insular, little concerned with what was happening outside Quebec, Canada, and our small social world. War with Germany didn't arouse much passion, enthusiasm, or interest.

In my case, because I had spent some time in Europe and especially in Germany during the summers, I was aware of what was going on in that country and what unpleasant human beings the Nazis were. In about 1935–6 I had met a number of young Nazis through an Austrian girlfriend named Titi von Granatstaten, who tried to teach me German, among other things. Titi was no Nazi, but her older sister most certainly was. Titi's sister and her Nazi friends openly expressed their hatred of Jews and their disdain for all 'non-Aryans.' In their minds, that included most Europeans and North Americans. They were an unattractive lot.

In 1939 Montreal was an interesting, lively, polyglot city, more European than most Canadian cities. The continuing disagreements between English and French were palpable. Hugh MacLennan's phrase 'two solitudes' aptly describes the atmosphere at the time. The coming of war did nothing to ease these tensions between the French and English communities. Indeed, given the highly emotional issue of recruiting for overseas service with the armed forces in the early 1940s, relations worsened. Such problems, however, were not uppermost in my mind, nor were they a factor in the thinking of most of my friends and peers.

When Allan Magee and I returned to Montreal we pursued our separate aims. Eventually, Allan joined the Royal Canadian Regiment, later serving with distinction in Italy and northern Europe and becoming, I believe, one of the youngest brigade majors in the Canadian army.

Achieving my desire to become a pilot in the RCAF proved more difficult than I had imagined. I turned to a favourite uncle, Frank (Bud) McCrea, who had been brought out of retirement to become an RCAF recruiting officer in Montreal, with the rank of flight-lieutenant (he had been with the Royal Flying Corps 1917–18, having first gone overseas with the McGill University artillery battery as a dispatch rider). I wanted to enlist as aircrew, but the medical officers declared my eyesight not sufficiently good for aircrew training. I was told that I could enlist only as ground crew. I refused the offer and applied instead to the Royal Canadian Navy (its recruiting office being only a couple of streets away). There were long line-ups, and we were told to come back in two or three weeks. Impatient, I abandoned this idea.

Eventually, I was accepted into the Royal Highland Regiment of Canada (Black Watch), in what was called the provisional officers' training school (POTS), with the grand rank of provisional second lieutenant. I counted myself lucky to have been admitted. Of the two hundred applicants for commissions in 1939–40, only seventy-seven were selected for the school's first class. Their acceptance, of course, was no guarantee that they would receive commissions. At the end of the first two months of the four-month training period, 25 per cent were weeded out. The remainder were then temporarily taken on the strength of the militia regiment. If they passed the rest of the course, they were posted to companies of the home regiment to await their turn to be sent as Black Watch reinforcements in the active army. These private recruiting efforts by the Black Watch were frowned on by the senior military authorities and eventually ceased in 1940, when all such recruits in the Montreal area had to be trained through McGill University or the active army's officers' training corps.

It transpired that no amount of such training made it possible for one to join the first battalion of the regiment, which had been placed on 'active duty' guarding the canals around Montreal, prior to being sent overseas. There were scores of qualified officers already in the regiment with prior claims.

On 9 September 1940 I was taken on strength as a second lieutenant and promoted the following day to lieutenant. Shortly thereafter I was appointed regimental adjutant, stationed in the armoury on Bleury Street, Montreal. Late in 1940 I was appointed weapons training officer (WTO) at Centre d'Entraînement 44 in St Jérôme, Quebec.

Our training in the Black Watch armoury left much to be desired. Our equipment was antiquated and in short supply. We used Ross rifles of First World War vintage, and the only machine-gun we had was a Lewis gun that had seen better days. I recall that one of the training methods used was to teach us how to 'strip' the Lewis gun and reassemble it as quickly as possible. Contests were held to see who best could perform the task blindfolded. The soldier in my unit who consistently won came from Frobisher Bay. He literally memorized each part, and where it fitted by touch. It was uncanny to watch.

During this time Colonel Paul Hutchison wrote on my behalf to Major-General Neil Ritchie, commander of the 51st Highland Division in Scotland (married to a Canadian), 'It would be a fine thing if we could have some of our young Canadians serving with the Imperials in that way. Two of our younger officers who, if given a chance, would gladly go over to the Regiment in Scotland are Major W.W. Oglivie and Lieut. J.K. Starnes. Both of these officers are very highly qualified. Ogilvie had four years at the Royal Military College. Starnes is a new young officer who has joined up since the war. For the past year he has been on full instructional duty loaned by us to one of the French Canadian training centres. He is completely bilingual. Both of these officers could finance the trip abroad.' To my disappointment, nothing whatsoever came of this *démarche*.

Being WTO in a training centre for conscripts under the National Resources Mobilization Act, 1940, was a novel experience. Most conscripts spoke only French, and I had plenty of opportunity to use the language. I also learned a good deal about French Canada. Most recruits came from rural and wilderness communities north of St Jérôme. Many had little or no formal education, but they showed natural aptitude for the weapons they were to use, and many proved expert marksmen, with a natural talent for fieldcraft. Most were considerably better potential soldiers than their city-bred confrères. They were a lively, interesting lot, some of whom I came to know and to like.

Helen and I married in Montreal on 10 May 1941, and then we were sent to Brockville, Ontario, where I attended a training school for infantry officers. Reasonable accommodation was difficult to find, and we ended up taking a room at the Manitona Hotel, as did a number of others on the course. Much of the training in midwinter seemed to involve lengthy, mind-numbing route marches, which usually ended up in one of the bedrooms in the hotel, with us sitting on the edge of the bath, our swollen feet soaking in lukewarm water heavily laced with Epsom salts, drinking whatever hard liquor was available.

I recall there being an unusually active mouse population in the hotel, an allegation that was vigorously denied by the management. Helen got the management to concede that there was a problem after she captured a large mouse that had fallen into a deep glass bowl half filled with popcorn, from which it could not escape. She added some gin to the bowl, which the poor mouse lapped up: Discreetly covering the bowl with a towel, she took it the reception desk and removed the cover. The terrified screams of the young receptionist quickly brought the manager, who, after removing the drunken rodent, agreed to place mouse traps in our room and to have the hotel cat patrol our floor.

At the end of the course, with apparently no prospects of being sent overseas with the Black Watch or some other infantry unit, I applied to join the Armoured Corps and was sent to Camp Borden for further training. The vehicles were ancient Valentine training tanks, provided by the British, which obviously were not designed for use in a harsh, northern climate.

Out of the blue, I received orders to report 'immediately' to the intelligence section at Military District No. 2 headquarters in Toronto. The section, run by Rodney Adamson, a former Conservative party stalwart, consisted of three people. My sole job was to clip newspapers concerning anything that smacked of threats to Canada's security. I was not very busy. After several weeks I was told that I had been selected to attend a German interrogation course in Cambridge, England. I had attended German-language courses at the university in Munich in the mid-1930s and had a certificate to prove it. In 1935 I had taken Spanish as a course for Ontario junior matriculation. I had studied German literature at Bishop's, and I was reasonably fluent in French, but by no stretch of the imagination could I have been considered a gifted linguist or the least bit knowledgable about intelligence or security. I assume that I was selected for the course in England solely on the basis of inadequate army records, since I never was questioned concerning my language abilities or indeed about anything. I was simply ordered to report to the course and to hold myself ready for embarkation within a short period of time.

In a letter to Helen from Halifax, dated June 1942, I identified our troopship as the *Duchess of York*, on which I met two others chosen for the course, Stuart Parker (48th Highlanders) and Felix Walter. I wrote: 'Walter is a Professor, about 35 or 40. Parker's German is about as good as mine! They think the course is one month, but they have had the intelligence part and I haven't, so I imagine something else is in store for me besides a straight interrogation course.'

'Eastbound – Somewhere on the Atlantic,' I wrote on 6 June 1942:

The North Atlantic, windswept and cold with brilliant sun making but small impression, a hurly-burly of Englishmen, Canadians, Americans, South Africans: soldiers, sailors, airmen. Men from Nottingham, Glasgow, London, Regina, Baltimore, New York, Cape Town, Toronto, Belfast, Cairo, Piraeus. Refugees from Czechoslovakia, deported in 1939, six times interned, the last for months in the Indian Ocean (by the British) and now on their way to London to join the Czech army.

There is one woman on board – a Wren [Women's Royal Naval Service]. One woman amongst a thousand men. But she is well guarded. First the navy does convoy duty, then the airforce. The army so far hasn't had a look-in. She will either become a nun or a prostitute by the time we land. Whichever it is she is a most interesting phenomenon. She has considerable charm in an English way.

I might have added that even had she opted for sex with some willing partner, there would literally have been no place in which to perform the act. Every cabin, every corner was occupied, twenty-four hours a day. Meals and everything else (such as lavatories) were by rota.

In Cambridge, Felix Walter and I were billeted together. From 7 St Peter's Terrace, Trumpington Street, on 16 July 1942, I wrote to Helen:

I am ensconsed in one of England's older colleges (Christ's College). We have a room and sitting room together and most comfortable. Tables, chairs, double leather lounge chair, fireplace (not used in summer unless exceptionally cold). The room overlooks the Hall and can only be reached by going through the main gate into a courtyard, through another gate, past the dining hall, through another semi-courtyard, past flower gardens, holly bushes and extremely old and very shady trees.

... I know one of the directing staff quite well, having gone through Brockville with him. His name is Sprung. You may remember my having mentioned his name. He was the one who confused the instructors by the length of the words he used.

Mervyn Sprung, known as 'Spike,' spoke fluent German as well, it being his mother tongue. I believe he had achieved a PhD, defending some abstruse philosophical thesis, at a university in Berlin in the early 1930s. He quickly mastered the many subtleties of German interrogation techniques, making a name for himself in the job. Good interrogators are born, not made. Sprung was one of these rare individuals. He could read the mind of the person he was interrogating. Sprung was an excellent instructor, and he was particularly helpful to me. After he left Cambridge, I believe the British used him for a while at the 'London cage' – one of their interrogation centres where they kept a number of their most important and interesting prisoners. He later won the Military Cross and finished the war as senior intelligence officer of the Canadian Far East Force.

Though I did not appreciate it at the time, I was extraordinarily fortunate to have Felix Walter as a flatmate, friend, and mentor. Through him

I met many interesting people. Despite the difference in our ages we got along well. He had a lively sense of humour, a quick intellect, and a great deal of knowledge and experience, which he generously and tactfully shared with me. He was of Swiss-German background, and his German, while not up to the standards required for interrogation, was good. I count myself as lucky that he took me under his wing in the 1940s.

It is clear from my letters that we were not suffering.

We are at lectures about 9.30, about five minutes walk from the town. At 11.30 we have fifteen minutes for coffee at a small place called The Peacock, run by a Czech refugee. The coffee is excellent, the counter laden with delicious hors d'oeuvres ... At 1 p.m. we have lunch. Afterwards, we usually read the newspapers and listen to the foreign news broadcasts (good practice). We are free until 4.30 p.m., but not, as you may imagine, 'free.' I have worked until 1 a.m. every morning so far and I still haven't 'clicked.' During the day all our serious work takes place in what is known as the Hawks Club on St. Peter's Terrace. We have dinner at 7.30 in Hall, for which I have to change to trews or kilt, etc.

Prior to the course, I recall, the matter of my dress had been discussed and regulated by some senior officer at Canadian Military Headquarters (CMHQ) in London. I was instructed to wear whatever uniform I had worn as a member of the Non-Permanent Active Militia. Influenced possibly by atavistic feelings and the fact that it was the only uniform I possessed, I was delighted to be authorized to continue to wear my kilt.

The first night Felix and I were invited to have dinner with the Master and his Fellows, which was quite an experience. We foregathered about 7.20 in the Combination Room, a very beautiful old room with a long ceiling, large beams and a huge fireplace. When the Master was ready we filed into the Hall where one of the undergraduates (there are about 35–50 in this college) said grace in sonorous Latin. I sat beside one lad of 70 and another of 75. They were extremely interesting. As you may imagine, we were still at the Boer War and the Fire of Chicago stage. The old fellow on my left confessed that he had been out after dark in Chicago when he was there forty years ago! However, they were nice and they were interesting. One of them showed me the Wine Book in which bets were made for bottles of wine (money bets are not allowed in the Combination Room). Several date back to the Battle of Waterloo, such as; 'I bet one bottle of claret that Napoleon will not be on the throne of France by November 18 1812 .'

Through his academic connections and background Walter introduced me to many interesting people I would not otherwise have met, such as 'Professor Glover of St. Johns College. He is about 75 but most entertaining – on the Stephen Leacockesque side. His son was a teacher at Trinity College School, Port Hope, Ontario for about six years. Hanes, a Canadian from Toronto, married to a South African, doing food research for the government. Another Canadian friend, with whom we are to stay next week-end, is the Very Reverend John Lowe, Dean of Christ's Church Cathedral, Oxford. I'll be a Bishop yet!'

On our way to Oxford by train, at a small station near Bletchley, we waited for an hour to change trains. At the time we were blissfully unaware that Bletchley Park was the place where the British were breaking German ciphers of all kinds. While waiting we made the acquaintance of a Major Wilberforce, who kindly invited us to have sherry in his rooms at All Souls, of which he was a fellow. We discovered later that he was involved in some kind of intelligence work. He had graduated with first-class honours in classics, was made a fellow, and subsequently became a barrister for the Privy Council.

With great good fortune, I was allotted a room by John Lowe overlooking the garden of the deanery. On 11 July 1942 I told Helen,

All three [Lowe] children, with a child's quick ear, have developed very pronounced English accents. They are all delightful, but Peggy, the youngest, is a gem. A more self-possesed, poised young lady I have never met. She holds complete sway over the family and thinks things through with amazing logic. She, incidentally, is a direct heir to the garden in which 'Alice' was wont to play. Lewis Carroll (can't remember his other name), then a professor of mathematics at Christ's, had his workroom in the library overlooking the garden. And, so the story goes, had fallen in love with the little girl and wrote Alice in Wonderland as a tribute to her. Peggy Lowe is the first small girl to play there since that time.

I could hardly have enjoyed better circumstances in which to be initiated to the delights of Oxford. I remember thinking how much I had missed by being an unsuccessful 1938 Rhodes scholarship candidate from Quebec.

Back in Cambridge, it didn't take me, or those running the course, long to realize that my German was not adequate for the demanding tasks of interrogation. 'They have decided to let me stay and fight it out, which pleases me tremendously, as you can imagine. The staff have been extremely helpful and kind. Unfortunately, they require a very high standard of excellence, so it has handicapped me somewhat. I have forgotten nearly all the German I knew. However, I'll have a crack at it. Hard work won't hurt anyone. Parker is being sent elsewhere and they are letting me stay on.'

Cambridge left a lasting impression on me.

Cambridge is very far from the war in many ways, although there is lots of evidence of the war (including an air raid shortly after we arrived) ... Cambridge still remains a sleepy little town dating back to God knows when. I think I have fallen in love with it and my only wish is that we may get a crack at it some other time when things are different.

You would love the buildings, the green parks, the river, the bridges, the churches, the small alleyways, the bistros, the shops, the market, the weeping willows trailing into the water, the punts and canoes, the bowling green and the Cambridge towers and its people. With all the foreign element here it resembles Paris' suburbs, Lyon or even Lausanne in spring. Very interesting. A light, heady flavour which seems to mix admirably with the heavy Yorkshire pudding and afternoon tea.

Some of my fascination with Cambridge resurfaced in my fifth spy novel, *Latonya*, published in New York in 1994.

When we were leaving Canada, Felix Walter, Stuart Parker, and I had had no clue as to what to expect in Cambridge. In fact and with hindsight, it is clear that the interrogation course was part of a very sophisticated and considerable effort by the British to gather intelligence about their enemies, principally the Germans. F.H. Hinsley's three-volume semi-official *British Intelligence in the Second World War* provides an admirably clear picture of the extent and depth of this effort, of which the systematic interrogation of prisoners of war was an important part.

The importance that the British attached to the course became evident from the kind of people whom they had assembled to direct it and the ratio of directing staff to students. From the group photograph I count twenty-two students and eleven directing staff. The commandant was Lieutenant-Colonel W.P.B. Aspinall. In his late forties, he had a background in MI 14 (responsible for information about the German order of battle). Other members of the directing staff were from the Norwegian, Polish, and Belgian armies. Spike Sprung was the only Canadian. At least one of the directing staff had had first-hand interrogation experience with the British Eighth Army in North Africa. Many of the staff were gifted instructors. One of the Norwegians, Captain Sverre Midtskau, I particularly liked, and we met again years later in London.

One of my first and most lasting impressions of the course was the great secrecy with which it was treated and the significance that the British attached to the 'need to know' principle. Sensitive, secret information was imparted only to those who were deemed to have a genuine need to know. Absolute secrecy and the need-to-know rule became so ingrained in me that it coloured my later life. Indeed, I believe I even developed a capacity to keep secrets from myself. Only recently have I been able to view the fetish about secrecy in a more objective, relaxed manner. We were solemnly warned to say nothing of what we had learned about the school, its staff, students, curriculum, or methods. With sound reason, since it transpired that we were told a good deal about the value in skilled interrogation of data derived from the interception of enemy communications and those derived from clandestine operations. We also were given some information about photographic intelligence and how it might assist interrogation work.

Most of us had little idea of Britain's extraordinary successes with photographic intelligence, particularly vastly improved photographic interpretation techniques. Some of these activities eventually formed the basis for the brilliant work done years later by the U.S. Photographic Interpretation Center in Washington, DC, with photographic images from satellites.

We were required to learn all we could about the German order of battle – army and divisional units, regiments, and specialized arms. We had to know the German army command structure, commanders, equipment, uniforms – especially uniforms and the changes constantly being made to them – rank structure, methods of communication, and training methods and techniques. While the main emphasis was on the army, we were required also to learn about the air force and navy. It was difficult to memorize the many kinds of uniform, colours, regimental insignia, and identification markings.

The linguistic aspects of the course I found especially difficult – regional dialects, accents, and local idiom, not to mention the complexities and subtleties of the written word, grammar and script. We were called on to know everything we could about German intelligence and security units, their roles, and their peculiarities, including the many SS units. It was a great deal to absorb in a few short weeks. At this stage, I probably knew more about the German army than I did about the Canadian!

Apart from the formal, obvious aspects of the curriculum, one learned at least as much by osmosis. Someone like Sverre Midtskau, despite being very discreet concerning his dangerous work, could make available valuable information and knowledge that could not be found in any textbook. In any event, it is easier to learn from someone with a delightful, quick, dry sense of humour.

'As you can see from the intermittent letter writing this has been a very hectic week,' I wrote on 10 July. 'In fact, it is the deciding one as far as passing or failing goes. So far, I don't know where I stand. The language still remains the prime obstacle although progress has been made. There are all kinds of other considerations: background (military and otherwise), character, personality, capability for this particular branch, which will enter into the decision.' The next day: 'Our results have just come out. Personally I am quite pleased. Firstly, Felix got through which pleases me for I really think he deserves it. They grade you A, B, C or D. A means qualified for this type of work. B means, could be qualified with further training in a certain branch, C means recommended for some special branch other than this and D is a failure. I received a B grade with the note that, "he be recommended for language refresher course."'

2

Secret Intelligence Work

Shortly after we learned our results, the course broke up. We reported to Canadian Military Headquarters (CMHQ) in London to be given our marching orders. We were received in what was known as the Military Operations and Intelligence Section (MO&I) by Captain Hugh Halbert, who was in the process of assuming command of the section from Major John Page (Toronto Scottish). To my surprise and pleasure, it turned out that Hugh was a member of the Canadian Black Watch. When we met he did not know the results and asked us what they were. From London I wrote to Helen on 19 July:

He chatted with each of us and finally disposed of everyone but me. He closed the door and we had a tête-à-tête, the outcome of which was I am to be employed as Hugh's right-hand-man in charge of the organizational set-up. After the interview (or what have you) we went across to the Canadian Officer's Club where we had tea. We then went to the YMCA officer's hotel, out Kensington way. Sprung slept on the couch, Felix in the best bed and I in a room with some English johnny. However, it was clean and cheap – five shillings and six pence the night, with breakfast. Sprung and Felix set off to their particular jobs, somewhere in London. I caught the train back to No. 1 Canadian General Reinforcement Unit (CGRU), near Aldershot where I had been instructed to report.

It is clear that I was in pleasant circumstances:

Tea in bed and the Sunday Times [20 July]. Breakfast at 8.00 and across Trafalgar Square, through the pigeons, to CMHQ and the first day's real work [which] I just spent seeing people and watching. Incidentally, Frank Fleury, who used to be Adjutant at Farnham [Quebec], was very decent and offered me the shelter of his apartment until I get squared around. He offered to share it with me as his present co-sharer, a Major Walker, is leaving. However, it costs $100 a month or twenty pounds and I think I can do better here. Here being the Constitutional Club, just off Trafalgar Square. It is a stronghold of English conservatism but extremely handy. I think I will become a member for two pounds and then I can get a room for two guineas a week. Forty dollars a month with meals extra. Sounds okay.

The Constitutional Club was quite an experience. I was very fortunate in having the support of Mr Barnard, the secretary. He obviously went to a good deal of trouble to help me out. I had a small room on the fifth floor, overlooking Northumberland Avenue. The club was a bastion of the Conservative party, the armed services, and male chauvinism. Ladies were admitted to the dining-rooms, but only through the back entrance, after threading their way through assorted garbage cans and climbing an unusually steep staircase, though there may have been a dilapidated lift.

The club's heating arrangements were non-existent. The lower rooms were supposed to be warmed by coal fires, and the bedrooms by electric heaters, into which one put shilling pieces with alarming frequency. The porter was a much-decorated former sergeant in the Royal Marines, who became a friend. The only name I knew him by was Harry. He seemed always to be on duty and remained cheerful no matter how late at night he was roused or how inebriated the person seeking entry. He was as tough as nails – a fountain of knowledge, gossip, and wisdom. He often helped me with good advice. There wasn't anything about London that he did not know.

On 20 July, I told Helen: 'Sunday I was up at 10.15 and had breakfast at the Canadian Officer's Club, opposite CMHQ. Nearly knocked over some old girl. She shook herself and I apologized. She was quite unruffled and said, "I don't believe I have met you. My name is Massey." I muttered, "mine is Starnes" and fled. Expect to be sent to Dachau by the High Commissioner any time now.' Vincent and Alice Massey had been in London since he was appointed high commissioner in 1935.

At the time I hadn't the foggiest notion of what might be involved in being Halbert's 'right-hand-man' or even what MO&I did, except for what its title suggested. I found that I had a curious, nondescript title – MI (X). The job involved bureaucratic responsibility for a slew of unrelated odd jobs that nobody else would touch, but for which Hugh was directly accountable to Major-General Price Montague or the Brigadier General Staff Elliott Rodger. Hugh became a good friend. I understood him better after he took me to meet his mother, who lived in a rambling cottage somewhere on the edge of the New Forest. She kept chickens, which were everywhere, inside and outside the house. One never sat down without first checking to be sure that there were no eggs among the cushions. She was a delightful, somewhat fey lady with a Scots accent I could barely understand. Working with Hugh was like being on a roller-coaster ride, never dull. He didn't suffer fools or laggards gladly and made no attempt to hide his feelings. He liked strong drink and could hold it reasonably well.

In fact, my job embraced a variety of tasks in the security and intelligence field not found among the usual duties of a Canadian military headquarters. These included irregular dealings with the British Secret Intelligence Service (MI 6) and the Special Operations Executive (SOE) in connection with the seconding of a number of Canadians (mainly francophones) with Royal Canadian Signals training to those organizations for specialized training and eventual use as British secret agents, mostly in western Europe, especially France. I was responsible for seeking out potential candidates from Canadian army units in England and, if they seemed to have the right qualifications and background (wireless operators, explosives experts, cryptographers, locksmiths, and linguists), to bring them to London to be interviewed by the British. The chief signals officer overseas, a brigadier, was very helpful in making the original selections. It involved me in an enormous amount of administrative work.

The section also had some responsibility for liaison with the British to try to arrange for a percentage of Canadians to attend intelligence training schools such as those at Cambridge and at Matlock in Derbyshire and to get on-the-job training at the excellent photographic interpretation centre at Medmenham in Buckinghamshire. The job also included making arrangements to have Canadian army personnel trained by the British (MI 8) – wireless intelligence in the latest techniques of the interception and deciphering of wireless traffic between units of the German armed forces.

I had to meet and deal with a wide range of British and American officers, most of them my senior in age, experience, and rank. Major Reginald Manningham-Buller, for example, who headed MI 8 at the War Office, was very helpful, and I learned a good deal from my contacts with him.

I also have a memory of visiting various RAF command and control centres, where the movements of fighter and other aircraft, friend and foe, were plotted. I believe that such visits were related to Canadian participation in intelligence gathering and very possibly to my involvement with the 8th U.S. Air Force, which I discuss later in this chapter.

So long after the events I find it difficult to place some of my deliberately cryptic comments to Helen in any sensible context. For example, on 3 August 1942:

Sunday was a great success. I met my friend the colonel and his counterpart from the near east. We travelled in his staff car to our destination. I met him about 10.30 and we had a pleasant drive through a very lovely part of the countryside, arriving in time for a spot of lunch. The colonel from the east was very interesting. He had quite a few stories about India and Egypt and such places. The laddie who met us showed us a very good lunch in a local pub, for 2/6 [i.e., 2 shillings 6 pence], hors d'oeuvres and all the trimmings. We spent the afternoon seeing what we were there for, leaving about 6.30, quite surprisingly, all worn out. The colonel wants me to go away for three days, either with him or alone, to another of these things. Might be interesting. I think you would like him.

The visits may have taken place under the auspices of what was generally known as SF (Special Forces), a secret British organization that carried out intelligence and sabotage work on the continent, in the Middle East, and eventually also in the Far East. SF dispatched secret agents (including some Canadians) to Nazi-occupied Europe to organize and arm local resistance movements and to help them in selected acts of sabotage.

A letter of 9 January 1943 signed by Lieutenant Colonel Julius Hanau and typed on embossed paper headed 'MO 1 (SP)' suggests that he may have been the mysterious colonel: 'Having discussed the matter you and I spoke about at our pleasant social meeting, I fear that under the prevailing circumstances it would be almost hopeless to try and get you into our "firm." My colleagues here best qualified to know, think that for reasons which you will readily understand, an application for your transfer might not be favourably looked upon. May I suggest that we leave matters as they are and perhaps later on when the atmosphere is more favourable, we might return to the charge.' Hanau, while on a mission in the Balkans, was caught by the Germans and eventually executed.

I recall also sporadic contacts with two Canadians of Russian background doing intelligence work in the War Office (MI 3[c]) – Nicholas

Ignatieff and Nick van Vliet. I liked them both, and they were very help-ful. I recollect as well some dealings at the Political Intelligence Direc-torate (covert) with Paul Lieven (Canadian army) – later Military Cross (MC) with bar.

In late 1942 or early 1943 there took place the strange series of events known in intelligence circles as 'John Starnes and his Indians.' In an undocumented report of December 1945 on links between CMHQ and British organizations, Felix Walter wrote:

The enterprise was conducted with great secrecy and for months the staff at CMHQ must have been mystified by the sight of swarthy-complexioned Cana-dian soldiers with high cheek-bones who travelled up in the elevators to the Conference Room on the 3rd floor, from which presently emerged sounds usu-ally associated with a tribal pow-wow.

Incredible diffficulties had to be surmounted as it was soon found that many of the so-called Indians had only a rudimenatry knowledge of their native lan-guages while the fact that these languages all differed one from the other to a radical extent made the adopting of a uniform code language almost insur-mountable.

Finally a selected batch of future signalmen were dispatched to High Wycombe for training under U.S. auspices ... Lt. Starnes was at that time the IO (X). His liaison duties had brought him in contact with a certain Capt. Lynn of the 8th U.S. Bomber Command. These two officers had read somewhere in a history of the last war that Canadian Indians had been successfully used as sig-nals operators at one stage of the campaign because their messages sent in their native language baffled the Kaiser's best code and cipher crackers. The plan was to repeat this experiment on a vaster scale!

I remember Captain Lynn – like me, a very junior officer – but I have no recollecion whatsoever that we discussed the history of the First World War in the way Walter describes it. The concept of using North American Indians aboard U.S. bombers for their voice communications (air to air and ground to air, and so on) in an effort to prevent the Ger-mans from understanding them was ingenious, but it was not mine. Walter was not at CMHQ when the idea was first broached and must have relied on hearsay or incomplete files (if there were any). Probably U.S. Air Force intelligence officers, unable to find sufficient suitable American Natives for the purpose, turned to the Canadians for help.

Eventually, as many as sixty or seventy signalmen from Canadian units were brought to London for testing and evaluation – not something a mere lieutenant could command! It was costly in money and time.

In the end, alcohol brought the project to an abrupt end. The dozen or so soldiers I turned over to the 8th U.S. Bomber Command had to be returned. The Americans had been too lax in their supervision of the men.

I also kept track of all the officers in the Canadian army who had intelligence duties. On a board covering an entire wall of the office I placed the names of intelligence officers in the different army formations. It proved to be a chore, since there were constant changes. It showed detailed information considered to be classified. Thus, when not in use, the display had to be kept under lock and key.

Hugh Halbert had a number of amusing contacts, although I don't believe that they entailed specific intelligence operations involving Canada. One of the more interesting was Dunderdale, a former commander in the Royal Navy, who appeared to be a deputy to 'C' (Menzies), head of MI 6. Dunderdale was a swashbuckling character who certainly fitted his part and with whom Halbert had established good rapport. I never found out exactly what he did, though he helped me on one or two occasions.

I was able to maintain some of my contacts from the Cambridge course. My letter of 29 July 1942 to Helen says: 'John Arnold, a Captain in British Intelligence and one of those who taught us at Cambridge, and I went out to dinner last night. As he is a former Londoner (he was a barrister here before the war) he took me to one of his old haunts, a delightful little restaurant up a side street, opposite the Savoy Hotel. A very good meal and quite reasonable too.'

The restaurant was Rules on Maiden Lane, which, years later I discovered, MI 6 sometimes used for entertaining 'visiting firemen,' like me. Indeed, at the time (probably the early 1970s) I suspected that some of the waiters were on their payroll, especially after the headwaiter addressed my host, Maurice Oldfield (then deputy head of MI 6) as 'General.' Oldfield grinned at me apologetically and gave a characteristic shrug. My first dealings with him had occurred when he was MI 6's representative in Washington in the 1960s, with visiting privileges in Ottawa.

Looking for potential British agents for Nazi-occupied Europe brought me into contact with a number of interesting characters. Selwyn Jepson had offices in the run-down, musty-smelling Northumberland Hotel, behind the War Office and almost opposite my 'digs.' The hotel had been requisitioned for SOE. It was there that I took potential recruits to meet Jepson. The atmosphere was quintessentially British, of the kind written about by E. Phillips Oppenheim and his contemporaries and even by Jepson himself, who had several 'thrillers' published between the wars.

Though small of stature and deceptively mousy in appearance, Jepson knew his business. For example, it was he who recruited Francis Cammaerts and Noor Inayat Khan as British secret agents. Their heroic exploits in France have been written about extensively.

M.R.D. Foot, in *SOE: An Outline History of the Special Operations Executive, 1940–46*, observed: 'Most of what is known of SOE's recruiting techniques comes from one of the most skilled craftsmen in this field, Selwyn Jepson, the author, who is able in old age to recall some of his triumphs and disasters of over forty years ago. As the recruiting officer for F, the independent French section, he conducted hundreds of interviews.'

By the time I began my duties as MI (X) in July 1942, Gustave Bieler, the first Canadian officer to serve with SOE, had been recruited by Maurice Buckmaster (eventually to head the French (or F) Section of SOE). A Canadian of Swiss origin, Bieler joined the latter organization in June for a trial period and by the the fall of 1942 had completed his training and was ready for service in France. I had the pleasure of getting to know him just before he was dispatched to France. He was dropped by parachute on 15 November 1942, near Montargie. His exploits, from November 1942 until he was executed by a firing squad in Flossenburg concentration camp in July 1944, are legendary.

Roy MacLaren's *Canadians behind Enemy Lines, 1939–1945* gives an excellent account of Bieler's work as a British agent and also of the other Canadians who served in this way. Felix Walter's official account, 'Cloak and Dagger,' gives a fuller rendering. Twenty-four Canadians saw service as special agents in France from 1942 to 1945, eighteen of them employed by SF and six with the Escaper Organization (MI 9).

According to Walter, the French Section of SF

was personally directed throughout the war by a British officer who had spent many years in Paris and had an intimate knowledge of France and French personalities. Gathered around him were a group of experts with similar qualifications who acted as his staff officers. Liaison between this technical staff and the French Resistance people varied throughout the period of hostilities. At times, particularly in the early stages of the war when the security-mindedness of General de Gaulle's organization was open to question, contact between the

French Section and the Resistance was on a purely local basis, but later the SF effort became more closely co-ordinated with the Allied overall plan ... The successes of 1944, however, were the fruit of bitter years of effort and partial failure and it is clear from a perusal of the reports of SF agents in France that the life of an Allied agent in that country in the summer of 1944 was almost a picnic compared to the existence of those of his colleagues 'dropped' a few years or even a few months previously.

Among Canadians involved in these unusual duties were Lucien Dumais, Guy Joly, Raymond Labrosse, Conrad Lafleur, and Robert Vanier (the escape and evasion organization), Beaudry (Political Intelligence Directorate – Covert), and Joseph Benoît, 'Gaby' Chartrand, and Frank Pickersgill (F Section of SOE), A.D. Yarich, who served with the escape organization in the Mediterranean theatre, and Steve Markos, among the first of the Canadians to join SOE.

Pickersgill was recruited directly by the British after he left France following the German invasion, where he had been a student. I ensured that he was commissioned into the Canadian army as a lieutenant and that all the administrative work for his transfer to SOE was completed. We met briefly before and after his special training and after his training was completed. Several weeks of special training had transformed his physique and mien. He had learned 'soft karate,' the samurai art of killing with the bare hands used by the Japanese and the Chinese. He showed me his hands; the sides were visibly hardened and felt like slabs of steel.

All were brave men, many being decorated for their dangerous work. I have retained the invitation that I received to the investiture at Buckingham Palace in March 1943 when Dumais, Lafleur, and Vanier, all veterans of the Dieppe raid, received the Military Medal (MM) from the king for their particularly daring escapes following capture by the Germans. Because of their experience in evading recapture, the British sought to employ them for their escape-and-evasion organization. All three volunteered to return to France, which took guts, since they would have known exactly what to expect if they were caught by the Gestapo. By the end of the war Lafleur had the MM, the Distinguished Conduct Medal, and the Croix de Guerre avec palme, and Vanier had the MM and bar and the MC.

At the beginning of the war the Canadian authorities were approached at different levels by the British to obtain agreement to recruit from the Canadian army volunters to be sent to Europe as British secret agents.

General McNaughton initially withheld approval, but eventually he agreed, with little enthusiasm.

At the outset, the problems of administering Canadian volunteers for special service with the British were complex. It was first considered that the best method was to discharge them from the Canadian army and to re-enlist them into the British. This was the method used for the very first Canadian volunteers: Yugoslavs recruited in 1941 by British Security Coordination (BSC) in New York City, then headed by a Canadian, Sir William Stephenson ('Intrepid').

Because the British organizations were operating with great secrecy, they sought to keep 'paper work' to a minimum. Some of the earliest volunteers were hired on the basis of a verbal rather than a written understanding. In some cases this led to unfortunate results for the men concerned and for their next-of-kin. By the time I became MI (X) it had become clear that a better system had to be devised. Eventually, agreement was reached that all such personnel should remain as members of the Canadian armed forces, 'on loan' to Britain's War Office (a convenient euphemism) for six-month periods, renewable as required.

Pay arrangements were unsatisfactory. There were different systems being employed, with each British organization using its own rates of pay and quite different accounting procedures. Efforts were made in 1942–3 to eliminate the resulting anomalies, but the problems were not resolved until 1944, when the Canadian Treasury Board accepted responsibility for the pay and allowances, at Canadian rates, of all Canadian service personnel loaned to the British for special services.

It was hoped that commissioned rank might confer some greater measure of protection on secret agents captured by the Germans, as well as improving their financial lot. All privates and non-commissioned officers (NCOs) were commissioned after they had passed their initial training and evaluation and the British had signified their willingness to employ them as secret agents. The Germans, however, treated them all as spies whatever their rank and usually, after torturing them, executed them. I don't think that any of those involved had any illusions about the protection that a commission, might offer.

One day late in 1942, Jepson asked me if I would be interested in volunteering to join SOE. I do not know what prompted him to consider me a possible candidate. He knew that my French was reasonably good, though I was not fluent. He knew also that I had learned the language in Switzerland and that my accent was European rather than North American. He would have had available to him the results of my German interrogation course in Cambridge. Probably more important, by mid-1942 the British were having great difficulties in finding suitable recruits, partly because of an assurance given by Churchill to de Gaulle that the British would not seek to use French citizens for such tasks.

In any event, I replied that I would be glad to volunteer. After a good deal of difficult negotiation with the Canadian authorities concerned, agreement was reached to release me.

I have retained a letter with the letterhead 'M.O.1 (S.P.), The War Office, Whitehall,' 15 February 1943:

To: Major J.D. Halbert, Canadian Military Headquarters, Cockspur Street. S.W. 1.

Lieutenant John Kennett Starnes,
Canadian Military Headquarters.

We understand that you very kindly agreed to release this officer's services for possible employment by this Branch.

We should therefore be most grateful if he could report to Captain Jepson on Monday, 15 Mar 43, if that date is convenient to you, for one month's attachment.

If, at the end of this trial period, he is considered suitable, we shall ask that he be loaned to us on the same terms as other officers of the C.A.S.F.

J.D. Kennedy
Lieut. Colonel

I made all my preparations (physical and mental) to report to Jepson in March 1943, but, for reasons that I never have been able to discover, at the very last moment the transfer was blocked 'somewhere up the line.' In retrospect, I have wondered if Halbert, despite his apparent agreement scotched the transfer at the last moment, for reasons of his own. Whatever the explanation, I was bitterly disappointed.

I don't imagine, however, that I would have got through the initial trial period, since, among other things, the idea of jumping from an aircraft, at a height of about three hundred feet, into the pitch black terrified me. If I had known about the survival rate of those in F Section of SOE, which became known only after the war, I might not have been so enthusiastic. Only one in four survived.

Not surprisingly, I was enjoined by the British to say absolutely nothing to anyone about my having volunteered to join F Section. It wasn't until I returned to Canada in 1943 to attend the war staff college in Kingston that I was able to inform Helen. I told nobody else.

It is clear from my letters to Helen that while I was fully occupied with these tasks I did not neglect the opportunities of being in London in wartime. For example, on 29 July 1942 I rhapsodized: 'The sky tonight was, oh so typically English. So crowded with clouds, so delicate with soft pastels, so faded in its blue, as if it were tired and old. Even the air, the one place one would expect to find free, was filled with birds migrating south, their wings fluttering – like the noise of rain on the trees. London is a lonely city. Big cities always have been lonely things to me anyway. Thousands of faces, a sea of faces. All intent about their business, each person wrapped in his or her own cocoon of daily life.'

On 18 July: 'Yesterday I had lunch at Mother Massey's, much to her delight. She thought I had gone to Sicily. No such luck! Now you know the reason for my last celebration with Allan [Magee]. He seemed in high spirits and very keen for the fray [In Italy]. He is a liaison officer, a difficult but good and interesting job. I was waiting with impatience for the news to break. However, everything seems to have gone very smoothly and at long last the Canadians are doing a job which they can do well.'

Another day:

I turned down Burlington Arcade the other day for the first time since 1935, principally, I suppose to see if the shop was still there where I used to buy lead soldiers. It was, but of course the soldiers aren't lead any more. They make them out of wood. They don't look nearly as nice but, better a lead bullet than toy lead soldiers.

... The most surprising thing is the suddeness with which you come upon one of those tremendous balloons, tugging lonesomely at its cables. Rounding some corner, crossing some quiet square, you come face to face with a giant elephant, shaking its head gently in the sun, its ears flapping noisily. Or, at night walking home, you come upon one of these strange, ghostly creatures, looming large in the blackness like some white elephant in the jungle, hungrily tugging at a patch of sweet grass. They are a part of this new London, a nice part of it. Huge and ungainly, amusing and very deadly.'

On another occasion I told Helen: 'On Saturday I went to hear the first performance of the BBC promenade concerts conducted by Sir

Henry Wood at the Royal Albert Hall. It was excellent and, if possible, I want to take in another.' The assistant conductors were Basil Cameron and Adrian Boult. The music included pieces by Beethoven, Handel, Saint-Saens, and Tchaikowsky. In small print at the bottom of the first page of the program are the words, 'In the event of an air raid warning the audience will be informed immediately, so that those who wish to take shelter, either in the building or in public shelters outside, may do so. The concert will then continue.'

'I start my "privilege leave" on Monday for seven days, which will be most welcome and interesting,' I informed Helen on 27 August 1944. 'I am spending it on attachment to the Royal Navy, either on a destroyer or MTB [motor torpedo boat].'

'Privilege leave' involved being temporarily stationed at HMS *Drake*, the Royal Navy barracks in Devonport. There, with two other Canadian soldiers, I underwent instruction in diving and accompanied an armed naval trawler providing escort to a gaggle of merchant ships carrying cargo from Plymouth to Falmouth. The small convoy, which averaged about seven knots, did not experience any really rough weather – enough, though, to make a landlubber regret having made the trip. If one could hold down one's food, the marvel was the cheapness of the gin – about two shillings and sixpence the bottle! The diving was more challenging and interesting.

We trotted down to the dockyard where we met 'Johnny,' a sub-Lieutenant (called a gunner). He is a deep-sea diver, in charge of diving instruction. Blond and blue-eyed, he was small of stature, wearing a dirty, torn and ragged naval coat, a still dirtier pair of dungarees, a large white (dirty grey) sweater pulled down to the knees for comfort. Needless to say, I immediately liked Johnny and all about him. We followed him on to a very old and dirty tug boat which took us out to the middle of the stream where we picked up two rather ancient look-ing barges with all the diving equipment aboard, helmets, life and air lines and old-fashioned air pumps (operated by hand).

Soon the skipper looked at his watch and said 'we better a get a move on.' We packed the cards, stripped off our battledress tops, tie, shoes, and gaiters and pulled on enormous sweaters ... From there on I placed complete confi-dence in these men. 'Sit down on the bench. Push your foot in. Now the other. Right. Stand up. No. One arm at a time.' That's when you begin to feel helpless. The suit is made of canvas, with openings only at the neck and around the wrists.

You climb through the neck, wiggle your hips into the body and shoot your feet into the bottom of the suit. Then, one hand at a time, you place the rubber ends in a bucket of water, slamming your hand through the sleeve. Then the other hand until only your head and hands are free. You stand up and shake the suit down. 'Leave lot's of room around the crotch otherwise you'll slice your cock off.' You then sit down and pull your head inside the suit until the top closes over you; front and bottom, back and top. They push and tug asking you to get down further. The air inside is stifling and you feel a wave of sheer claustrophobia. You pull yourself together. 'Alright, come up.' You push your head joyfully through the hole. Somebody places a metal ring over your head. 'Hold it, here, with your hands. Watch your chin.' The rubber holes are snapped over metal lugs on the disc, then two half-circles of metal are clamped over the lugs.

Now the shoes. Great, weighted things with tremendous cords and leather thongs. You stand rooted to the deck. God, you could never get out of this; buried alive in twenty feet of water. Nonsense! What the hell's the matter. Scared? Shake your head. Tell yourself you're not, you liar! Now the helmet. 'Duck your head.' A quick twist and a wrench and the thing's in place. Only a small hole left where they will screw on the face plate. Somebody leans close. 'When you get down the ladder turn the water valve on the left, down and adjust your air intake. When we put the weights on we won't keep you standing around. Remember, getting on to the ladder, swing your feet, don't lift them. Right, hold the front weight.' ... A tap on the helmet. Somebody comes close, the chap who went to Russia. 'Alright? Remember to lean forward against the current.' You ask a million questions in a flurry. He laughs and says, 'If you forget everything you'll do well.'

In another note from HMS *Drake* I wrote rather cryptically: 'I've been trying to arrange a look at the counterpart to our branch. I think it's about done. Should be interesting.' I was seeking access to a Royal Navy secret intelligence establishment near Devonport, which continuously plotted the movement of any shipping detected in the English Channel. (I believe that Halbert's mysterious contact Dunderdale was helpful to me in this regard.) It turned out to be a large Royal Navy operations room completely staffed and run by Wrens, working round the clock. I believe that the centre was linked to the series of radar stations maintained along the coasts and with other such facilities, including wireless interception stations and direction-finding equipment. Apart from being extremely efficient, some of the Wrens were smashingly good-looking!

'Tonight [28 January 1943], before going to Mother Massey's, I'm meeting Charles Ritchie (Canada House), a former beau of Willa's. We are to have a quick drink at the Carlton. You can see that the social ramifications of life are many.' 'Mother Massey's' was the nickname for the Canadian Officers Club. Willa Magee Walker, Helen's first cousin, later became head of the RCAF Women's Division.

By the summer of 1943 I was informed that I had been nominated to attend the 8th Canadian War Staff College course in Kingston, Ontario, which surprised and delighted me since it meant that I would be reunited with Helen and would meet our son Colin for the first time (born August 1942). Since I had little or no regimental or staff experience, except my curious staff duties, it was thought that I should be seconded to various units for short periods to fill in the serious gaps in my military knowledge.

During the summer I was seconded, in quick succession, to the 21st Canadian Armoured Regiment (GGFG), the 8th Canadian Reconnaissance Regiment, the 8th Canadian Infantry Brigade Company (Royal Canadian Army Service Corps), and the 3rd Royal Canadian Corps of Signals. On 24 August I informed Helen: 'Going to London on Saturday to try to arrange a couple of attachments to artillery units, if time permits.' Time did not permit.

It was difficult to learn much that was likely to be of use to me at the war staff college, but I enjoyed the experiences and the people I met. For example, while with the 8th Recce Regiment I was able to attend a 'commando-type' course which the unit had been authorized to set up and run. Since it entailed use of live ammunition on expropriated rather than Crown land, permission to conduct training had to be sought from both British and Canadian authorities. On 11 August I noted; 'On Friday night as we had no water laid on we took the gang down to the sea for a swim. The first swim in the sea I've had since I've been in England. The water was warm and the sun was glorious. What more could one ask? ... Sunday, after a ten mile route march and a "scheme" [military training exercise], we headed for the beach in the afternoon. This time the tide was high and the breakers came dashing in ... a beach with lovely white sand.'

We weren't far from Portsmouth, where occasionally we would end up in the evening. On one such night I saw, in one of those bright red telephone booths with glass windows in the lobby of some hotel, an obviously vigorous, young British sailor copulating with a scantily clad, red-haired young woman. It was an astonishing feat, considering the size of the booth. Even more astonishing, none of the many passersby seemed to pay any attention! Perhaps the innate good manners of the English prevented them from staring.

Before I returned to Canada I took some leave in Ireland. The contrast with wartime London was a shock. From the Royal Hibernian Hotel in Dublin I wrote Helen on 24 September 1943:

Imagine if you can, after nearly twenty months of blackout, seeing harbour lights twinkling in the distance, a flashing beacon stabbing hot and bright into the darkness. Then swiftly the shore lights take form and lights along the waterfront and in shop windows can be seen. One can make out motorcars driving about. It's a very moving sight I can tell you and a memory I will always cherish, symbolic of many things.

Imagine too after severe, although by no means unbearable rationing, finding oneself thrust into a world where food is plentiful. Where bananas and oranges, and figs are sold freely. The plentitude and the range of food staggers me somewhat I must admit. Fresh eggs, chops, steaks, onions, milk, butter, cream, marmalade, chocolates, lobsters, crabs, kippers, real meat sausages, lemons, melons, sardines, and excellent sherries and wonderful liqueurs.

The people too have a different air about them. Prosperous, healthy and happy. Well dressed and well washed. Everyone has a clean, soapy smell about them. After English girls the Irish girls are a change. They look more like Canadian girls. They hold themselves as if they owned the world and don't care who knows it. For the most part they seem, if not beautiful, strong featured, but there are an extraordinary number of good looking and well-groomed women. Invariably they have wonderfully clear eyes and clear, wide foreheads, with either black or red hair. Some blondes but they seem scarce.

I know now where the McCreas come from. I saw a woman the other day who was so like my mother I nearly spoke to her. The same features, the same eyes and the same red hair and freckles. Later, in the art gallery there was a painting of an 'Irish Lady' which was the spitting image of my mother when she was younger.

My trip to Dublin was made so much more pleasant as a result of introductions from friends in London. For example: 'I met Tony Werner in the courtyard of Trinity College and we went along to the Irish Parliament buildings where I met a Mr. Briscoe, T.D. We had a most interesting lunch. Across the room was De Valera and some members of his cabinet. I met the Secretary of State for External Affairs, the Minister of Agriculture and others whose names I can't remember. The lunch was excellent and Briscoe, who, incidentally, is Jewish, with a broad Irish accent, was intensely interesting. Widely read and travelled, he was well able to answer my spate of questions. After lunch he took us all over the House, the Senate chamber and the committee rooms. The House, built around 1745 by either the 1st or the 2nd Duke of Leicester, is a very lovely example of Georgian architecture.'

3

War Staff College

Returning to Canada in 1943 proved an unexpected cultural shock. Though there was some rationing in Canada, the contrast with England was startling. Canadian shops and markets were cornucopias by comparison with England's. The lack of blackout restrictions and the absence of serious rationing for gasoline, tires, and oil products accentuated the differences.

With some difficulty Helen and I found a small place to rent in Kingston. Whatever the shortcomings of the apartment, we were happy simply to be together again. Our landlady was a harridan, but, since she appeared to like young officers, we got along quite well. Sitting on the bathroom seat one could fry eggs on the two-burner electric stove, and, there being no refrigerator, we had to keep important things like beer and butter on the window ledge, trying to remember not to let them freeze solid.

I spent all my time during the day and often many nights at Royal Military College (RMC) trying to master the numerous subjects we were taught in the War Staff College course, many of which were complete Greek to me. Our instructors were excellent. Indeed, the poor British army major, Reggie Walters, who had me under his wing should have been decorated for his patience and kindness. Many of the other students were friends of long standing. In some lectures I was fortunate to be paired with Mike Dare – we shared a desk. He saved me on several occasions from my ignorance and inexperience. Years later he succeeded me as director-general of the RCMP Security Service.

It was clear that I did not have sufficient military experience and background to benefit fully from the course. Its best feature for me was that it enabled me to be reunited with Helen. I believe that it did broaden my military knowledge, but whether it helped the Canadian war effort is difficult for me to judge. Eventually it led to an increase in Canada's population.

In March 1944, while still at RMC, I received two letters that surprised and pleased me. The first was from Don Matthews, chief administrative officer in External Affairs, enclosing a copy of a letter signed by Norman Robertson and sent to my Montreal address, which read:

As a result of the very great expansion that the war has brought to the work of the Department of External Affairs, we have immediate need of additional staff in the diplomatic ranks. The work of the Department will undoubtedly expand further after the termination of hostilities and, therefore, we are anxious to recruit at the present time persons who have had overseas service with the armed forces, who will be eligible for permanent appointment rather than make temporary appointments of persons not having had overseas service, who probably would not be able to continue with us after the war.

Having this situation in mind, we have gone over our lists of persons with overseas service, who have expressed an interest in joining the ranks of this Department and have recommended your name for consideration by the Civil Service Commission, who makes these appointments. The Civil Service Commission will, shortly, be asking you to report for an interview. It is expected that immediate appointments will be made to the position of probationary Third Secretary and that the persons so appointed will be eligible for permanent appointment after one year's satisfactory probationary service.

The scale of remuneration for these appointments is still under discussion but it is expected that the starting salary will be $2400 per annum and, after permanent appointment, increases for satisfactory service amounting to $180 per annum can be granted at the end of each year to a maximum of $3000 per annum. From that point on, persons will be eligible for promotion to the senior grades of the diplomatic service.

Under these circumstances, I hope that you will be interested in seeking one of these appointmments and will arrange to be present at the interview when requested by the Civil Service Commission. It is not anticipated at the present time, that there will be any formal examination for these appointments.

In the same mail came a letter from G. Saunders, secretary of the Civil Service Commission, asking me to present myself for an 'Oral Board to be held in room 205, East Block [of the Parliament Buildings], Ottawa on Friday afternoon the 17th of March at 3.00 p.m.' However, 'I regret that no fund is voted to defray the cost of travelling expenses in connection with interviews.'

Arriving at the East Block for the interview I met another candidate in uniform, Jean Fournier, then a major in the artillery. We were interviewed separately, Jean going first in order to catch the afternoon train to Montreal. The composition of the board was impressive, even intimidating, though Norman Robertson went out of his way to put us at our ease. Robertson acted as chairman, assisted by Laurent Beaudry, Stuart Hemsley, Hugh Keenleyside, John Read, and Hume Wrong. Two were representing the Civil Service Commission.

As one might have expected, Norman Robertson and Hume Wrong's questions were subtle, catholic, and interesting. My interview took about forty-five minutes, but the time seemed to fly. I enjoyed the experience. Certainly, the questions were unlike those being asked at the staff college.

In March 1944 I wrote to Norman Robertson: 'As my month's embarkation leave is nearly ended I was wondering if you could give me some indication as to what the decision is to be as, quite naturally, it will make considerable differences to any personal arrangements I must make. As I indicated during my interview on 17 March, granted the opportunity, it has always been my wish to enter Canada's diplomatic service, but since the outbreak of war it never occurred to me to leave the army even if the opportunity arose, and my own wishes, if there were any means of fulfilling them, would be to have a period of further service with the army, but on *active* operations.'

On 24 March I received the following telegram: 'I have received your letter of March 22nd. I have written to General Letson asking him whether he can arrange for your release to this department at the earliest possible date. As I have previously pointed out to you and to General Letson I consider this transfer would be fully warranted. I fully appreciate your statement that the transfer will not be owing to any efforts on your part but solely as a result of consultations between myself and General Letson.'

I immediately responded, and, not long before reporting in Halifax for embarkation, I received the following reply: 'I have received your letter of March 31st concerning your decision to remain with the Army until the end of the war. While I am sorry that you have felt it necessary to take this decision, I fully appreciate your reasons for doing so and want to assure you that your decision will in no way prejudice your chances of appointment at a later date. I hope you will advise this department as soon as you will be available for consideration for appointment to its staff.'

I remember thinking that Robertson was extraordinarily persistent in this matter. It is only recently that I have discovered, in talking to other former members of External Affairs in the same circumstances, that he pressed them too to leave the armed forces and join External Affairs.

During the staff course or on my embarkation leave, I carried out some chores for Felix Walter, by then head of the Canadian Intelligence Corps Overseas. One of the tasks was to visit the military organization that intercepted and deciphered enemy and other wireless communications, in the La Salle Academy on Guiges Street, off Sussex Drive. There I first met Ed Drake (then a captain), who later headed the Communications Branch of the National Research Council (CBNRC) and with whom I was to have close contact.

Writing to Helen on 6 May 1944, en route to England, I observed: 'Six swans flew overhead, winging their way north somewhere on the west coast of Scotland. A herald of things to come perhaps? The King's birds. The first time [on a troopship going overseas] one feels that everything is very real and earnest. This time there is almost a magical, unreal quality about the whole affair.'

After languishing for several days in Aldershot at the intelligence reinforcement unit, under Major Bob Raymont, I was ordered to report to Felix Walter in London. I told Helen:

Frank Fleury is the new boss-man when it comes to people like myself. He showed me my report from the staff college in Kingston. Not exactly a good report but I feel it an honest appraisal. It stated, 'Starnes is neat and apparently physically fit. He will take the initiative when the course is clear. He shows average application in his work but loses interest and requires occasional checking. He works well in a team but prefers to work alone. He is polite and respectful and has an equitable temperament. He speaks French and German. He has a good vocabulary but is hesitant and mumbles when he speaks. His written work is quite adequate. He is an average learner but his grasp of new ideas is sometimes incomplete, due to lack of experience.

'He has both the infantry and the armoured corps but his knowledge of these arms is weak due to lack of field experience. His knowledge of other arms is limited. He has experience in intelligence work. He has a fair knowledge of staff work. His appreciations and decisions are not always sound as he is inclined to miss major factors and, due to lack of experience, his knowledge of the principles of administration is weak and he does not understand their application. He is not considered suitable for any third grade staff appointment at present, due to lack of experience in the field. He is considered adequate for a third grade intelligence appointment.'

A pretty good summing-up I must admit. All in all I think they did not overestimate or undervalue my military capabilities. Frank Fleury feels it would be foolish for me to do anything other than intelligence work and Felix has such a job for Tim and me almost immediately. ['Tim' was John Timmerman, a former member of the RCMP, later responsible for security in External Affairs.] We became friends when I was working in Canadian Military Headquarters in London and he was working in Aldershot ... Felix Walter, however, was very upset that I had turned down External Affairs. He feels, as does Frank Fleury, that I might be seconded from the army to External Affairs.

I had the impression that Hugh Halbert and Felix Walter did not admire each other. Certainly they were quite dissimilar. Hugh was impulsive and quick to reach conclusions. Felix was far more cerebral and deliberate with people and problems. I was not present at the handover of responsibility for MO&I, but it cannot have been easy, especially in matters related to British 'cloak and dagger' organizations.

It took some time before Timmerman and I were told what to do. By the end of May 1944, however, we had been seconded to G 2 (Air), 21 Army Group, Main Headquarters, on the western outskirts of London. Our immediate bosses were an Englishman and an American, both ranked as majors. Our principal tasks involved collation of intelligence from many different sources, photo interpretation, wireless interception, secret agent's reports from SOE, MI 6, Ministry of Economic Warfare, and so on, with the aim of identifying targets on the continent for possible air strikes.

Not long after being seconded to 21 Army Group (Air) headquarters I was asked to see Norman Robertson at Canada House. Norman was accompanying Prime Minister William Lyon Mackenzie King to London for a meeting of Commonwealth prime ministers in May 1944 and informed me that the army had proposed to second me to External Affairs with my existing rank (captain). He said that he intended to have me appointed immediately as third secretary at the Canadian Legation to the Allied Governments-in-Exile in London.

4

On Foot in the Blackout

Being seconded to the Canadian Legation to the Allied Governments-in-Exile in London, which I was on 25 May 1944, appeared not much different from being seconded to the main headquarters of 21 Army Group (Air) on the western outskirts of London. Both involved administrative work in intelligence, and neither brought me any closer to action at the very moment when it was obvious that the Allies were about to launch an all-out attack against the Germans in Europe. The preparations for 'Overlord' were everywhere to be seen, and as a recent member of the intelligence staff at 21 Army Group headquarters, I knew more than the average person about what might be involved, though none of the vital secrets.

To my surprise, the job at the legation represented a sea change. Not only was the work unfamiliar, but I was ignorant of the basic rules. Moreover, I knew almost nothing of the corporate ethos of the Department of External Affairs except for what I had picked up by osmosis from the few members I happened to know, such as Charles Ritchie. The organization seemed like a small men's club, with a flavour about it not unlike that of the Constitutional Club! I remember hoping that I was wrong, and, of course, I was. It was a small club, but possessed of intellectual novelty, vigour, and freshness.

On 27 May 1944 I informed Helen: 'I had a chat with Pierre Dupuy who will be, or I should say now is my boss officially, since I was seconded with effect the 25th of this month. A spot of difficulty has arisen over my dress. For obvious reasons, Pierre does not want me in uniform on certain occasions. So, I shall have to get a suit of sombre hue. A suit made here is still far above anything I could get made in Canada. Coupons are the only snag but I imagine I can get special coupons for the occasion. I actually am taking over from Chris Eberts' (a friend from school and university).

Twelve days later I described the job: 'We must serve the interests of Canada in relation to the countries to which we are accredited and, of course, in the larger sense, we must ensure cooperation amongst them as allies.' The legation was accredited to Belgium, Czechoslovakia, Holland, Norway, and Poland, but not Vichy France. All these governments-in-exile hated the Nazis and desperately wanted to free their peoples and lands from German occupation. I found the Poles and the Czechs the most fascinating. I had been in both countries very briefly in the late 1930s but knew little about them.

'Today,' as I told Helen on 28 July, 'has been busy. We now have another government. That of the Yugoslavs. Something else to confuse my reeling brain. Just as I was getting the historical, ethnological, geographical and political vagaries of Poland, Czechoslovakia, Holland, Belgium and Norway straightened away in my mind. Just as I had the Curzon Line fixed in my mind, now I must learn the political and geographical significance of Ljubljana, Mount Blegos, Trieste, Gorizia, Mount Maggiore, etc., ad nauseam. However, I really don't mind. In fact, I'm revelling in it, simply loving it. Every bit of it, the good with the bad. The boring with the exciting.'

The legation's offices at 14 Berkeley Street, in the west end, were adequate and not gaudy. However, since we relied on Canada House in Trafalgar Square for secure communications – machine-cipher equipment, trained communications staff, professional diplomatic couriers, and all manner of other vital administrative support – we continually wished we were nearer. Most of our authoritative, reliable background material came from the Foreign Office, through Canada House – excellent 'country papers' and copies of some dispatches and telegrams exchanged with missions around the world, invariably well written and informative. The British did all this in part because Canada was an 'old commonwealth' country but also out of enlightened self-interest. Helping Canada in this and other ways might pay off. Certainly it made us more sympathetic and supportive of their policies in matters great and small.

Peter Wright (author of *Spy Catcher*) made an interesting indiscretion during a top-secret conference of the heads of the security and intelligence agencies of CAZAB (Canada, Australia, New Zealand, 'America,' and Britain) held in Montebello, Quebec, in the 1970s. He told us that throughout the war the British, as a matter of course, had been 'reading' all Canada's military and diplomatic communications exchanged with England, 'just to be sure what the Canadians were up to.'

Occasionally, to our delight, Wright would commit such indiscretions, usually after a good lunch or some late-night poker game. There is no doubt that the British had the capability to intercept and 'read' our communications, especially as they had helped provide the special equipment and the machine ciphers used at Canada House and had complete access to the transatlantic cable system. The volume of such wartime traffic, of course, would have been considerable. I assume that the British did not then possess 'search engines' capable of extracting specific information from masses of messages, since computers then were in their infancy. However they managed it, they obviously had the ability to cope with the mass of Japanese, German, Italian, and other intercepted communications traffic, quickly extracting the specific items that were of use to them.

A large, unwieldy 'code book' issued by the British enabled us to compose our own 'coded' messages to be sent through the post office. It was a simple substitution system of the kind used between the wars for transmitting commmercial traffic, not a high-grade encrytpion system. To compose even a short message took hours, especially if one had little practice. We seldom, if ever, resorted to it, able as we were to rely on the excellent system at Canada House.

Apart from Pierre Dupuy, the chargé d'affaires ad interim, Charlie Hebert, the military attaché, and me, the only other members of the legation were an arthritic 'orderly' (General Georges Vanier's title for him) – a refugee from the legation in Paris who, though born an Englishman, was more fluent in French and spoke English with a pronounced French accent – and four efficient, cheerful, locally engaged women doing essential administrative chores.

'It goes without saying, of course,' I wrote Helen on 27 June 1944,

that you should treat anything that I do put on paper as extremely confidential and not for anyone else's edification but solely and simply for your own. Firstly Pierre. He has been twenty-two years in the service and never seems to be able to forget it, which I feel does him incalculable harm. Most of that time has been spent in service in France, with the exception of a short period when he was recalled to Ottawa. At that time, following the fall of France, he was Chargé d'Affaires in Vichy. He was implicated with the underground movement in many ways. [Surely I must have meant 'involved,' not 'implicated'?] Taking what, for the average person, let alone a diplomat, were extreme risks. However, he managed to handle all his affairs. When we severed relations with Vichy he came to this country, setting up the legation in London. He brought his mistress with him from France and has set her up in style, living with her quite openly at his house in Maidenhead.

He is a very good personal friend of the Prime Minister, who appears to set much store by what he has to say. I feel sure that any advancement he has had is due in no small measure to the P.M.'s willingness to listen to what he has to say. Pierre is in the habit of writing personal notes to the P.M. which has the effect of irritating people in External no end. If he cannot get satisfaction on some point or other he will use the simple expedient of writing to the P.M. direct. His standing with the department cannot be very high because he is essentially a career diplomat and yet he only holds the rank of counsellor in the service, mainly I feel because men like Robertson feel that he is apt to be biased in his political outlook – which is very [Roman] catholic and consequently very anti-Soviet.

... I like little Pierre. Most of the things that I have said are facts; I have not expressed many opinions. I like him and I do feel that he is a damn good Canadian representative, a good diplomat and a very clever man. He does play politics, but that is part of his nature. Despite his obvious man-of-the-world outlook on things generally, he is remarkably naïve about some things. For instance, when seeking promotion (which I must admit, technically he is due) he writes directly to the Prime Minister and asks for it, stating his case rather crudely, little realizing that the P.M. would have to refer the matter to his under-secretary of state (Norman Robertson).

... Pierre has very strong interests in French politics. He views them as a Frenchman rather than as a Canadian, which is another reason for the department being somewhat leery of his opinions. When he was recalled in 1941 and [Georges] Vanier was appointed Minister it was then obvious that the French Provisional Government would be moving to Algiers and that a Canadian representative would naturally have to be appointed there. Both he and Vanier intrigued and fought for the job. Vanier won and Pierre was made Chargé d'Affaires ad interim [in London]. In theory, Vanier holds the appointment while in Algiers as representative to the French, the Greeks and the Yugoslavs. The rivalry still exists and, from time to time, there are definite signs of it reappearing in odd, unexpected corners. The result of all this feuding has been a divided office.

Though I liked Dupuy, I found his security practices appalling. For example, he had the bad habit of opening the diplomatic pouch on his own and of disposing of the contents in a haphazard manner. His idea of safeguarding secret papers was to place them in the drawer in his desk. Happily, if the need arose, such documents could be easily recovered, using a bent paper-clip to open the cheap lock. We would sometimes receive an urgent message from Ottawa asking questions that could be answered only if we referred to the documents Pierre had hidden.

In my letter of 27 June 1944 I went on: 'As to the department itself, Norman Robertson is the man behind the wheel, along with my friend Hume Wrong. Both are extremely able men who do a good job. There are others equally clever such as Mike Pearson in Washington, Dana Wilgress in Moscow, who writes truly masterly despatches, [Jack] Pickersgill in Ottawa, Leighton McCarthy in Washington, and Charles Ritchie in London. Some of the men they have are extremely brilliant. I have a very high regard for the manner in which they keep the government informed.'

I was able to visit Paris in May 1945. Georges and Pauline Vanier asked me to lunch in their apartment in a hotel. Afterwards, wanting to show me some paper stored in the mission safe, Georges went through an elaborate routine involving a small key to an escritoire that was concealed under a corner of a large rug in the living-room. In the escritoire was hidden a big, heavy key to an antiquated-looking metal safe. The safe was quite small, embellished with painted curlicues of muted colours – the kind that Hollywood uses in classic western movies. Even if the ruse had remained undiscovered, the safe could quite easily have been opened by professionals. The whole scene could have been from one of Peter Sellers's movies.

On 17 June 1945 I informed Helen:

Felix's corps [Canadian Intelligence Corps Overseas] has now grown to alarming proportions and he calls himself ADMI. All this would not be possible if he had not systematically built up a fantastic organization. Everything that the British and the Americans do we must do too, even if it means that we are unable to do it properly. The excuse used by army authorities, that Canada must be completely sovereign in her dealings with her allies is perfectly correct perhaps in relation to matters diplomatic, but the army has made it the excuse to create a fabulous number of jobs. Canada with but five divisions has sought representation on almost everything going. The principle is good and I for one would like to see Canada play an ever growing rôle in the planning of world security and in helping to maintain peace, but for God's sake, in moderation!

I have tried to give you a short summary of some of the things which actually make the wheels turn. Personalities play such an important part in all the things that we do. To me they give the true background to any story. I have left out much that even I do not want to put to paper, but that can wait until we meet. Rest assured I won't forget any of it.

That, of course, was nonsense.

The effects of the Allied invasion of Europe were quickly evident in the number of Canadians in all three services posted as missing in action, wounded, or killed. I had lunch with Massey Beveridge, a friend from Montreal who was flying for the RAF. I believe that he flew a Beaufort fighter that also could be equipped for aerial photography. Two days later he was posted as missing. Eventually he was listed as killed in action.

In an undated missive to Helen I wrote: 'No news of Jack [Martin] or Allan [Magee].' Word had come via the military grapevine that they both had been wounded or were missing, Martin in Normandy, and Magee in Italy. In fact, Allan turned out to be alive and well, but Jack Martin, who had been best man at our wedding and with whom I had played hockey and football and shared in many extracurricular activities at university, was badly wounded near Caen while serving with the Canadian Black Watch.

News of these and other wartime casualties and deaths made a deep and lasting impression on me, especially when they were very close friends. One had a feeling of utter helplessness.

On 11 August 1944 I apologized to Helen: 'If this seems slightly confused I hope you will forgive me. I have just arrived back from seeing Jack at the 17th Canadian General Hospital. In addition to seeing Jack I saw Phil MacKenzie and had dinner with Harry Scott. The amputation on [Jack's] right leg is well below the knee. I was struck by his remarkably good morale and, considering what he has been through, his healthy appearance. He has lost some weight, quite naturally. But his frame being large, it really isn't noticeable unless one knew him before when he looked like a minor edition of a Percheron stallion.'

Since my wife and Jack's were close friends, I wrote in as great detail as I could, including sketches, to be passed on to her. The official notification would provide only the barest outlines of his injuries and little about his prospects:

Understandably [Jack] wants to talk of his seventeen days which, from his description were hell. His first time into the forward zone brought him into the midst of a German attack while in charge of 40 reinforcements who were entirely green. Jack apparently found himself in the center of all this dressed in Sam Browne belt and kilt, with a greatcoat over his arm! He told me he learned, after the event, that a German 88mm gun had fixed its sights along the road down which their 30 hundred weight truck drove. They were sitting ducks!

There goes the bloody siren! God, I could kill the whole bloody German race with my bare hands. It isn't so much that they have crippled someone we know and like but someone who above all loved his freedom, loved to use his limbs.

What good purpose can be served by killing young children and women? God. [I was now referring to the recent incident of a V-1 rocket landing somewhere in Chelsea.] If you had only seen the blackened, charred bodies – six of them laid out side by side on the road – With a torn, tattered newspaper to cover their horror. A newspaper which flapped idly in the early morning breeze, revealing under one corner, a young girl. One side of her face half torn away, bones white and splintered. There is NO point in it. Christ! What can that girl have done to deserve such a fate?

While raids on London by Luftwaffe aircraft were rare, the Germans began attacking with V-1s and later with V-2s. Although these assaults were unnerving and dangerous, daily life continued. Without completely ignoring 'buzz-bombs' one got used to them and soon became able to calculate where they were likely to land.

Fourteen Berkeley Street did not get off completely unscathed. On 24 August 1944 I told Helen:

Coming back to Berkeley Street about 12.45 on a week-end, lo and behold the salvage trucks were outside and the street was closed. I then remembered a particularly loud bang. It was a near miss. All the windows were out or, I should say, in. I was overjoyed to notice that the only ones left intact were mine. I always leave them open, top and bottom and it seemed to have worked. I got into the building and put in a priority call to Maidenhead to tell Pierre what had transpired.

Finally, after picking up glass and whatnot and salvaging bits of the flying bomb for the 'incident officer' (trust the English, anyone else would call them Explosion Officers or something similarly explicit). In Pierre's absence, I sent off a cable to Ottawa about the 'buzz bomb.' Enclose some swanky stickers that are affixed to letters addressed to me from some pals I used to know, who let me have the odd bit of interesting news now and then.

I believe that the envelopes were from contacts in Special Operations Executive (SOE) or MI 6. From time to time they sent me background material about some of the countries to which we were accredited, usually in envelopes festooned with shocking-red top-secret stickers.

I added: 'Paris has freed herself. What wonderful words. Paris free at last, after four hard years of unrelenting struggle to retain dignity and to keep alive a faint flicker of freedom. Paris stands for all that one loves in European culture. It somehow symbolizes a large and generous way of living which few other capitals of the world have been able to emulate. Long may she enjoy her new-found liberty!'

The same day I had lunch with Frijhof Jacobsen of the Norwegian Ministry of Foreign Affairs, who was active in his country's underground. He returned home a couple of times on political missions that must have been very dangerous. Many years later he became ambassador to Canada, then permanent under-secretary in the Norwegian Foreign Office, and subsequently ambassador in Moscow. He was a clever, self-effacing, and exceptionally talented man.

Apparently 30 August 1944

was a fantastically busy day and today promises to be be even more so. Met Ivo Ducachek of the Czech ministry of foreign affairs for a quick drink and a talk before lunch. Took Jean van den Bosch of the Belgian ministry of foreign affairs to lunch at the Royal Automobile Club and then took Peter Aylen of the CBC to see the head man in Radio Orange. Along with what seemed a thousand annoying little things, such as issuing visas, it was a busy day. Today, I have to take Aylen to see the Belgians and the Norwegians and to have lunch with the Poles at the Ritz. I also have to see Saul Rae, who is on his way to Paris to set up shop there once again – re-opening the legation, etc. Charles Hebert left by the early morning plane for France. He won't be back until sometime tomorrow, the lucky dog! I have to take Aylen to see the Czechs and to attend some function of the Netherlands government in Regent's Park. What they can have in Regent's Park I can't imagine. Perhaps the dear old queen will be indulging in a spot of tap dancing for the troops.

Ivo Ducachek was one of a number of Czechs I came to know in London, married at the time to Francine, a Frenchwoman from Nice. He helped me understand the intricacies of the Czech government-in-exile. When the Nazis occupied Prague he was a lawyer who had turned to journalism for a living, specializing in foreign affairs. He managed to escape in 1940, making his way to London, where he was active in the Czech underground until 1945, when he was seconded to the U.S. Third Army under General Patton. When the war ended he returned to Pilsen and was elected to parliament, where he was a vigorous leader in the anti-communist, pro-Western movement. After the Communist take-over he fled to the United States, where he joined the faculty at Yale.

On 4 September 1944 I wrote,

My first intimation that something was cooking came in a telephone call from Charles Ritchie. Pierre received a cable instructing him to proceed to Brussels at once, or as soon as the government returns. He is to be the chargé d'affaires. Tommy Stone to take over here in Pierre's place. Charlie Hebert (now in Paris) is to join Pierre and yours truly is to remain here with Stone. Pierre at the moment has arranged for a plane, through Air Marshal Breadner, and may be going to Europe tomorrow about noon. As he intends only to make a flying visit, returning to London in a few days, he has made arrangements that Tommy Stone will not take over until he leaves London for good, which leaves me in charge while Pierre is in Belgium.

Planes, communications, ciphers, accommodation, foreign currency, cable facilities between Ottawa, Brussels and London, permission from Eisenhower, permission from everyone, including God. Events have moved quickly.

On 7 September 1944 I followed up:

Mr. Morrison, the Home Secretary has announced relaxation of black-out restrictions, the end of fire guard duties on a compulsory basis and the last parade, as it were, for the Home Guard. Now, instead of having to have blackouts on every window, the lights need only be screened. In other words, no glare is allowed and ordinary curtains suffice. In addition street lighting is to be improved and cars can turn up their lights. Railway sidings and factories are permitted bags of light. You have no idea what a mental and physical relief this will bring to the people. After all, five years is a long while. Imagine, there are some children who have never seen the lights!'

I probably knew London better than any city in which I have lived, simply because, like millions of others, I learned to find my way unerringly on foot in the blackout. Almost without thinking, I knew exactly where the curbs were and how many steps in each stairway or stairwell. In many ways the senses other than sight were every bit as important in finding one's way in the pitch black. Smell, sound, and touch proved invaluable. For example, I always knew when I was near a greengrocer's, a butcher's shop, or a pub. Sometimes I could even identify them by the smells they gave off. Certainly it was possible to know a pub by the delicious aromas it exuded – whether it was a purveyor of Watney's, Younger's, or Whitbread's ales. For example, The Bag o' Nails at the back of Buckingham Palace could be detected from quite a distance, depending on the direction of the wind. It served a Younger's that I particularly liked. Also, it was not far from where Tommy Stone had rented a mews flat.

Bombed-out churches, shops, and ruined buildings each had their own special smell, especially those that had burned. Similarly, it was not too difficult to tell where one was on the darkened streets from the fetid, hot air blowing up through the ventilators from the underground; each line seemed to have its own distinctive smell.

There were even moments of sheer magic during the blackout. Crossing Green Park, Hyde Park, or St James' Park under a full moon could be very beautiful. Often the only distinctive sound would be the wind strumming through the steel cables holding the anti-aircraft balloons tethered overhead.

Rain seemed to affect the quality of the blackout. It seemed to make everything blacker, more opaque, possibly because it seemed to reduce smells. Fog sometimes had similar effects. I recall on one occasion being completely disoriented at about ten o'clock in the morning in the middle of Trafalgar Square, in a yellow 'pea-soup' fog. Sounds, sights, and smells, except the smell of diesel oil, were completely dampened, and I could not see more than a foot in any direction. In fact, I completely lost all sense of direction. Eventually, I got down on my hands and knees and felt my way to the curb, or some recognizable, immovable object.

Continuing my letter to Helen of 7 September: 'Tommy Stone came in this afternoon and I spent most of the time explaining the set-up. Happily, I have been preparing for the eventuality for the past three months, so things are all set to get cracking immediately as far as I am concerned. The full story of the V-1's is now being told. 92% of all the buzz bombs casualities were in the London region. The battle of London, as the papers call it, is over or at least we hope it is. Mr. Duncan Sandys has given the following figures. Over 8000 flying bombs were launched, an average of 800 a day. Of these, 2,300 got through to the London area. This number did not include many which came to grief in France.'

The Germans continued to attack the city with V-2s until the rocket launch-sites were overrun by Allied forces. The V-2s carried a larger warhead of high explosives, and were more unnerving, since they could be heard, if at all, only split-seconds before they hit. I think it was a toss-up between the V-1 and the V-2 as to which was worse from a psychological standpoint – probably the V-2.

Helen and I had hoped that she and the children would join me in London. With that in mind I had looked at length for suitable accommodation. Finally, however, the chief administrative officer, Don Matthews, informed me that, 'At the present time the future of the Legation to the Allied Governments and personnel at that legation is doubtful and it is highly probable that in the very near future missions will have to follow at least some of the Allied Governments back to their own countries and presumably the staff in London will be moved along with those missions. I am doubtful, therefore, whether, quite apart from the conditions in London, it would be wise to consider having your wife join you immediately. Should you be moved to some place other than London, we will agree to her transfer at the earliest possible moment.'

I had met Tommy Stone through contacts at Canada House but did not know him well. I was aware that he had been involved in intelligence work in Ottawa, mainly in communications and postal censorship. What I did not know then, because he was very tight-lipped about such matters, was that early in 1940 External Affairs had made him responsible for all aspects of economic warfare, which involved using information obtained from censorship operations and any other available sources of intelligence. Neither was I aware that Tommy had obtained Norman Robertson's enthusiastic support to establish a cryptographic unit in Canada.

In his history of the CBNRC, Kevin O'Neill says,

Not content to let the subject lapse completely, early in 1941 Captain Drake and Lt. Herbert Little of the Directorate of Naval Intelligence (DNI) took up with Tommy Stone the possibility of External Affairs sponsoring a cryptographic unit in Canada. Mr. Stone and his superior Norman Robertson were quite keen, particularly in view of the War Office [British] suggestion about the Vichy codes [that Canada should attempt on its own hook to decrypt], and the latter proposed NRC as a suitable and less conspicuous place for housing such a project ... Dr. C.J. Mackenzie, then acting President of NRC, was not unwilling to consider such a proposal, especially as NRC had recently received a private contribution of $200,000 for the 'war effort,' which came to be known as the 'Banting Fund.'

When Tommy Stone and I met in September he was, I believe, working full-time with the British on psychological warfare. Stone was a colourful character who in the 1930s married into an old U.S. Southern family. Pierre Dupuy was quite different from Stone, in temperament, background, and financial means. There was no love lost between them, and neither made any effort to disguise the fact. Any attempt to bring them together was a complete waste of time.

At the time I was unaware that Tommy Stone and Lester ('Mike') Pearson had been friends since boyhood in Chatham, Ontario. Stone had been brought up there, and Pearson's father became the Methodist pastor at Park Street Church in 1914. Stone thus was a charter member of the brilliant group of men around Pearson who subsequently helped develop the Canadian foreign service.

It is easy to forget or even to be unaware that by the end of 1944 the Soviet Union's intelligence service had gained quite extraordinary access to the most closely guarded British and American military and political secrets. Despite ingenious and apparently comprehensive security measures to protect such secrets as the British–American project to manufacture an atomic bomb, and Britain's breaking of German military and diplomatic ciphers, John Cairncross, recruited by the Russians in the late 1930s, made a complete mockery of British security. His numerous acts of treachery were discovered by British security authorities only years later. Their discovery harmed Britain's intelligence and security arrangements with the United States and other allies.

While acting as Lord Hankey's private secretary, Cairncross informed the NKVD – the Soviet security police – that the British and Americans had been working on an atomic weapon since late 1940. Hankey had presided over several commissions on defence, security, and scientific research and received all manner of highly classified information, to which Cairncross had access and which he promptly handed over to 'Henry,' his NKVD controller. In *My Five Cambridge Friends* (i.e., Anthony Blunt, Guy Burgess, Cairncross, Donald Maclean, and Kim Philby), Yuri Modin states that Cairncross forwarded copies of thousands of highly classified British documents to Moscow, including Hankey's very accurate personal forecasts of the progress of the war. In 1942, Cairncross's NKVD controller suggested that he try to penetrate the Government Code and Cipher School at Bletchley Park. Cairncross managed to join the school, despite its extraordinary security arrangements, and was employed there analysing intercepted Luftwaffe messages.

Through Cairncross the Soviets eventually gained access to much communications intelligence hitherto kept completely secret even from Britain's closest allies. They considered the material so valuable that they decorated Cairncross with the Order of the Red Banner, one of their highest honours. 'Henry' – Anatoly Borisovich Gorsky – managed to show Cairncross the actual decoration in London.

While accredited to the Allied governments-in-exile in London I had no inkling of the extent and seriousness of the Soviet Union's intelligence activities directed against the Western Allies. Given the relative ease with which the 'Cambridge five' were able to acquire top-secret information of all kinds, the Soviets probably had access to everything that the British produced concerning relations with the Allied governments-in-exile. Certainly they had a great interest in the ability of these governments to re-establish themselves in Europe. We now know the extent to which they went to ensure that the Allied governments of bordering countries came under their control. Jan Masaryk's defenestration in Prague is but a crude example. Blunt, Burgess, Maclean, and Philby were quite capable of handing over very valuable information about British and American efforts to help these governments re-establish themselves and create anti-communist regimes in Prague, Warsaw, and Belgrade. Soviet espionage hurt all the countries of the Western alliance, exacerbated by the near-negligence of some Allied officials and politicians.

Canada was no exception. At least until Igor Gouzenko's defection in 1945, most Canadians believed themselves unaffected by such threats. Thus their attitudes to espionage were dangerously unrealistic. There were officials such as Norman Robertson, Hume Wrong, and Arnold Heeney, and politicians such as Mike Pearson and Douglas Abbott, who clearly understood the problems but were unable to change others' attitudes quickly enough to avoid damage.

Apart from two or three short periods when I was on my own, for the remainder of my time at the Canadian Legation to the Allied governments-in-exile in London in 1944–5 I worked under Tommy Stone.

Unfortunately, much of the time he suffered agonizing bouts of sinus infection, which was not helped by the dry martinis he so enjoyed. Several operations to cure the sinus condition brought little relief. When he was feeling well, however, Stone was great fun, and a joy to work with. He was gregarious, amusing, quick-witted, brilliant, shrewd, and disarmingly frank. He played the piano well, improvising to suit his mood or that of his audience; 'Take the hair from any old chair,' was a rude ditty he delighted in playing. His repertoire of such numbers seemed inexhaustible.

I was asked to spend Christmas 1944 with Helen's cousin, Willa (Magee) Walker, at their home, 'Over Rankeillour,' near Cupar, Fife. In 1940 Willa's husband, David, while serving with the Imperial Black Watch in France, was taken a prisoner-of-war. In different prisons, he planned and took part in a number of daring attempts to escape. Two days after Christmas I reported to Helen: 'Without any exaggeration it was the best Christmas I have ever spent away from home.' For Christmas the family included the Walkers' daughter Huldah and her children, Elizabeth and David, aged ten and eight, respectively.

In the afternoon Willa and I, Mr. Walker and Elizabeth walked over towards 'the mountain' (1,000 feet) which forms part of their land. As this totals about 800 acres you have an idea of its size. Elizabeth and I ate rose berries, looked in the burn, and smelled the dead stoat which the keeper had hung up some weeks past.

On Boxing Day I took the children out and pulled them across frost covered fields on a sled with iron runners. There is a maid and a cook, a gardener, a gamekeeper, and a couple of farmers. I was enchanted by Over Rankeillour. The house is so huge that we had to help the maid by doing the dishes and making beds.

The house was unbelievably cold throughout.

I saw the 1945 New Year in at a party given by Tommy Stone in his mews flat in London. 'Had a bang-up party. Lieutenant-General Brooks and his wife, Vi and her 15 year old child. The mother looks about that age herself. Alison Grant [later married to George Ignatieff], Mary Greye, Vladimir Rybar and wife (Rybar is Under-Secretary of State for Foreign Affairs in the Yugoslav Ministry for Foreign Affairs), Ansim McKim, Ivo and Francine Ducachek, Charlie Hebert, Anne Gordon, Graham Spry and a couple of odd souls whom I did not know.'

Rybar was an interesting man, a tough cookie, who, despite being the most senior official in King Peter's foreign office, was certainly no royalist. Madame Rybar was a handsome, statuesque woman, whom Stone, with his penchant for picturesque language, might have described as 'a real lolapalooza.'

Two days later:

Things may be developing much more swiftly than we anticipated. Despite the fact that the general war picture in Europe has not improved, the governments of at least some of 'our' countries may be returning shortly. Whether Tommy and I are to remain until the bitter end we do not know. I personally am keen on being sent to Prague. Whether they will see fit to appoint me there I do not know. I can only hope so. Czechoslovakia to me offers the most interesting post in Europe at this time, standing as it does between Russia and Germany and, following as it does, a policy of cooperation with Russia in the east and the U.K. and the U.S. in the west. Czechoslovakia undoubtedly is a test case for Europe and more particularly the Balkans. It will be the sounding board of Europe.

On 7 January 1945 I wrote home:

From the complexion of events it looks as if the next week will be even more hectic. Tommy has had a recurrence of his sinus trouble and his doctor has ordered him to ease up. He has to have some of his teeth pulled out (in my estimation his teeth are the root of his illness) and to take treatment for his sinus, after which the doctor has ordered him to convalesce for a reasonable period. The result, twice as much work and worry.

Our bailiwick, as you will have perceived from press reports, is having a particularly active period. The Poles are all but committed to suicide, the Czechoslovaks are making plans for departure, the Yugoslavs can't seem to convince their King he should relinquish his jewelled crown, the Dutch are dying rapidly and in water up to their chimneys. The Norwegians are sharing a common frontier with Russia and two or three hundred thousand of their people are suffering the Norwegian winter without either sufficient food or clothing after being forcibly evacuated from their homes, most of which were burned to the ground or simply blown up. In the North American parlance our governments are bitched, buggered and bewildered and, by consequence, so are we.

Yesterday, Tommy gave a lunch at his house for Prince Bernhard and Princess Juliana. Present were Mary Greye [working for SOE], Anne Macdonnell [one of Jim Macdonnell's daughters], their highnesses' personal adviser, van

Tets, Col. Nigel Sutton, Tommy, Alison Grant [working for SOE], Harrowich of the Bank of England, their H's and your husband. The lunch went off with éclat. Everyone, even their H's, seemed to enjoy themselves.

Bernhardt is very charming. I had a quite a chat with him about the relative merits of skiing at Mont Tremblant and Villars s/Ollon [sur Ollon]. They eventually had to leave as they had a call booked for Ottawa. God, if they would only make me a prince for a couple of hours. I'd be on the bleeding 'phone for the whole period. Later, when all the guests had departed, Tommy, Alison and I went to the legation and Tommy sent off a couple of cables about something Bernhardt had told him. On Tuesday I have asked Francine and Ivo Ducachek to have lunch at Claridges. Tuesday evening, the Bank of England johnnie has asked Tommy and me to a cocktail party. On Friday I have asked Librach of the Polish government to have lunch with me at the RAC. Socially, I am rich, financially I shall be poor, but what the hell! Canada's relations will at least remain good, I hope – depending on the quality of the meals.

Yesterday morning one of those damn rockets [V-1] landed about 500 yards from home, whilst I was in the delicate act of shaving. Hell of a whumpf, but at least it would be swift. The explosion stove in many windows. Luckily I was not on the windward side. The stinkers seem to be getting more accurate. As you will have seen, a TCA plane crashed in the Atlantic and we understand one of our diplomatic bags was aboard so I expect some of your letters will be lost. Tonight I am supposed to be having dinner with Sam and Helen Hughes in their flat. Should be interesting.

Sam Hughes and I shared office space when we were in MO&I Section at CMHQ in 1942. He was the grandson of Sir Sam Hughes of First World War fame. Whatever Hughes's regiment, the uniform called for a broad red band around the hat, almost indistinguishable from that worn by officers of full colonel rank and up. Walking out in London's streets in his company was a gas. Senior and sometimes obviously elderly officers in various armies would throw salutes as soon as Hughes hove into sight, which he returned with polished ease and obvious delight.

Eventually, Tommy Stone's hectic life and serious medical problems caught up with him, and he was obliged to return to the United States for treatment. In a postscript to a letter (27 January 1945), I added: 'I saw Charles Ritchie, Jack Wheeler-Bennett and Tommy off on the 8.30 p.m. train for Glasgow. Ansim McKim and Crosby Noyes, Tommy's step-son-in law, also were there. A sad affair!'

Before he left London, Stone had sent a letter to Norman Robertson:

It is perhaps appropriate that, at the end of 1944, I should make some report on the work of John Starnes. In view of the excellence of his work it gives me great pleasure to do so. Starnes is a knowledgeable young man who, in my view, shows great promise in the Service. He has the ability to make friendly and wide contacts and on more than one occasion I have had confirmation of the accuracy of his reporting. He works regularly and hard to keep abreast of the papers and documents which go through this Legation which, since there are only two of us to do it, demands a certain number of his evenings. I notice also during the four months that I have been at this Legation a steady improvement in his drafting.

Starnes is very well thought of by the officials of the various Foreign Offices with whom this Legation deals. Many of these officials, who are much senior to him, have spoken to me about him in terms of high praise. They obviously enjoy seeing him and talking with him.

It may be of some help to the Department in deciding on Starnes' future moves to know that of the five countries to which this Legation is accredited Czechoslovakia interests him most. He has several Czech friends with whom he is on intimate terms and he has on more than one occasion told me that, at the moment, he would rather go to Prague than to any other European capital. He is actually studying Czech at present and making some progress. His French, as you know, is excellent.

I might add that Starnes was responsible for the despatch which I sent forward the other day reviewing Czechoslovak affairs for the year 1944, and one which I regarded as a very good job of work.

Stone's showing me his report on my work was most unusual. It taught me a lesson that I did not forget, and in the 1960s, while at External Affairs, I found that I was able to help confirm this practice.

During this period, through my contacts in the Czech Foreign Office I came to know and admire Charles Katek, an American working for the Office of Strategic Services (OSS). His parents had been born in Czechosolvakia. OSS had recruited him to act as a secret agent in Czechoslovakia, a dangerous, difficult task that he took on with enthusiasm and a certain devil-may-care attitude. During this time he made his way to and from that country with great frequency and apparent ease.

On 26 January 1945

I attended the annual and at the same time the farewell party of the Czechs, given by Dr. Ripka [a senior minister in the government]. There must have been some 300 people present – all the diplomatic corps. Francine Ducachek was wearing the most enormous hat I have ever set eyes on. Some friend of hers had brought it from Paris. She assured me it had a Scotch motif for my benefit. You would like Francine. She is parisienne and full of life. The Russkies were there in force – perhaps seven or eight military people and two or three of their diplomatic staff. The only thing that startled me was to be announced in a loud voice as 'the Canadian Chargé d'Affaires.'

5

Chargé d'Affaires

After Tommy Stone's departure in January 1945, the work of the Canadian Legation to the Allied Governments-in-Exile in London continued apace. On 29 January, 'just as I was leaving, John Holmes, who has taken Charlie Ritchie's place at Canada House, turned up. We had a good dinner at the Traveller's Club where we were joined by a laddie who was in Canada working as a vice-consul and doing work for the Ministry of Information. He knew almost everybody in the club and many people in Canada. Somewhat like a walking encyclopedia – very amusing bloke.'

My friendship with Holmes lasted many years. He was a homosexual, and for that reason he was targeted by the Soviet NKVD in an attempt to coerce him into assisting it. All this came to light, apparently through a Russian defector, when I was head (1958–61) of Defence Liaison Division (2), dealing with security and intelligence at External Affairs. I was completely surprised to learn of Holmes's sexual orientation and very upset to discover that because of this he had attracted the Soviets' attention. Norman Robertson delegated me to take Holmes to RCMP headquarters for questioning, but I was not present, of course, during the interview. Exhaustive inquiries found absolutely nothing to suggest that Soviet intelligence had succeeded in recruiting John or that he had been disloyal in any way. Under the provisions of cabinet documents, Robertson, as Holmes's deputy minister, had to decide his future. With Holmes's concurrence, he decided to look for employment for him outside External Affairs. Robertson quickly found him a post in academic life, where he soon became a respected commentator on many aspects of foreign affairs and a distinguished author.

Holmes served for a number of years with distinction on the council of the International Institute for Strategic Studies (IISS), with head-quarters in London. When his term at the IISS expired in the 1970s, and after I had resigned from the public service, he suggested to Alistair Buchan, the director, that I succeed him. I had already been a member of the institute for ten years and eventually was elected to the council, where I served for eight years. I had the impression, however, that some on the council, notably the Americans, were not enthusiastic about my mid-term re-election and would have been happier to have had someone of their choice in my place. I remain grateful to Holmes for making it possible for me to succeed him on this interesting, unusual international body.

Holmes was a great Canadian. In my opinion, he was one of two mem-bers of Canada's fledgling foreign service during the formative postwar years whose ideas and initiatives had valuable and lasting effects. (The other was Gerry Riddell.) A recent article by John Hadwen in the Sum-mer 1996 issue of *bout de papier* neatly captures the spirit of the man.

Since vetting of public servants is such an arcane matter, long shrouded in secrecy, a number of observers tend to blame the RCMP for the government's regulations dealing with security clearances, par-ticularly for the denial of access to classified information for those deemed to have a 'character weakness.' Some commentators have criticized the RCMP for its 'Cold War security mania about homo-sexuals as security risks.' The force may have displayed unnecessary zeal in pursuing homosexuals in the public service who posed poten-tial security risks, but it was doing no more than following the explicit directives laid down by the cabinet, revised from time to time during the 1950s and 1960s, and practised throughout the public service.

My letters to Helen during the period in 1944–5 when I was in London with the Canadian Legation to the Allied Governments-in-Exile seem to dwell unduly on the representational side of my work. In fact, how-ever, the legation did what any small diplomatic mission does. Because for much of the time I was the only person there, represented Canada at diplomatic functions arranged by the Allied governments to which I was accredited. I soon found this aspect of the job a pain in the neck. I wrote to Helen about these events because I thought it would amuse and interest her, and I had to keep so much of my work confidential. Many official reports have since been declassified and are obtainable from the National Archives of Canada, in Ottawa, but they add little of historical interest about the Allied governments-in-exile in London, their day-to-day business, or the personalities involved.

Apart from the normal political and economic reporting there was of course some consular activity – enough to swamp me at times. For example, Tomas Bata was living in London, trying to make plans to extend the family business to Canada and elsewhere. After the war his family company made its headquarters in Canada. Because of Bata's Czech connection, I became involved in trying to assist these efforts, and he eventually became a friend of mine.

I occasionally got some exercise. 'Although our hockey team did not make the finals,' I reported on 1 February 1945, 'we have had a challenge. If I feel fit, I will play on Sunday. However, if I feel only half as bad as I do now I won't be playing.' At the beginning of my assignment to Canadian Military Headquarters (CMHQ) in London in 1942, one of the NCOs playing hockey for the CMHQ team had asked me to join the group – we had played together in St Jérôme, Quebec, when I was stationed there in the army in 1940. The St Jérôme team had some unlikely name like 'les vagabonds,' and usually a respectable number of supporters showed up. While the game was in progress, modest amounts of money would be stuffed into our shoes in the dressing room, presumably by the management.

About the only other exercise I got in London was walking, and I welcomed the chance to join the CMHQ team. I continued to play while at the legation. I am not sure what External Affairs would have said!

On 7 February 1945,

I attended a very pleasant luncheon at Claridges, given by the Norwegian Foreign Minister, Mr. Trygve Lie [later the first UN secretary general]. The King of Norway [Haakon VII] was there and I had a few words with him. He is indeed a very impressive man. Dressed in the field-grey Norwegian uniform with high collar he cuts a very fine figure. The lunch was made up of some 30 people – mostly of the dip corps ...

Mr. Lie was embarrassed by the unexpected arrival of Mr. Hugh Dalton, head of the U.K. Board of Trade and he had to ask me if I would mind being moved from Canada's traditional seat of honour as senior dominion. I assured him it was a pleasure to sit anywhere at his table. In any case I found two interesting people in the Aarskuits. She was by far the most beautiful lady present, so I actually blessed Mr. Dalton.

'I'm convinced,' I wrote two days later, 'that very little more can happen to me now in my capacity of Chargé d'Affaires. The Netherlands government resigned yesterday afternoon! I think all these governments have been deliberately waiting until the moment when they knew I would be alone and undefended. This morning I had to see Sir Neville Bland, the British Ambassador to the Netherlands. I am getting rather adept at hanging my exceedingly dirty raincoat on ambassadorial coat-hooks. I can't get it cleaned as it is the only one I possess and it rains continually.'

A week later I went to a very interesting luncheon given at the Dorchester

to meet the Canadian representatives on the Commonwealth Relations Conference and the Trades Union Congress.

The latter has just finished, the former is just beginning. Some of Canada's noblest sons were there; Victor Sifton, Millard, McGuire, Graham Spry, Beverly Baxter, Lord Greenwood, Lord Winterton, Sir Edward Peacock, Lt.-General Price Montague, Admiral White, Houghton, the new head of the Canadian Navy overseas, a Mr. Armstrong, the Agent General for Ontario. Altogether a most amusing little bun fight.

As you may have seen, one of my governments has gone. The Yugoslavs arrived in Belgrade yesterday.

Demotion soon followed. 'Well me luv [I wrote on 5 March] I am no longer the exalted chargé d'affaires – in fact with the arrival of "Temp" Feaver I am now twice removed from the position. He showed up this morning after a short trip of eleven hours transatlantic. His appointment is as First Secretary to the Legation to the Netherlands government, and he is to proceed with Pierre to The Hague when Pierre takes up his post there as Minister. In the meantime he is another body to help in the general work of the legation to the Allied governments, although we are fast losing them.'

By 4 April I had

come to some very clear idea of what I think is wrong with our approach to the international security organization, etc. [United Nations] ... science has outpaced us many, many times over. We can perform virtual miracles. We can in fact do almost anything on the face of the earth . Our knowledge is prodigous in certain fields. Strangely enough, in the most important field of all we have lagged sadly – in our relations one with the other and, on a bigger scale, one community with another. We know for instance that one language can be taught throughout the world. We know that it would do more than anything else to break down the thousand barriers which exist between nations and peoples, but we can't seem to teach our children such a language, one sure way of providing security for our children and their children.

I ended on a more practical note: 'Your perfume should be in Montreal before this letter – kindness of Herman van Royen, a member of the Netherlands delegation to San Francisco. Nice chap. Hope you meet him.'

On 9/10 April I apologized to my wife:

I'm afraid that my letter which immediately preceded this will upset you – you may even think your children have a godless father. To reassure you I refer you to page 18 of the April issue of the Reader's Digest which contains a condensed version of Elton Trueblood's book 'The Predicament of Modern Man.' In my roundabout fashion I was trying to establish that in my estimation the proposed united nations organization, by completely overlooking the spiritual problems facing the world, is ignoring one of the primary ailments of our age. I thoroughly endorse Trueblood's ideas, just as I welcome the idea behind an international organization for the establishment of lasting peace, but I do not think there is sufficient, if any realization of the close relationship that should and must exist between any such an organization and the spiritual beliefs of the peoples of the world. I take issue with all those who tend to view the problems separately. I also take issue with all those who will not recognize the fact that the ills of India, China, the Mississippi valley or the Danube basin are in point of fact the ills, ipso facto, of the whole world.

I informed Helen on 17 April:

On Saturday, after having written you I received a telephone call from John Holmes to say that Hume Wrong wanted to see me. So I broke a date with the Poles or rather stalled them off, and saw him at Canada House about 12.30. The conversation lasted about 15 minutes during which we discussed the problems attendant upon moving personnel to the many and various missions abroad and then more particularly about my own possible future. He said he understood that I was interested in going to Prague, etc. He asked me why and I told him I thought that it would probably be the hub of events in Europe, etc. In the same conversation he asked me how I would like to go to Belgrade and also explained that there might even be a remote chance that I would go to Washington, given certain conditions. The conditions apparently being that they now have two French speaking men [French Canadians] in Washington, one of whom they would like to move. However, he indicated that our date of the end of August was a sensible date to shoot at and he thought it would work out alright, maybe one or two weeks either way. He then ended up with a lot of complimentary things about my work. Well, as you can see from this we still are working in the dark, so I plan to continue as planned. I told him you were beginning to send things over and what a difference it made to our planning, etc. So, I think we shall simply go on the assumption that you and the children will join me towards the end of August. If there is a change well it's just too god-damned bad – the department can pay the expense.

About this time, to my surprise and pleasure, I received a letter from Norman Robertson, dated 19 March 1945:

Now that you have handed over as Chargé d'Affaires to the Allied Governments in London, I think that it is in order for me to send you a note of appreciation of the way in which you have carried on between Mr. Stone's departure and Mr. Dupuy's arrival. You have certainly had an unexpected and unusual load of responsibility thrust upon you in the light of your short service in the department and you have acquitted yourself with credit. I should like to mention especially the report in your despatch No. 92 of February 15th of your discussions on the Yalta decision with Sir Owen O'Malley and Mr. Mikolajczyk. This was a very good piece of reporting with the addition of a shrewd commentary of your own.

Stanisław Mikołajczyk, the prime minister of the Polish government-in-exile, was a most interesting and likeable man. I believe that the flat where we met to discuss the Yalta agreement probably had been found for him by the British. I was admitted by a dark-haired woman, who joined in our discussion. I assumed that she was his mistress, about whom I had heard a good deal. Mikołajczyk answered my questions carefully and with great patience. Indeed, I was surprised that he replied so readily and with such frankness.

He understood the risks he was taking in agreeing to return to Poland to join the Soviet-sponsored provisional government in Lublin, eventually to become the Polish Government of National Unity, recognized by Britain and the United States. He was well aware that the Soviets would attempt to eliminate him and his Peasant party as soon as they could. He was a brave man.

In a letter dated 27 April 1945 I wrote,

Although the war news seems to be good I can't say the diplomatic front seems to be flourishing. The peace arrangements, if one is to believe the papers, seem to be meeting with many more difficulties than the war measures. I read a very interesting and good little pamphlet published by the Wartime Information Board, written by Hazen Sise, called 'A Peace to Live With.' It is not a bad effort. I also recommend a book by Leopold Schwarzschild called 'Primer of the Coming World' and another book by Vansittart called 'The Bones of Contention' and one by Wm. Beveridge called 'The Price of Peace.' All are pithy reading, worth any thinking person's attention.

Just the kind of thing for a young mother with two active young boys, in the throes of arranging to transport them to Europe!
My epistle of 1 May read:

Seems strange to think that the war in Europe may end tomorrow or the day after. At long last it looks as if the end is only a few days off. I'm afraid that to most of the people in the UK it will pass without much change or without much notice. Many of the restrictions imposed in wartime are to remain for many, many months yet. Things in the shops and throughout the whole country will still be in very short supply, food will be as scarce as ever and any semblance of the pre-1939 life seems out of the question for a number of years yet. There appears to be a lively appreciation amongst the broad mass of the people that a difficult and precarious time lies ahead. A beaten Germany and a ravaged Europe are problems which will have to be solved apart from, and even in spite of, the present experiment [the UN] taking place at San Francisco. Happily, our future does not rest entirely upon the successful outcome of that gallant venture. The people here realize that they have a very full rôle to play in policing Germany for the next 60 years – in fact until the year 2000. All these and many other reasons will I think tend to make Victory Day a bit flat and something of an anti-climax.
    ... War has not only left its mark on the buildings and the countryside of Britain, it has has etched its story on the character and heart of nearly every man and woman who has lived through it. There are many vacant chairs around the dining-room tables in many houses across the length and breadth of the land. Chairs, which no amount of wishing can fill once more. Men and women have been living new and different lives these past six years. Their outlook on life has broadened, their experience has become enriched. They no longer will be able to to fit themselves calmly into the pre-war niches they occupied. New and bigger, sometimes even better niches, will be required. It will be interesting to see how they go about it.
    I hope to be in Paris on the 25th for about a week, depending, of course, on a

lot of things. This I realize will probably be the last straw [for Helen, who knew Paris and loved it] and I will expect to see you over here with the children in time to join me. However, the time will undoubtedly be when you are thoroughly fed up with living in strange cities and travelling, travelling, travelling, endlessly.

The tenth of May, our wedding anniversary, was quieter than the previous days:

This is following upon VE Day so anything I write should not be held against me. To give you an idea of the rejoicing which has taken place here these past three days is quite impossible at this moment. I shall try to put it all down into a coherent story as soon as I can collect myself together. I must say here though that I have never seen such a spontaneous and heart-warming display of sheer joy and glorious happiness anywhere or at any time. The scenes last night and Tuesday night will be forever etched on my mind. The Palace, the King and Queen, the floodlights, the crowds, the singing, the flaming torches all down the Pall Mall, the National Gallery floodlit. St. Martins-in-the-Field with soft lights playing up its columns, Big Ben alight, the searchlights, the music, the bonfires in Trafalgar Square, the fountain outside the Dorchester Hotel, Battersea power station, floodlit. The gay, tri-coloured rosettes, the orange, blue, green, red and yellow hats, the horns, the Bow Bells and, above all the thousands upon thousands of people. We had a grand and memorable time. Something I shall, never, never forget.

On 15 May I wrote again:

Yesterday, in conversation with John Holmes at Canada House he mentioned how nice it was that you were coming over. I said 'What the hell do you mean?' He said, 'Haven't you seen the cable about it' I said, 'No.' According to John, Canada House received a cable stating that you and the children would be coming over. No dates were mentioned. T'any rate he is looking into the matter and will let me know. If it's true I'm overjoyed as it means the department have definitely made up their minds which is at least something.

... I know now that I should have written about VE-Day almost immediately after it happened. Some of the more amusing things I heard and saw; the little black and white dog going up Edgeware Road with a British and an American flag jutting out of both sides of his mouth and some unidentifiable flag draped over his back. He solemnly stopped his parade to sedately lift a leg against a nearby tree. It is to his credit, I think, that the flags still fluttered proudly over the homely scene.

The very drunk RCAF officer and his even drunker companion, a pretty little WAAF, on the number 11 bus on VE-Day afternoon. Picture the bus thundering along its accustomed route, swaying and pitching from side to side. The Canadian holding onto the upright at the entrance to the bus with one hand and onto the WAAF with the other. She, poor girl, being violently ill. All this to shouted instructions from the 10 or 15 passengers in the bus. 'Hold her head higher,' 'press her stomach,' 'mind she doesn't slip,' 'lie her down' (this one I thought a little bawdy), 'a ruddy shaime,' 'hold her nose,' etc. The crowning remark was made by some well-meaning old girl as the pair were disembarking at Victoria Station. 'When yer get off dearie, you just lie down on the grass and put yer laigs up.'

In front of Buckingham Palace at 10.30, the Palace brilliantly floodlit, the seething mass of the crowd. In relative darkness, after the King and Queen had come out on the balcony and had retired, a girl next to me turned to her companion and asked; 'Do yer fink 'e sar me?'

On 17 May 1945 I informed Helen: 'Had lunch with Felix the other day. He is, as usual, full of news. He hops back and forth between Germany and England like the Lt-Col. he is. He now sports the title DDMI. Some fun! I think M.I. Section CMHQ already is planning some kind of post-war work. At least they should be good for another ten years' ... I am going down to get the MO at CMHQ to fill in my medical papers for permanent employment in the Civil Service. God knows why, as they could get a complete medical record on me from the army, if they thought to ask.'

I concluded on 18 May: 'The past few days have been positively hectic! But Pierre 'phoned through from Brussels to say he is coming back this afternoon. He wasn't, as I think I mentioned previously, coming back until Sunday. I expect there was a hitch in his plans to go to Dachau. Probably it being in the American Zone he wasn't able to proceed without permission from SHAEF. You have probably seen that the Dutch cabinet have resigned again, so perhaps that may have had some faint bearing on the problem.'

En route to Switzerland for a brief holiday I stayed a few days in Paris in the same hotel as Saul and Lois Rae. Saul made the hotel reservation for me. On the Sunday morning, to give them time to themselves, I offered to take their children out to a small park nearby. To my pleasure, I found that the park was given over that morning to stamp collectors, but my small charges, Jennifer and Bobby Rae, were bored stiff, though too small and young to protest effectively.

After returning to London from the continent I wrote Helen on 9 June:

There has been a blackout of news since my departure for the continent on 25 May. I apologize but I think you will appreciate the reasons thereof. I did write from Villars, Switzerland by ordinary post but the letters won't reach you for some considerable time. I will try and collect my story together over the weekend and make it readable. You will be amused to hear that in a circular from the Department of External Affairs the 3rd secretary competition is discussed at some length. There were 201 competitors and, your husband apparently was sixth, in order of merit. This I might say is the first indication that I have ever had that I even passed the examination.

Apparently the department still was unable to decide what to do with me and eventually, after a good deal of effort, through the good offices of Cyril Donnelly of the British Foreign Office, I was able to find a suitable house in Hampstead and to sign a lease. The rent was to be six guineas per week. The going price for similar houses was ten guineas and up. The landlord and his wife went to great lengths to be helpful.

My missive of 23 June enclosed 'a letter I have written to George Glazebrook about my trip to Switzerland. It was non-official and, therefore, I think I am within my rights in sending it on to you. At any rate you might find it of interest as it will show you the kind of things which arouse my curiosity.'

'I will be leaving Sloane Avenue Mansions on Monday, July 9,' I wrote on 2 July, 'and I will take up residence at No. 5 Constable Close. Once installed, if I ever am, I will endeavour to whip the house and surroundings into some kind of shape. I am at the moment sounding out the possibilities of finding either a permanent or part-time woman who could come in each day and clean up or, better still, a cook whom I could nail semi-permanently.'

By the middle of July, however, our plans changed completely, and my sojourn in London came to an abrupt end. In terms of moving families around, External Affairs proved to be not unlike the army, except that the army made decisions relatively quickly and implemented them efficiently. Thus, up until the very last moment in the summer of 1945, when many of the allied governments-in-exile were making plans to return to their capitals, the powers that be had made no decisions about what they wanted me to do.

On Bastille Day 1945 I wrote to Helen:

Never a dull moment in the service of the Department of External Affairs. Yesterday, I cabled you to say that I expect, weather permitting, to be at Dorval on Sunday. I am scheduled to leave Prestwick on Sunday morning and, with the six hour difference in time, I should be in Montreal Sunday night, some time after 7 p.m. If this works out I suggest we stay in Montreal Sunday evening, catching the afternoon plane to Ottawa on Monday. We can stay in the Château and, after business is done, I figure that a little leave in Knowlton [where my parents had a cottage and where the children were] would be in order.

The change in plans has not, as you can imagine, made things any simpler. I still have a house for which I have paid one month's rent and the whole affair has cost a considerable number of pounds. However, the department is agreeable to continuing my rent allowance, presumably until I recoup my losses. However, if my arrangements have been complicated I imagine yours are ten times worse. I do apologize for the extreme lack of logical commonsense which the department has displayed. However, one must expect such things in such a racket.

The actual move pleases me tremendously as I will have a good opportunity of learning something of the internal workings of the East Block and of the people in it! It is a great disadvantage to have to cater for people who are only names instead of personalities – departments instead of people. Will bring Patrick's christening present with me as well as a birthday present for Colin.

Our few problems paled by comparison with those of hundreds of Canadian servicemen and their families still scattered across the world. Many of these men had been wounded or taken prisoner and had little hope of being repatriated for a long time. I was heading home.

Part Two:
External Affairs
1945–1969

6

Robertson, Pearson, St Laurent

I could hardly have had a better vantage point from which to learn the ropes at External Affairs and to meet the small coterie of officers then working in the East Block of the Parliament Buildings in Ottawa in 1945. I formed many friendships at this time, some of which lasted a lifetime, with people such as Bill Crean, Evan Gill, George Glazebrook, Terry MacDermot, Bert Mackay, Gerry Riddell, John Teakles, and John Watkins.

While External Affairs was still actively recruiting, it was probably Felix Walter who first suggested Watkins as a likely recruit. I believe that Walter, through his many academic connections, had come to know and admire the man who was at the University of Manitoba. Hume Wrong, then an assistant under-secretary of state, contacted Watkins and eventually persuaded the reluctant candidate to take the Canadian foreign service examination. In September 1946 Watkins was offered and accepted a position as a foreign service officer (grade 4), serving initially as first secretary in the European Division. Watkins was erudite without being the least bit pompous, and he had a delightful sense of humour. He was a gifted linguist; before his posting as chargé d'affaires to Moscow (in 1948) he knew a bit of Russian, but he soon became almost fluent in the language, written and spoken. By January 1951, however, Watkins's health had deteriorated to the point that he had to be repatriated on sick leave, and he was replaced by Robert Ford.

During this period, Soviet intelligence tried unsuccessfully to entrap Watkins because of his homosexual leanings, as I found out only when I was ambassador to Germany in 1962–6. I was as surprised and shocked at the unwelcome news as any of John's friends. He showed great courage and fortitude in facing the ordeal created by the Soviet machinations. Both of the experienced RCMP investigators, Harry Brandes and Jim Bennett, reported that there was no evidence to suggest that Watkins had been a traitor. Several books have described the affair. Among the better accounts is *Moscow Despatches: Inside Cold War Russia*, edited by Dean Beeby and William Kaplan, which contains examples of Watkins's delightful prose and describes the tragedy briefly, clearly, and with compassion.

Norman Robertson arranged for several of the newcomers in 1945 and 1946 to meet the minister, William Lyon Mackenzie King. We assembled in one of the larger offices on the ground floor of the East Block, for sherry or tea – I think the latter. The under-secretary presented each of us to Mr King. Norman introduced me as 'F.N. McCrea's grandson' – his information about people was exhaustive!

What Robertson did not know, however, was that King did not like my grandfather, Liberal MP (1911–25) for Sherbrooke, Quebec, and that the feeling was mutual. In 1924 McCrea denounced the government for betraying industry and voted against the budget; he had already voted against it on the tariff, railway freight rates, the Home Bank, pensions for civil servants, and several other, lesser matters. The Montreal *Gazette* commented: 'Few will be found to question Mr. McCrea's wisdom when he declared that it was better to defeat a government than to ruin a country. When such a declaration comes from a man who has to make such a sacrifice and to take such a risk as the Sherbrooke member did to utter it, his motives are beyond question and beyond praise.' In 1925 my grandfather decided to run as an independent 'liberal-protectionist' but then withdrew, his health having deteriorated. The shabby political machinations within the Liberal party leading to his decision were unattractive. The last time I saw him was on his deathbed, in October 1926. I was eight years old then and regret very much that I did not have a chance to know him better.

A self-made man, he had remained on his father's farm in South Durham, Quebec, until he was twenty-one and then, against his father's wishes, went into the bark and lumber business. Family lore has it that father and son fought like cat and dog. Of McCrea's many interventions in the House of Commons I like best a phrase he used (8 June 1925) when opposing the government's intention to reimburse the depositors of the Home Bank, which failed because it was badly managed: 'The man who puts his money in a bank does so in order that he may receive a revenue from it without doing any work; but the man who invests his money in industrial and other enterprises very often does so for the purpose of developing the country rather than for the revenue he may take out of it.' Though he thought it scandalous that one could make money without having to work for it, he skilfully used the banking system and the legerdemain of compound interest to make money for himself!

To my relief, King showed no interest whatsoever when I was introduced to him. Obviously my fears had been exaggerated, fed by family gossip about the enmity between the two men.

The only other occasion I met King was in June 1947, when I was asked by Mike Pearson to take a statement concerning the engagement of Princess Elizabeth to Lieutenant Philip Mountbatten, RN, prepared at External Affairs, to King's office in the Parliament Buildings for his approval. Jack Pickersgill ushered me into the presence. I sat well in the background while the prime minister considered the text of what he was being asked to say in the House later that day.

King was in his shirt sleeves and suspenders, with a couple of strands of what little hair he had falling across his damp forehead. His shirt sleeeves were held by two rather ugly, well-worn, silver and copper-coloured flexible metal arm bands. He wasted no time in attacking the draft statement, using the stub of a pencil to scratch through various words. The authors of the statement evidently had included some polite words about Mountbatten. King objected, angrily crossing out the laudatory words, exclaiming, 'I don't give a darn about him.' He incorporated these changes into his statement to the House.

I believe that Bill Crean was the only member of the department with professional credentials in security matters. The only other person in Ottawa with a similar security/intelligence background was Terry Guernsey. As a member of the Security and Intelligence Directorate of the RCMP, he had received training in London from MI 5, which led eventually to establishment of the RCMP Watcher Service and a Canadian professional counter-espionage capability, which has stood us in good stead over the years.

Bill Crean and I seemed to share a sense of the ridiculous (of which there was no lack in the department at the time), a love of history and literature, and a mutual interest in security and intelligence, though he had far greater knowledge and experience. He had served with the

British army in Norway and North Africa, doing both security and intelligence work, and latterly with MI 5. I learned much from him, and we had great fun in the process. One night we took him with us to a cricket club dance in Ottawa and introduced him to a beautiful, young Scot from Edinburgh, Elizabeth Grant, whom he later wed.

In 1946, while working closely with George Glazebrook, Crean established a professional capability for dealing with hidden electronic listening devices. In the labyrinths of the basement in the East Block, Room 77, he set up a sophisticated, top-secret training facility for 'sweep teams' and for personnel being posted abroad. It contained all the latest in audio-surveillance equipment used by Soviet intelligence and other, now-hostile intelligence services (lent to us by the British and the Americans). Apart from its general educational role, Room 77 offered professional training for 'sweepers' employed to ensure that diplomatic missions abroad remained free of such devices. Bill also provided our missions with tamper-proof steel shells for the safe storage of classified documents.

At the same time he drafted the first physical and personnel security regulations. Some of the latter eventually became part of a cabinet document that laid out the criteria for the granting of security clearances in the public service. I believe that Louis St Laurent, while our minister, personally approved the precise wording of at least parts of the regulations. Crean also helped establish a professional corps of diplomatic couriers and facilitated acquisition of secure machine ciphers from the British. He did a great deal to bring Canada's foreign service into the twentieth century, though few of his colleagues were aware of this.

Crean's English accent was the object of criticism by some of his peers, and this made his job more difficult. He had taken some legal training in London prior to the war and then served in the British army. There was a certain silly chauvinism in Ottawa at that time, but it did not affect the way in which Pearson or Robertson or most of the other senior officers treated him or his job.

Indeed Robertson and Wrong, and later Pearson, gave their full support to his work. Many in the diplomatic service – some newcomers, and some ministers – simply didn't believe that such measures were necessary! This kind of thinking appears more recently to have led the department to abandon a good deal of its caution in the course of launching a computer-based communications system.

I succeeded Jean Chapdelaine as Norman Robertson's assistant in mid-1946. It seemed to be common knowledge that Pearson was to succeed Robertson, and the changeover took place on 5 September 1946. Robertson and I seemed to get along reasonably well, though I found him rather intimidating. His mind was like quicksilver, and his knowledge encyclopaedic. His sense of humour was delightful, and he could link apparently disparate matters – such as the Australian wool industry and Canadian mining activity north of the fiftieth parallel – in a breathtaking way.

Running a tidy office and keeping a clean desk were not Robertson's style. His office was almost entirely taken up with files of all shapes, sizes, and security classifications. Some had been there for weeks, even months. To search for and find any particular piece of paper was a major task, requiring patience, knowledge, and luck, which assistants Sybil Rump and Marjorie McKenzie possessed to a high degree. Without their skills and dedication, the system would not have worked at all! I think that Robertson viewed with tolerant amusement my sporadic, amateur efforts to create some sort of order out of the apparent chaos.

Wisely, as it often turned out, when he had doubts about some proposition or wished to avoid a lengthy discussion with some eager sponsor of a bright idea, he would simply put the file aside. Subsequently seemingly urgent problems often simply dissolved. Norman would return the file to the grateful author with a benevolent smile, sometimes having to do no more than initial the document in question. Seldom did he comment in writing.

The departmental filing system was almost non-existent. At the outbreak of the war a file classification system of sorts was imposed, which remained unchanged well into the 1950s. This inflexible, unprofessional framework was quite incapable of containing the explosion of documentation that occurred with the war and immediately thereafter. Moreover, individual officers created files of those matters for which they were responsible. Such documents were neither registered nor filed in a central repository, and so one could never be certain that all the relevant documentation was available or even where it might be located.

This became true especially of sensitive material, such as the papers relating to Igor Gouzenko, his defection in 1945, and its complicated aftermath. For a number of years they were kept in Robertson's office in an empty carton, which had originally contained a dozen bottles of Corby's Canadian Whiskey. When I became Robertson's personal assistant, their custodian was Marjorie McKenzie, who jealously guarded them somewhere in the office, along with numerous other cartons stuffed with papers dealing with the strange cases of Otto Strasser and his brother. In part as a measure of security, the Gouzenko affair often was referred to in open correspondence as 'the Corby case.' No doubt this baffled Soviet intelligence.

During the few months working for Robertson in 1946 I learned a lot about his approaches to various problems – information that was to stand me in good stead many years later when I again reported directly to him. I quickly learned that he knew a great deal about intelligence and security matters. I think that he found them interesting and sometimes even intellectually challenging – a relief from the usual round of bureaucratic intercourse.

Robertson had his critics, particularly concerning his perceived shortcomings as a manager. Such people, however, failed to appreciate that while his procrastinations were obvious (and deliberate), he got through an enormous quantity of detailed work each day. For every file or document he sidetracked he read and dealt with a dozen, and seldom were his decisions faulty. Jack Pickersgill was aware of the enormous pressures of Robertson's job. Indeed, fearing that they were harming his health and might even kill him, he spoke to Mackenzie King to get him to agree to move Robertson out of Ottawa.

When Robertson left to become high commissioner in London in the autumn of 1946 and Pearson succeeded him as deputy minister, I was delighted to be asked to continue in my job. I found Pearson a very different sort of person to work for. I think that both men had a similar basic philosophy and that this was one of the subtle aspects of the relationship which enabled them to get along so well for so many years. Pearson was no less complicated than Robertson, and in many ways it was more difficult to work for him. He knew exactly what he wanted, and he knew how to get it. I found some of his judgments about people surprisingly harsh, not lacking in compassion but sometimes based on impatience rather than conviction. Pearson wrote most of his own speeches in a long, flowing, rounded hand. Unlike Robertson, he was superb in handling his relations with journalists. He obviously enjoyed these contacts and being able to 'manage' them to his own purposes.

Probaby by this time King had indicated to Pearson that he hoped he would become a member of the Liberal party and perhaps eventually prime minister. King planned various steps to further this idea. For example, several months after he became deputy minister Pearson spoke to a joint assembly of members of the Senate and the House of Commons in the Railway Committee Room about Canada's emerging role in foreign affairs. Pearson did some preparation, but not as much as he often did. When we turned up, the committee room was filled to capacity. Pearson, who had given no sign of uneasiness, was nervous as a cat. His hands, which he held tightly beneath the table, were shaking uncontrollably. The moment he got to his feet to speak, however, he was in control. He had the complete attention of his audience. The speech was a *tour de force* and, I think, marked the launching of his political career.

Louis St Laurent moved to External Affairs as minister on 4 September 1946, the day before Pearson became deputy minister. As Pearson's personal assistant, I acted as a kind of liaison with St Laurent's office. Each day Parliament was sitting I would get material to the new minister in time for him to use it in the House of Commons – usually before 3 p.m. I would trot over to St Laurent's office with a bundle of papers, most signed or initialled by Pearson.

St Laurent's training as a corporation lawyer and his intellect made him an extraordinarily, quick learner. Often I would find him perched on the arm of one of the large, black leather chairs in his room, having a sandwich and a glass of milk. He would accept the papers and go through them methodically and very quickly. At first I didn't see how it was possible for anyone to read so quickly and to absorb the very detailed information many of the documents contained. He would get up in the House a few minutes later and speak without so much as glancing at his briefing notes. He also was a most kind and considerate boss – something about which some of his successors as minister could have learned!

Occasionally, St Laurent would ask me what I thought about some of the material I took to him. Most of the time I would have to say that I knew little or nothing about it and hesitated to express an opinion. He never once expressed irritation or made me feel guilty for my ignorance. The range of subject-matter was great, much of it well beyond my competence.

My work for him in this way was one of the most rewarding periods of my career. He was a great man, one of nature's gentlemen. It was only later that I realized how fortunate Canadians were in having the St Laurent–Pearson team. The two men shared a broad, humane view of Canada's place in the world and of the role it should play. They complemented each other in quite extraordinary ways. The relationship was based on mutual respect and understanding rather than rivalry and mistrust. However, by the time St Laurent made his prime ministerial world tour in the mid-1950s it had become obvious that his physical and mental powers had deteriorated markedly. I was working at the Canadian embassy in Bonn when he visited Germany, and the contrast with the considerably older Konrad Adenauer was sadly obvious.

Early in 1947 Mike Pearson and his wife, Maryon, tried to assist and enliven the lot of the junior members of the rapidly expanding Department of External Affairs and, more particularly, of their spouses. At the suggestion of Maryon Pearson, Joyce Wrong, and Yetty Robertson, and under their direction, a number of younger wives prepared a 'Foreign Service Wives' Manual.' Helen and I recently found a copy. Apart from its intrinsic historical value, it illustrates the enormous differences between today's diplomatic culture and that which existed nearly fifty years ago. It also indicates the radical changes in Canadian mores since then.

Under the heading 'Obligations upon Posting,' the manual stated: 'Upon receiving notification of posting, an officer should immediately telephone an officer of equivalent rank (unless he personally knows one of senior rank) of the mission of the country to which he is going for the purpose of expressing his delight and good fortune and asking if he might call. He might, at the same time, state that, should the Ambassador happen to be free at the time of his call at the embassy, he would be most honoured to present his respects. Such telephone call and personal visit is frequently productive of an invitation from the embassy to some entertainment function.'

The 'Wives Manual' contains housekeeping advice and is vaguely reminiscent of Lawrence Durrell's *Esprit de Corps: Sketches from Diplomatic Life.* Some of the advice about diplomatic etiquette and protocol was not always welcomed by the younger officers and their wives, but it was helpful and it was acted on. But some strictures were bizarre. For example, 'In many of our smaller missions you may find that from time to time you ride in your Head of Mission's car with him. The ranking person sits on the right hand seat, the next in rank on the left side. A third person in the middle and the fourth person on a small seat if there is one behind the driver or beside him if there is not.' What happened if there was a fifth person? The trunk, I imagine.

Not long after I started working for him, Mike Pearson asked me to take on a peculiar task. Apparently, Lionel Chevrier, as minister of transport, had asked him if External Affairs could use its influence to assist his department in recovering from the United States hundreds (it may even have been thousands) of Canadian-owned railway box cars.

Knowing little or nothing about how long rolling stock could be kept and used before being returned to the country of origin, I soon found myself dealing on the telephone with some hard-bitten colonel in the U.S. Army Corps of Engineers in some place like Des Moines, Iowa. I don't think that we had any leverage whatsoever. However, in due course, our box cars began returning, easing some of the pressure on Canada's railways.

After the crisis passed, when I was reporting to Chevrier on some related matter, he asked me if I had ever contemplated entering politics. If I had such ambitions, he said, he would be glad to help me realize them. It was clear that he had in mind my standing as a Liberal candidate in some riding. I replied that I had entertained political ambitions (as is clear from some of my wartime letters to Helen), but I no longer was attracted to the idea. I did not tell him that I had been disgusted by some of the political manoeuvring I had witnessed and felt that life as a public servant suited me better. This was not the last such approach I was to have. It gave me cause, however, to reflect on the delicate relationship between public servants and politicians, something about which I became acutely aware years later, especially during the hearings of the Keable and McDonald commissions in the late 1970s and early 1980s.

Perhaps in early 1946 I was invited for the first time to one of the annual Parliamentary Press Club dinners, probably at Mike Pearson's instigation. Through my work for Pearson I had come to know quite a few members of the press gallery, and I enjoyed myself tremendously. When the dinner was over, Brooke Claxton, a long-time friend of my father, kindly offered me a lift home. I welcomed the offer. We lived in a small apartment at 7 Echo Drive, overlooking the Rideau Canal, and there was no bus service. It was only when I got into Claxton's car (some kind of Ford or Chevrolet roadster) and we waltzed across Laurier Avenue bridge, that I realized that he was drunk. The roads were very icy. It was a hair-raising drive. Mercifully, at that hour there was almost no traffic, and there were no police in sight. I was relieved when he deposited me before our front door!

About the same time Pearson mentioned to me that Arnold Heeney, then secretary to the cabinet, was looking for someone to replace George Ignatieff as secretary to the Advisory Panel on Atomic Energy, of which C.D. Howe was titular chairman. Pearson said that he had suggested my name to Heeney. I was of course pleased and fascinated. Among other things, it gave me an opportunity to work closely with Heeney, which turned out to be a revelation and a pleasure. His brother-in-law, Arthur Yuile, and I had been at the same school in Montreal. Heeney was very patient and helpful and taught me a great deal. It also gave me an unusual, early opportunity to learn something about atomic energy, about Canada's part in the development of the first atomic weapon, and about the Canadian role in the Combined Policy Committee (CPC) and the activities of the Combined Development Trust, in which C.D. Howe was involved. These bodies were concerned, among other things, with the provision of uranium ore.

A 'top secret' memorandum from Heeney to Pearson, dated 31 January 1946 and released under the Access to Information Act, 1989, concerned cabinet consideration of a draft agreement with the Americans and the British on peaceful uses of atomic energy. Heeney wrote, 'This represents a step forward but I am rather concerned, nevertheless, for, apart from Mr. Howe, none of the Ministers (including the P.M.) has any clear understanding of what is involved. Certainly, before the documents are approved for signature there will have to be further discussion in Cabinet. Meantime you at least have confirmation that the government are satisfied to have the drafts go forward to the CPC.'

I believe that a subcommittee of the CPC was set up as a result of meetings between Churchill, Roosevelt and King in Quebec City in 1943. It met only rarely, at places such as Los Alamos, New Mexico; Oak Ridge, Tennessee; and Stanford University (Palo Alto, California). I recall that James Chadwick, a British physicist who received the Nobel Prize in 1935 for his discovery of the neutron, represented Canada at some of these meetings. He had worked at the Cavendish Laboratory in Cambridge under the Nobel laureate Ernest Rutherford, who had taught at McGill University, which Canadian connections I assume account for the ZEEP atomic reactor's being built at Chalk River, Ontario – the first such plant to be put up outside the United States.

Also among the papers released to me is a 'top secret' memorandum entitled 'Atomic Warfare' initialled by Pearson and dated 8 November 1945. Clearly Pearson was the author. It is his style of drafting – clear, unequivocal, and persuasive:

Before any sound policy, national or international, can be laid down in respect of the development, manufacture and use of atomic energy for warlike purposes, the following assumptions must be confirmed:

1) That the atomic bomb is not merely a new weapon in a long succession of weapons, since man first began to fight with clubs, but something revolutionary and unprecedented; a new departure in destruction and annihilation in effect.

2) That the atomic bomb dropped on Japan, if development is not controlled, is only the beginning, not the end, of the use of atomic energy for destruction; that even more devastating bombs are being or could be developed which will be to the present bomb as a machine gun is to a breech-loader.

3) That the secret of the atomic bomb cannot be kept and that within, say, five years a country like the U.S.S.R., will know all about it.

4) That the manufacture of the bomb is possible in any industrial state which knows the secret.

5) That projection of rockets with accuracy over great distances is now or shortly will be possible.

Pearson's appreciation was extraordinarily prescient. We now know that the Soviet Union, through its aggressive espionage activities and atomic research, already had the 'secret' of manufacturing an atomic bomb and then began building its own device.

As we now know, by early 1945 the Soviet NKVD had two valuable secret agents – Allan Nunn May and Bruno Pontecorvo – within the Anglo-Canadian nuclear research team headed by Professor John Cockcroft, director of the Atomic Energy Division of the National Research Council in Montreal. Nunn May was a British scientist who began to work on the plans aimed at the production of an atomic bomb (code-named 'Tube Alloys Project') in 1942 and soon afterwards contacted the GRU (the intelligence directorate of the Soviet General Staff). Nunn May joined Cockcroft's research group in Montreal in January 1943 and not long afterwards handed to Pavel Angelov of the GRU residency in Ottawa two samples of enriched uranium (U-235). Angelov's boss, Colonel Nikolai Zabotin, the legal GRU resident in Ottawa, considered the material so important that he instructed his deputy to take it immediately by hand to Moscow.

Bruno Pontecorvo was a brilliant Italian émigré physicist. He worked in Montreal as a nuclear scientist and a Soviet secret agent until he was transferred to the British atomic research establishment at Hartwell early in 1949. Soviet intelligence officers acquainted with the espionage cases later said that they rated Pontecorvo's work almost as highly as that of Klaus Fuchs, another Soviet secret agent who also joined the Tube Alloys Project in December 1943.

In his 'Atomic Warfare' paper Pearson went on:

It is assumed that the above statements are substantially true. If this assumption is correct, then no government has the right to give its people a feeling of security, which can only be false, by basing its policy on the opposite assumption, that a national or three-country monopoly of development and production is possible. Even if, for some years at least, such a monopoly were possible, its value to enforce peace would not be great because other countries would know perfectly well that Anglo-Saxon public opinion would not permit the preventative use of such a terrible weapon ... It follows, therefore, that any constructive solution of this problem of the war use of atomic energy, must be international – not national. There is, in fact, no national solution ... It has to be said that the discovery of atomic weapons is the most revolutionary event in human history since Noah launched the Ark. In sober fact, its significance for the future can hardly be exaggerated. It presents us with the greatest threat to man's existence ever conceived, and, paradoxically, the greatest opportunity to realize world peace ... The atomic bomb, finally, may force the United Nations to become an effective association for peace. This, however, can only happen if the problem it has posed is approached and solved internationally. No other solution is, in fact, possible, and the effort to find one will be fruitless – and worse.

Also among the documents released to me was my 'top secret' letter, dated 6 November 1946, to George Ignatieff at the Canadian delegation to the UN Atomic Energy Commission, Hotel Biltmore, New York. It is a lengthy document concerning a visit I had made to Chalk River:

I would first of all like to impress upon you how important I feel it is for everyone dealing with atomic energy problems to have an opportunity of visiting such a plant. Lacking such knowledge, I have found it difficult, and you no doubt have experienced the same problems [in dealing with such matters] which are now before the [UN] Atomic Energy Commission, without actually having seen a plant. My views, for instance, concerning controls have been considerably modified in the light of what I saw at Chalk River. Having seen something of the extreme difficulties of control attendant upon the production of plutonium in all its intricate phases, I am in some doubt that international control through inspection is in fact a practical proposition. As you are aware, my understanding of the technical processes is extremely limited, nevertheless I saw enough to realize that control by inspection is a far more complex problem than one would be led to believe from following the discussions in the [UN] Atomic Energy Commission. It is clear to me now that it would require a good number of experienced inspectors even in a plant such as that at Chalk River.

It seems to me that a more practical approach to the problem of control has been made to us by the United States delegation in proposing that all matters pertaining to atomic energy production should be under the aegis of an international authority. I am more inclined now to think that the present discussions at the U.N. in New York are academic in nature and that controls to be really effective must go beyond *national* inspection. I do not see how controls can possibly succeed unless there is some form of international authority, responsible for the design and construction of plants, and the production and mining of fissionable material ...

I was told, however, by Sir George Thompson that atomic energy plants could be constructed in such a way that the possibility of effective inspection would be well nigh impossible.

... I left Ottawa yesterday morning in company with Roger Makins of the United Kingdom Embassy in Washington, as neither Mike nor Arnold were able to go with him. We travelled by car and arrived at Chalk River about 12.15, in time to join Dr. Lewis, Sir George Thomson, Dr. Mann and Dr. Lawrence for lunch. Immediately afterwards we visited the new [atomic] pile which is still in the process of construction. For the sake of convenience our party split in two – Sir George being conducted around by Dr. Lewis (U.K.), who is Director at Chalk River, and Roger Makins and myself were ably conducted by Dr. Lawrence and a Mr. Wiggins, who is an expert on the engineering side.'

My powers of description are insufficient to give you an idea of the magnitude and the complexity of the undertaking at Chalk River. I think it is safe to say that the construction of the plant alone represents a major engineering feat ... The underside of the pile is a vast complex of wires, controls and safety devices. It is here that the cooling system, which plays such an important part in the operation, is controlled ... Some of the additional problems in connection with control of the plant arise out of the peculiar nature of the operation ... It is necessary, for instance, to keep the building which houses the pile, completely free of all dust and impurities in the air. Consequently the entire building has to be vacuumed and all the air coming into the building has to be purified. An accurate measure of the radiations being given off by the pile has to be constantly maintained to safeguard the health of the workers in the plant. For instance, there are gamma ray and neutron counters inside the building which indicate the intensity of the radiations being emitted by the pile, and which sound an alarm if the intensity of the radiations becomes high enough to endanger human life ...

In discussions which took place between Dr. Lewis, Sir George Thomson and some of the other scientists present, I gained the impression that 'cheating' would be a fairly easy operation. That is, it would be quite possible to falsify the mechanical records, which are the only means they possess at present of estimating the output of the plant. I gather that there are many stages in the production at which 'cheating' could be successfully accomplished over a period. Dr. Lewis claims that it would be a simple operation to change some connection, or to falsify the output of the automatic recording machines. He also stated incidentally that it would be child's play to commit serious sabotage at a plant such as the one at Chalk River ... There was, I believe, a suggestion put forward by General McNaughton that some members of the commission [UN Atomic Energy Commission, including the Soviet Union] might visit the Chalk River enterprise in order to acquaint themselves with the workings of a plant. While this would be something which would have to have the approval of the cabinet, I am uncertain of the wisdom of such a proposal from the point of view of security. It seems to me that any scientist proceeding to Chalk River could gain a great deal of valuable information concerning dimensions of the pile, the techniques involved and the general layout of the plant. [Omond] Solandt, with whom I have discussed this point feels, however, there would be little of real value which a group of visitors could carry away. He even went so far as to suggest that the construction of the Chalk River plant might prove misleading. I am not, of course, qualified to dispute his contention, but I think we should carefully consider the matter before committing ourselves, bearing in mind that it would probably have to be a subject for cabinet consideration.

My concerns about the security of the plant now seem rather silly, since, the Russians already had obtained a great deal of information concerning the techniques of producing fissionable material through espionage and from their own independent atomic research.

One of my duties as Pearson's personal assistant was to receive communications intelligence material which it was thought he should see. Pearson was very knowledgeable about our communications intelligence-gathering activities. For example, during the war External Affairs had been sending intercepted Vichy–Ottawa traffic to the War Office in London for deciphering. In returning some of these decrypted messages to Ottawa, Pearson, then first secretary in London, quoted a War Office official: 'We are wondering whether your people in Ottawa have any idea of setting up a cryptographic bureau of their own; if so we think we could be of considerable help to you.' Pearson commented: 'It looks as if the War Office are having some reluctance to continue to decode these telegrams.'

There were very strict security procedures for the handling of all such material and special security – SA (Special Access) – clearances to internationally agreed standards required for all those so indoctrinated. The material was carried by hand, and the recipient had to sign for it and ensure that it was returned by hand to the distributing authority – in External Affairs, Defence Liaison Division (2). I would arrange for the intercepts to be seen by Pearson, who dealt with them promptly. Usually they were returned the same day. I do not know how valuable he found this type of information. Clearly, its value depended on the subject-matter and timeliness. (By mid-1946 Soviet intelligence was receiving identical material through its networks in Britain – the 'Cambridge Five.')

My job with Pearson came to an end when I was posted to the Canadian Permanent Delegation to the UN in New York, following Canada's election to the Security Council in 1947 and General A.G.L. McNaughton's appointment as the head of delegation. Initially I served with the Canadian Delegation to the UN Atomic Energy Commission. I had liked working for Pearson and had learned a great deal, but it was clear to me that to continue would involve a greater personal political commitment than I was willing to assume.

7

New York and Frisco, Bonn and Paris

It proved to be an exciting time serving on the fledgling Canadian delegation to the United Nations. George Ignatieff was the senior adviser, doing an extraordinarily good job keeping McNaughton happy and out of trouble – a time-consuming task since the general did not always agree with the instructions he received continuously from Ottawa. There were relatively junior advisers from External Affairs, including Harry Carter, Sidney Friefeld, and George Grande, and me, and special advisers Harry Lewis (from National Defence) and Jack Babbitt (from the National Research Council). External Affairs provided administrative support. Fortunately, from time to time the delegation was strengthened by the temporary assignment of officers sent from Ottawa for specific purposes, such as Gerry Riddell and John Holmes.

I had had my only previous, very brief contact with McNaughton in 1942 as a very junior military intelligence liaison officer. This was during a military training exercise in southern England called 'Spartan,' intended to test the capabilities of various British and Canadian military formations, especially at the command level. My simple task was to gather information from more junior commands and to convey it by hand to army headquarters, where it was transferred from my small map to a huge map. I was only one of several such liaison officers. It was believed that transmitting information in this way enabled the military formations concerned to maintain radio silence. For the purpose, liaison officers were provided with motorbicycles. Mine was a small, nifty BSA rather than the large, powerful, and unwieldy Harley-Davidson which the Canadian army favoured but which, in my brief experience, was difficult to handle on the narrow English roads, especially in the blackout.

I found myself an embarrassed bystander to a sharp disagreement between McNaughton and Brigadier Simmonds, then the Brigadier General Staff at Canadian Army Headquarters, concerning the disposition of certain Canadian formations. I believe that some relatively large formation was 'lost' for several hours, and the two officers seemed to be trying to ascribe blame. While knowing nothing about the dispute I remember feeling sorry for McNaughton, who seemed to be getting the worst of the argument. Simmonds struck me as being a very smart cookie.

A few years later I came to know and to admire the general. He was a quick learner and good negotiator, though it sometimes took a good deal of persuasion to get him to change his mind once it was made up (something at which Ignatieff became very expert). McNaughton was always very considerate of his staff and appreciative of anything members did for him. His wife treated all of us as kindly and warmly as if we were her children.

Not long after McNaughton's term as president of the Security Council had ended, he was present for a meeting of the council during an interminable discussion of the Palestine question. At some point he appeared to experience difficulty in making his fountain pen work. In no time, he had cleared a space before him at the semi-circular council table and methodically began to dismantle the pen, using a set of small tools that he always carried in his vestcoat pocket – screwdrivers, pliers, and so on. Gradually, as the repairs progressed, the attention of the audience in the visitor's gallery became focused on McNaughton instead of the Palestine question. He was quite oblivious to this. Thus, when the pen was repaired and he was able to write with it again, he was quite unconscious of the audible sigh of satisfaction that went up from the crowded gallery of onlookers.

It was no wonder that we all liked him. He was completely without side or affectation of any kind.

Some time after we were moved to the Canadian Permanent Delegation to the United Nations in New York, the UN decided to hold the next General Assembly meeting in Paris. This meant that the Canadian office in New York would have little or nothing to do for several weeks. Those advisers on the delegation in New York who were not needed in Paris were to be usefully employed elsewhere for the period. Since I was not assigned to Paris, I was instructed in 1948 to return to Ottawa to assist with the production of that year's report on the activities of the UN and Canada's part in them. Helen and the children would remain in New York and I would be in Ottawa – a further separation that neither of us welcomed.

My irritation with the arrangement shows through in my letter to Helen. Probably in late November 1948, on Château Laurier note paper, I wrote:

From what I have seen and heard the department is in a state of chaos but out of it will come a good organization. It was a great thrill to see in operation at last all the things I recommended, the Personnel Planning Board is an institution – the new records system for personnel records is set up – my 'cards' are functioning, the file covers I designed are being used, a centralized records establishment is now going – a beginning has been made on the new cypher equipment to make London the nodal point for European communications.

My main job is to be one of production and editing. This morning I am going over to the East Block to write an atomic energy critique on a suggestion by NAR – a crazy one. Yesterday saw Mike [Pearson], Hume Wright, Terry [MacDermot], George [Ignatieff], Don Matthews and Jim George.

Two days later I wrote: 'After dinner, at nine p.m. I taxied to Mike's house [Pearson] and helped Alison Ignatieff with Michael, getting them on the train to Toronto. George left after dinner this evening to go to Chalk River. It was the least I could do.' In a few days I told Helen: 'Left the East Block with Archie Day to hoist a quick one. We found the town was dry. Civic elections! So we had dinner together in the Belle Clair.' Day was a brilliant, mercurial character with great charm and wit, who used his erudition like a rapier. Unfortunately, he had a very low tolerance for alcohol. Pearson recognized Day's unusual literary talents and often turned to him for assistance.

When I had been working in External Affairs for the first time, George Glazebrook was briefly my boss in Political Division 1. A cultivated, erudite, tough-minded academic historian, he had an obvious interest in intelligence and security matters not unlike Norman Robertson's – they both found the unexpected complexities an irresistible intellectual challenge. One of Glazebrook's favourite writers was Dashiell Hammett, creator of the hard-boiled New York private-eye Sam Spade. He could quote the dialogue with ease and with almost a Brooklyn accent. Unfortunately, he was not universally admired, particularly by some of the military in intelligence and security work. He did not have a high opinion of their intellectual and literary abilities and sometimes made this obvious, which made for uneasy relations between External Affairs and National Defence.

George Ignatieff and I sometimes disagreed. He was not good at delegating responsibilities, and this led to occasional clashes. We differed over how the 1948 report on the UN should be prepared. In a letter about this time I wrote, 'The biggest joke of all is that, after all the urgency attached to the production of the report, it is discovered that the King's Printer, after promising to return typescript material in galley-proof form 72 hours after receiving it, is not able to do it in under two weeks! The department never learns. The stupidity of it all.'

Ignatieff was amusing, urbane, intelligent, and companionable. Moreover, he was a good cook.

One day I wrote Helen:

Today has been a foggy, foggy dew and still is. Had lunch with Bill [Crean], Terry [MacDermot], and George [Ignatieff]. Amusing, but nothing amuses me greatly these days, least of all this so-called department of government.

I enclose a copy of a memo which I handed to Terry following a talk I had with him this morning. I didn't express myself as violently as I did in my letter to you last night, but I made my case plain. I really dislike the job I have been asked to do. The thing which gets my goat is the constant changing of ideas and the difficulties of getting the stuff to suit everybody's tastes. I don't know what the trouble is, but I can't come to grips with the job and I'm damned if it is really consuming all my energies. It seems to consume my time, but it doesn't appear to be really taxing my energy. You know what I mean. A day in Mike's office or a day in Personnel Division took more real work than a week at this job. In short I don't like the preparation of 'Canada and the UN, 1948.'

Another day I recounted:

Had an interesting evening with Bill Crean and got to bed about 11.30. There are big things doing in the department. For your own ear and nobody else's, Norman is going to be High Commissioner in London, Hume [Wrong] is to go to Washington [as ambassador] and Mike is to become the Under Secretary [minister]. This within the next month or so! [Victor] Odlum has been offered South Africa in the hope that he can be forgotten in Pretoria and there are a number of other changes of a major character contemplated.

I spoke to Jack Pickersgill this morning and he thinks I should have been sent down to Chile a month ago! He agrees there is a possibility that I may not go now. I personally feel there is a very good chance that we will go. Jack was also doubtful about Mike becoming undersec. [minister]. As he said, one good speech by Mike and the P.M. will begin to suffer pangs of jealousy. As Jack says, however, he [Pearson] can do a lot in the first month or so of office and, with a new Secty of State for External Affairs, it might be as near perfection as we will ever get.

In a further note I continued: 'There have been suggestions of an oblique character that you and I might remain in N.Y. after 1 Jan 1950 – presumably to run the permanent delegation, which would suit me perfectly. I am satisfied that this is not the time to return to Ottawa and I hope that I am not moved back. Terry [MacDermot], by the way, has been asked if he would like to move to N.Y. as Consul-General! He is thinking it over and my guess is that he will take it, probably within the next 12 months. I think Arnold Heeney will be the next under-secretary (no inside dope, just intuition.)' A few days later: 'I'm guessing that Arnold Heeney is to be the under-secretary – a good thing.'

One undated letter reads: 'The general [McNaughton] showed up in Ottawa today – He is a dear. The first thing he said was, "where is your wife and family?" I said, "New York." He said "how long?" I said, "two months." He said, "Bloody awful." I said "Yes." He is a thoughtful old codger at times.' The same letter refers to the 'Three Crowns letter.' Tommy Stone appeared in New York, probably in November 1949, on the weekend I was permitted to return briefly to New York. He insisted on taking us with him for 'a drink' with Sir William Stephenson ('Intrepid') at his apartment in Manhattan, not far from Rockefeller Center, where the delegation had its offices.

The apartment was large and attractively decorated; the living-room was two storeys high. Stephenson and his wife, Mary French Simmons of Tennessee, were delightful hosts. Under Stone's skilful guidance, the conversation proved lively, indiscreet, and fascinating, made the more so by lethal dry martinis served in large brandy snifters. When the three of us took our leave we were still able to walk, but barely. We soon found a Scandinavian restaurant called the Three Crowns, where we had an excellent smorgasbord and began to sober up. I have no recollection of how we got home.

While the UN General Assembly was still meeting in Europe, I was sent from Ottawa for about ten days as part of the Canadian delegation to

the 31st Session of the International Labour Organization (ILO), held
in San Francisco from 17 June to 10 July 1948. The very beautiful countryside around San Francisco, the excellent weather, the atmosphere of
the city, the people, the buildings, and the restaurants were a revelation. The Canadian delegates were congenial and competent. I already
knew and liked the secretary of the delegation, John Mainwaring. I
have a particularly fond memory of Paul Goulet, the most senior
Department of Labour official. In an espionage novel entitled *Latonya*
(1994) I tried to capture some of my impressions of the city.

   We stayed at the Palace Hotel.

I should have made more time to write to you. My only excuse is the city. It's a
wonderful place ... I wish you were here to share it with me. Nob Hill at sun-
down, the view from the Top of the Mark [a bar atop the Mark Hopkins Hotel],
which is sheer heaven. Never have I drunk with such a feeling of grandeur. For
65 cents you get not a single but a double, the view providing the other ounce-
and-one-half ... For my money this part of the world has it.

   ... Paul Goulet came in and I have just finished coding a telegram which I
drafted. The time is 12.30, Saturday. The Governing Body met in the afternoon.
Paul Goulet asked me to take the chair for the government [*sic*], which I did. I'll
admit I got a great kick out of it and spoke twice. It's not like the UN. There are
no microphones. You get up on your hind legs and address the assembled mul-
titude in stentorian tones. I hate to repeat the old refrain but I think I really was
the youngest representative by ten years. I don't mind admitting I was as nervous as hell but I wouldn't have missed the chance for anything in the world!
Paul tells me that if he goes back to Ottawa (which he may have to do later on)
the Department of Labour and External want me to head the delegation which,
considering I know damn all about the ILO, pleases me no end ... I've been to a
rodeo, eaten barbequed steak, got a hell of a sunburn and I'm going to turn in
... Jesú, but this boy has had his fill today.

   In a follow-up letter I wrote: 'I can't recall a week which has been so
crowded. The work has now reached a furious tempo, with committees
and plenary sessions and group meetings all going ahead at the same
time, much in the manner of Mr. Barnum & Mr. Bailey's shows. One of
my preoccupations has been the completion of a report on the work of
the Governing Body which I have finished – usually the report is submitted two or three months after the meetings but to hell with that!'

   The Governing Body was to select a secretary-general of the ILO. The
principal candidates were British and American. The British candidate,

a knight with a Welsh name, told us that it was our duty, as members of the 'British Commonwealth,' and in Canada's interest, to support him. His ham-fisted, patronizing demeanour merely irritated us, and we supported the American, who won. Our instructions allowed us to act as we thought would serve Canada's best interests. The British were furious but had only themselves to blame.

From New York I was sent back to Ottawa in 1950, to head up a newly created Establishments and Organization Division, dealing with the unglamorous but practical problems of maintaining a far-flung foreign service. It dealt with salaries, allowances, conditions of work, departmental regulations, and the like. The division was given responsibility for pulling together all the increasingly numerous rules and regulations, including those touching on security.

My immediate boss was Herb Moran. He was tough-minded and efficient, sometimes holding strong opinions but invariably fair, provided that you didn't make too many mistakes. I learned a lot from working closely with Moran. Arnold Heeney was the deputy minister, and a very good one. He and Mike Pearson worked well together. Having been secretary to the cabinet for a number of years, Heeney knew all the ministers involved and, equally important, how the system worked and why it didn't work. From my standpoint the best feature of the job was to have Marcel Cadieux as a fellow head of division with whom I did a good deal of business. Cadieux then headed the Personnel Division, running a tight, efficient operation.

During this time I persuaded Pearson (with Moran's agreement) to assist us in getting Treasury Board officials to agree to provide financial help for members of the foreign service and their families in parts of the world where living conditions were difficult. We were trying to obtain financial assistance to enable staff members with infant children to purchase pasteurization equipment for use in countries where the milk was considered a health hazard.

Pearson had not been enthusiastic about appearing before his cabinet colleagues on the Treasury Board to argue the case, and his reluctance soon proved justified. One of the members was Jimmy Gardiner, minister of agriculture, who proceeded to pour scorn on our idea, saying that when he had been brought up in western Canada they had pasteurized their milk on the kitchen stove. Why was some fancy equipment required by these lily-livered diplomats, and so on? Pearson lost the argument and was angry at me for having put him in that position. Some time later, when Gardiner had left the board, we returned and got agreement for such expenses to be met by the department.

At the end of my three-year stint on the adminstrative side of the department's work, Herb Moran asked if I would like to go to Bonn to replace Jean Chapdelaine as number two at the embassy. I was pleased with the idea, since it meant more responsibility and an opportunity to use what little German I still had and my pre-war knowledge of the country.

When we arrived in Bonn in the summer of 1953 the Federal Republic of Germany (West Germany) was being run by the Allied High Commission – in effect the British, the Americans, and the French, each with their own zone of responsibility. Berlin was under quadripartite control, with East Germany being the Soviet zone. Thus Canada's representatives in Bonn were accredited to the Allied High Commisssion, and most of our dealings were with the British. For example, our extremely comfortable house on Im Etzental Strasse had been built with occupation funds for the use of the British. Through a deal which the Canadian ambassador, Tommy Davis, made with Sir Ivone Kirkpatrick, the British high commissioner, the Canadians rented the house on very reasonable terms. Such accommodation was at a premium. The house placed us in the middle of a British *Siedlung* (settlement). We were surrounded by 'Brits,' most of them senior members of the British high commission, and formed friendships in this way, many of which have lasted over the years.

The three occupying nations had extraordinary 'reserve powers.' For example, in security and intelligence they retained control over a wide variety of such activities, including clandestine interception of telephone and other communications. Thus in these matters we often dealt directly with the British, many of them our neighbours. The contacts I made in the British security and intelligence community later proved invaluable.

Tommy Davis's bluff, undiplomatic manner, loud voice, and a certain earthiness were deceptive. He was by no means as gauche or naïve as he sometimes appeared. A political appointee with strong Liberal affiliations, he was intelligent, shrewd, and successful as an ambassador. After Davis's term ended, he was replaced by Charles Ritchie, who has written in his inimitable style about the period in *Diplomatic Passport* (1981). By the time Ritchie took over, we had a first-rate team of administrative staff and officers, some of whom became heads of mission. It was a happy embassy and produced its share of useful, relevant reporting. Ritchie was a delightful boss – never a dull moment. Thanks to Bill Crean, Bonn, along with Brussels, London, New York, Paris, and Rome, had modern, secure cipher machines and specially trained communications staff to run them. The mission's products were quickly and securely communicated, as were Ottawa's instructions to us. Invaluable, for example, during the lengthy negotiations concerning the presence in the Federal Republic of Canadian armed forces and their families.

In the spring of 1956 Charles Ritchie received a telegram from Jules Léger, deputy minister at External Affairs, proposing that I be posted to the NATO international staff as deputy-executive secretary to the North Atlantic Council, replacing an American, Luke Battle. A few years later, when I was Canadian ambassador in Egypt, Battle was the U.S. ambassador there. Unfortunately, his term in Egypt was ending as we arrived. Several years later he became an administrator of the imaginative Rockefeller-sponsored restoration of Williamsburg, the old royal capital of Virginia.

In the NATO secretariat I was a general dog's-body to The Lord Coleridge (he insisted on being addressed as *The* Lord Coleridge), secretary to the council. Richard Coleridge, a former Royal Navy captain, didn't suffer fools gladly and made no attempt to disguise his distrust of anyone who wasn't English. He ran a tight ship and managed to bring order out of even the most confused council discussions, which they often became, especially when they involved senior ministers. His considerable skills in drafting documents perhaps owed something to his forebear, the poet Samuel Taylor Coleridge.

Coleridge had previously known and worked for NATO's secretary-general, Lord Ismay ('Pug'). They were on a first-name basis, working well together, with Coleridge given free rein to arrange the council's agendas, to keep well-written, accurate and clear minutes, and to give effect promptly to decisions taken. His language often appeared to have its origins on the quarterdeck of an eighteenth-century British naval vessel, but most of the non-Englishmen who worked for him liked him and cooperated fully. They did not seem to mind being called 'wops,' 'frogs,' and 'bloody Turks.' Some of his methods may have been crude, but he got results.

Some member countries on the council quite shamelessly used their nationals to pursue national interests. This unfortunate habit weakened the secretariat as an instrument for pursuing policies that reflected the collective views of its members. It also made day-to-day business tiresome and at times tricky, especially when NATO members disagreed.

In due course, Ismay was replaced as secretary-general by Paul-Henri Spaak, the Belgian statesman. Richard Coleridge's command of French was reasonably good, but those of us who knew him well wondered how he would fit in with Spaak, who was quite unlike Ismay in background, temperament, training, and outlook. To our surprise Coleridge hit it off with Spaak and the organization continued to run smoothly. Credit for this must be given to both men!

Coleridge had built up a very efficient staff. The administrative underpinnings were sound, owing much to his genius for putting in place a 'no-frills' administrative infrastructure, capable of being quickly adjusted to take account of unforeseen events such as the interminable rows between the Turks and the Greeks over Cyprus. He was also responsible for ensuring that adequate security measures were in place and constantly observed in order to protect NATO's many secrets – a vain attempt, as we now know. Unknown to NATO's authorities, the Russians had penetrated many of its most closely guarded secrets. We now know that by 1958 the KGB (successor to the NKVD) had achieved several such successes through Kim Philby et al. and through espionage operations designed for use against the French.

We managed to find an apartment in the 16th arrondissement on rue de Boulainvilliers, off the Place de la Muette. I could easily walk to NATO's headquarters in the Palais de Chaillot, and the neighbourhood was fascinating, filled with delightful bars, bistros, elegant shops, and excellent restaurants and open-air markets. An added pleasure was the Bois de Boulogne, only a short drive away.

All good things come to an end, however, and about the middle of 1958 I was instructed to return to Ottawa to head Defence Liaison Division (2) at External Affairs, in succession to Bill Crean. Before I could be released by the NATO secretariat, however, Crean was posted to one of our missions in Europe. In the interim, Hamilton Southam headed the division.

8

A Rotten, Stinking, Depressing Job

Though I had acquired quite a bit of background in intelligence and security affairs, heading Defence Liaison Division (2) meant that I would be taking over security and intelligence in External Affairs at the height of the Cold War, at a time when the Russians and their allies had mounted a series of successful intelligence operations against NATO countries, including Canada. As we are now aware, those operations were even more extensive and damaging than we imagined.

I was pleased that I would be reporting directly to Norman Robertson, who had become deputy minister earlier in 1958. Knowing the strains associated with his job, I suggested that he might prefer to have me report directly to someone else. He made it quite clear that he wanted the head of Defence Liaison Division (2) reporting directly to him. He had great knowledge of security and intelligence affairs, and they fascinated him. As well, the department was experiencing personnel security problems, some of them complex and worrying, and all of them involving human tragedies in varying degrees. Invariably Robertson had to make difficult decisions, some of which affected life-long friends and close colleagues. He carried out this most unpleasant aspect of the job promptly and with scrupulous fairness. He never complained, though clearly he hated the task.

Deputy ministers personally decided whether to grant or withold security clearance for personnel in their department. In a department such as External Affairs, where so much material was classified, without a top-secret or higher security clearance (for communications intelligence material) it was impossible to work, especially on top-secret intelligence reports from our allies, which entailed rigid restrictions on handling and dissemination.

When I reported for duty in Ottawa, Hamilton Southam already had his hands full as chairman of the Joint Intelligence Committee (JIC) and as director of communications security (DCS) – a pseudonym for the person responsible for providing policy guidance to Communications Branch, National Research Council (CBNRC), concerning gathering of communications intelligence and communications security activities. These were to become my jobs.

Southam asked me to take on a pile of personnel security files that had accumulated since he took over from Bill Crean. I did the work, but not with enthusiasm, since I knew what to expect. It was a collection of sad, often tragic stories, involving foreign service personnel of all ranks of both sexes who, for one reason or another (sexual desire, drug or alcohol abuse, cupidity, or plain stupidity) had attracted the interest of the Russian intelligence services and their allies, which tried to ensnare them into commiting acts of espionage. Fortunately, in only a few instances was the primary motivation to commit treason ideological, as in the cases of the British officials Blunt, Burgess, Cairncross, Maclean, and Philby.

Each situation was different and had to be dealt with on its merits. The process of establishing the truth of an allegation was tortuous, time-consuming, and difficult, and sometimes the results turned out to be frustratingly inconclusive. The privacy of individuals and their families became involved, making it extremely difficult to have such cases dealt with in some fair, impartial manner that might also ensure that their identity did not become widely known.

Norman Robertson was extraordinary in dealing with such matters. He managed to do so with compassion, intelligence, and dispatch and in such a manner as to avoid criticsm from our allies and from Canadian and other security authorities, while also protecting the individuals concerned and their families. Unfortunately we were now dealing not merely with a dozen or so such cases but with scores, from security guards to ambassadors. The majority were directly attributable to KGB mischief-making, though some were the result of Eastern European intelligence services working with the Soviets. I have no doubt that having to deal with these problems took years off Norman Robertson's life. Few of even his closest colleagues ever were aware of the facts.

I have found it very difficult to write about these matters and do so only in cases that already have received publicity – for example, those of John Holmes and John Watkins, discussed above. To discuss some particular case may conceivably lead to the identification of other individuals, some of whom may never have realized that there were grounds for believing that they had been targeted by the Soviet Union. In the handling of personnel security cases I believed that I had and still have a clear responsibility also to protect the privacy of the people involved. In most cases the matter revolved not around 'national security' but rather the no-less-important issue of preserving the privacy of individuals and their families.

It amazed me how Robertson managed to deal with these horrible problems while at the same time regularly occupying himself with so many complicated matters of substance, such as nuclear proliferation. In addition, Prime Minister John Diefenbaker treated him with undisguised suspicion because of his close personal and professional associations with Pearson and other Liberal supporters. Somehow Robertson retained his delightful sense of humour and showed no loss of the skills that won him a reputation for making excellent dry martinis.

When Hamilton Southam finally left Defence Liaison Division (2) in 1959 to become ambassador to Poland, I found my plate pretty full. Working directly for Robertson, however, made all the difference. Because of him, a rotten, stinking, sometimes depressing job became only a rotten job. Dealing with personnel problems was made much easier by having John Timmerman to assist me. He was a realist, and though he could be tough when it was required, he handled the job with compassion and great common sense. While I was still with NATO, Crean had cabled to Paris to ask me if I could recommend someone for the job, and I had suggested Timmerman.

Personnel security problems aside, other aspects of the job were fascinating. Chairing the Joint Intelligence Committee (JIC) took a great deal of my time, with interminable meetings on minuscule but not necessarily unimportant points of detail. It was astonishing how much time JIC gatherings could take up trying to decide how many Russian ICBMs could be balanced on the tip of the North Pole, as it were. Also consuming large chunks of time were interdepartmental intelligence-gathering and security matters generally.

Being chairman of the JIC should not have been as time-consuming for me as it sometimes proved to be. It was not a run-of-the-mill interdepartmental committee. For one thing it was one of the few government offices equipped to receive, send, store, and handle top-secret intelligence material derived from intercepted communications of all kinds. It was linked by dedicated, secure landlines and transatlantic undersea cables to London, Washington, NORAD headquarters, and elsewhere. The JIC was created in November 1942 by a decision of the Chiefs of Staff Committee and consisted of the directors of intelligence of the three armed forces services. Initially, it concentrated on wartime security. Thus its discussions did not deal with intelligence matters as such, though it did produce the occasional intelligence assessment paper.

After receiving a briefing from the British about how their JIC operated and its connections with the Foreign Office (whence its chairman invariably came), it had been agreed that some formal connections between Canada's JIC and the Department of External Affairs might be useful. The British had some extraordinarily able people serving on their JIC, particularly among its assessment staff. Some of their papers, on a whole range of subjects, were of very high quality. Many of the papers that the Canadians produced suffered by comparison, but four that I recently discovered reveal the evolving cooperation between British and Canadian military intelligence during the Second World War (see Appendix A, below).

The connections on intelligence matters betweeen External Affairs and DND were slow to form, and it wasn't until July 1945 that the Chiefs of Staff Committee (CSC) approved a recommendation that representatives from External Affairs and the RCMP be invited to participate in all meetings of the Joint Intelligence Committee (JIC). George Glazebrook became the External Affairs representative.

By the summer of 1946, when the chairmanship of the JIC was rotational, Glazebrook took the chair. When he left Ottawa to return to academic life he was replaced by David Johnson (later to become ambassador in Moscow). Shortly therafter Johnson was replaced by Gerry Riddell, who, until his untimely death not long afterwards, acted as a special adviser to Pearson while he was secretary of state for external affairs. There appears to be no written record of why in 1946 the chairmanship of the JIC passed permanently into the hands of External Affairs. I believe that it was as a result of earlier private discussions between Norman Robertson and Charles Foulkes, chairman of the CSC. When Robertson thought it necessary, he could be quite persuasive, even intimidating, and this was a matter on which he had strong views.

At this point it may help readers to be given a bit of the background to the creation of what turned out to be one of the most important intelligence-gathering activities carried out by the Canadian government – the Communications Branch of the National Research Council (CBNRC).

During the war, consideration had been given to a proposal by Captain Drake for a joint cryptographic bureau run by the three services. CSC turned down the proposal in 1940. Their decision read as follows: 'The Committee decided that they were unable to recommend the institution of a Cryptographic Branch in Canada, and felt that we should continue to use the United Kingdom facilities for this work. In the event of these being seriously interfered with by enemy action, a similar organization exists in the U.S.A. which would be available to assist in the event of the United States' entry into the war. They also considered that the cost of such an organization could not be justified at the present time.'

Yet there was action on other fronts:

About the same time Hugh Keenleyside of the Department of External Affairs and Dr. C.J. Mackenzie, Acting President of the National Research Council also were discussing the creation of a Canadian cryptographic bureau. Captain E.S. Brand, Director of Naval Intelligence, learned of their interest and in a terse note to Keenleyside in January 1941 informed him the Chiefs of Staff already had rejected the idea. Fortunately, the matter did not rest there, Keenleyside and Mackenzie pursued it. Keenleyside in February 1941 wrote Mackenzie, 'If this [the CSC's] decision is to be taken as final, the only remaining aspect of the programme which I had in mind would be the construction of a new code for the use of the Canadian Government ... Perhaps we might consider the possibility of going ahead on this line alone if the remainder of the project is to be dropped.

Eventually, the question of gathering communications intelligence in peacetime led to the creation on 1 September 1946 of the CBNRC. The proposal was sponsored by three ministers – C.D. Howe, Louis St Laurent (External Affairs), and Douglas Abbott (DND) – in a submission dated 13 April 1946, also signed by W.L. Mackenzie King. Thus the new body was created by a Treasury Board minute and an order-in-council.

Unfortunately, an External Affairs officer was to be director of communications security (DCS) at CBNRC. The arrangement was a hangover from the days when Norman Robertson and Mike Pearson had a considerable interest in Canada's intelligence-gathering activities and had insisted that these should be conducted by External Affairs officers.

Some time later, in 1970–1, when a search was instituted to find a successor for Drake as director of CBNRC, Gordon Robertson, then secretary to the cabinet, sought my views. He said that there was a feeling that Drake's successor should be a Canadian rather than someone with an English background, like Kevin O'Neill. I said that apart from the fact that O'Neill was Irish, it seemed to me that at that particular juncture in the agency's development it was important to appoint the most professionally qualified person available. Whatever O'Neill's perceived shortcomings on other grounds, I thought that he filled the bill. In 1934 O'Neill won a scholarship to Oxford University, where from 1935 to 1939 he studied classics and philosophy, graduating with an honours BA. He had served in the British army, enlisting in the Royal Fusiliers in June 1940 as a private. He was discharged in August 1946 with the rank of major, having done intelligence work from 1942 to 1946.

As well as working at essentially domestic activities, I was responsible for keeping our intelligence and security relations with our principal allies and friendly third parties on an even keel. I also tried to avoid secret commitments unless they had an obvious Canadian purpose or advantage – for example, to agree to help secret agents of some country in return for information about KGB espionage activities directed against Canada. The immediately following story about the security guard in Tel Aviv is a good example. I found the international aspects of the job tricky, interesting, and tiresome. For one thing, they involved a great deal of wearying travel.

I recall one particular espionage case. The Israeli authorities informed us that, while carrying out surveillance in Tel Aviv of a known KGB agent, they had observed him to be in contact with an unknown male. Further investigation showed the unknown man to be a security guard at the Canadian embassy in Tel Aviv. The story proved to be long and complicated. Eventually, the man confessed to having worked for the KGB in Tel Aviv, but it wasn't until some years later, when I was director-general of the RCMP Security Service, that we learned that the woman the KGB used to ensnare the man was available for questioning in a friendly European country. From her we learned that the man's earlier confession had only been partial. In fact, he had been recruited by the KGB some years prior to being in Israel, while a security guard at the Canadian embassy in Moscow. At that time, among other acts of treachery, he had provided the KGB with easy access to the chancellery building one evening while he was the only person on duty. The KGB obtained the embassy ciphers, which enabled it to read all the incoming and outgoing communications the following several months. At the time (1948–9) the Israelis had suggested no *quid pro quo*, and we were grateful to accept their help.

One had to be constantly on guard. Our allies were just that, but some were not above taking advantage of our ignorance or naïveté. On this particular score Norman Robertson was very helpful. He was seldom fooled by some apparently innocent request for assistance or some offer to provide us with useful intelligence, with no apparent strings attached. He usually was able to spot such ploys and to turn some potentially awkward situation to our advantage with a deft suggestion or a clever turn of thought.

My job also entailed welcoming a constant stream of visitors. For example, in 1960 or 1961 Allen Dulles, then head of the CIA, visited Canada. We welcomed the chance to show him something of Canada's communications intelligence-gathering activities in the Arctic and the problems of maintaining posts there. His visit was arranged to coincide with the Department of National Defence's (DND's) annual resupply of its installations in the north, including SIGINT stations such as that at Alert, on the Arctic Ocean.

I had already dealt with Dulles during visits to Washington. I liked him, though I didn't know him well. He seemed favourably disposed towards Canada and reasonably knowledgeable about us. For his visit, DND made space available on an RCAF North Star aircraft. Since Doug Harkness, minister of national defence, also was a passenger, we received royal treatment. The journey was, however, tedious and long. The aircraft was slow and extremely noisy. Whether or not we wanted to, we got to know one another.

Our first landing was at Alert, where DND manned a listening post on behalf of CBNRC. The greatest part of the intercepted communications traffic was Soviet military, providing a great deal of information about military and related activities in the Soviet arctic. The Americans regarded the information as useful, particularly in terms of assessing the threat from Soviet ICBM attacks on North America. Our geography gave us unique access to this kind of information. Hence Dulles's interest in making the trip.

Among the passengers was another minister, the Reverend Brown, from Newfoundland. To while away the long hours of flying across the featureless, frozen landscape, Dulles and some of the others, including Brown, arranged to play bridge. When we put down at some place in the western Arctic I recall Dulles drawing me aside and saying in an aggrieved tone: 'That Father Brown of yours. He cheats, you know.'

About half-way through the trip Dulles made a show of reading a fat-looking file marked top-secret, with my name clearly printed on the cover, saying in a rather avuncular manner: 'My people give me good reports on you.' I don't know what reaction he expected, but I suppressed my irritation and avoided comment. Despite his unintentionally patronizing attitude, I found that I liked Dulles and I think that the feeling was mutual. Certainly he had had a wealth of experience in dealing with espionage matters during the Second World War.

We ended our tour with a quick visit to some U.S. military intelligence installation near Anchorage, Alaska, and headed back to Ottawa. I don't know how useful the trip was from Dulles's standpoint. I learned a lot about our own Arctic installations and their problems, and I certainly knew Dulles better than I had before we set off. I liked to think that it resulted in our receiving preferential treatment from the CIA in the following years, but I cannot offer proof.

Another such visitor was a former U.S. airforce general, Charles Pearre Cabell, then deputy director of the CIA. He arrived in Canada flying his own aircraft. The head of the CIA station in Ottawa, George McManus, and his South African wife, Lindsay, together with secretarial staff from the embassy and me, boarded the aircraft in Ottawa and flew to Quebec City, with Cabell at the controls. Mrs Cabell, a devout Roman Catholic, had expressed an interest in visiting the shrine at Ste Anne de Beaupré, near Quebec City. Through the officer commanding the Royal 22nd Regiment, Cabell was invited to be guest of honour at a mess dinner in the Citadel – a great honour.

The regiment put on a real show. The candle-lit setting in the mess was magnificent with the silver candelabra, the beautiful, highly polished mahogany table, the regimental cutlery and china, the colourful mess jackets, and the regimental mascot – a handsome, odorous billy-goat. I believe that Cabell was impressed and a bit bewildered when he found himself surrounded by hosts who spoke only rapid-fire French. He must have wondered whether he had been transported to some regimental mess in seventeenth-century France.

When we landed in Quebec City it was a beautiful evening – not a cloud in the sky, and the temperature crisp but not cold. We no sooner got the Cabells safely ensconced in their rooms in the Château Frontenac Hotel than it began to snow, at first, softly. But gradually a wind out of the northeast began to blow, and the snow came down in earnest. It soon developed into one of those blinding snowstorms for which Quebce City is renowned.

Knowing that the Cabells were snugly in their hotel, we sallied forth for dinner, finally finding a likely-looking restaurant near the hotel. The dining-room, on the second floor, was crowded. The dinner was excellent, and we enjoyed ourselves. Afterwards, George McManus, in his easy-going, gregarious way, wandered among the diners. When he rejoined us I was horrified to discover that he had a number of wallets belonging to some of our fellow-guests. I had visions of the Quebec police being called and a first-class diplomatic incident developing. I made it plain that somehow he had to return the articles. Unfazed, he made another friendly round of the rooms and, in due course, reported back with a big grin – 'They're all back.' I don't know how he was able to do it without creating a ruckus, but he did. I was angry as hell but very relieved that the incident hadn't developed into a nasty scene.

Needless to say, McManus was not a desk man, though I never heard any complaints about the way he carried out his liaison duties. I think that most of his considerable service had been in active operations. It took experience, charm, and extraordinary sleight-of-hand to do what he had done that evening. Such escapades aside, he was very likeable and proved a good liaison officer during his tour of duty in Canada.

A notable development in the Canadian intelligence community was the birth of the Joint Intelligence Bureau (JIB), eventually to be headed by a delightful, talented Welshman, Ivor Bowen, who had had considerable experience in the British JIB. Maurice Oldfield (a future head of MI 6) and Bowen had been at university together and were good friends, which proved helpful to our work in intelligence and to future relations with the British intelligence community.

I took over as chairman of the JIC from Hamilton Southam some time early in 1959. In 1958 the JIC had been reorganizing itself to improve its methods of work and its products. Rejigging of the secretariat was intended to resolve the differences between those favouring a broader, civilian approach to the JIC's work and those wanting continued emphasis on military problems. A compromise, proposed by Bowen, eventually was accepted.

A member of the Joint Intelligence Staff (JIS) who, because of his experience and writing skills, made a notable contribution to the JIC's work was Jack Trotman, who has made a name for himself, under the *nom de plume* John Penn, as the author of a series of excellent mystery stories.

About this time there was a flurry of excitement caused by the cutting of several transatlantic telephone and telegraph cables. Such sudden breaks had occurred before, apparently caused by icebergs, but not on the scale then being reported. These latest breaks appeared more serious. The Americans believed that the cuts had been deliberately made by Soviet trawlers. Interruption of these vital, secure communications links with Europe was considered a reliable indicator of impending Soviet military action in Europe. Some of these events moreover coincided with renewed crises over Berlin and some radio-jamming activity by the Russians in Europe. In due course, however, the excitement died down.

The Privy Council Office (PCO) sometimes requested JIC papers dealing with economic and political intelligence. Until this time the PCO had not shown much interest in intelligence matters, though it was involved in security policy. In this case the interest was sparked by Bob Bryce, secretary to the cabinet, who took a lively and informed interest in such matters. By this time British and American representatives attended some Canadian JIC meetings, and there was similar, reciprocal Canadian participation in London and Washington.

As for a proposal for dealing more adequately with economic intelligence, at Norman Robertson's request I discussed it with Charles Foulkes and Robert Bryce. In 1959 Robertson suggested creation of a senior interdepartmental group of officials from External Affairs, Trade and Commerce, and the Bank of Canada to which the JIC would report on economic intelligence matters. It took time to give effect to the proposal. About a year later, four or five senior officials from the interested agencies, chaired by Ivor Bowen, formed the Economic Intelligence Committee (EIC), with the JIB providing the secretariat.

The effort was not very successful, partly because the senior, very busy officials involved simply were unable to give it proper attention. There was also a limited understanding outside the intelligence community of what 'intelligence' could and could not provide. By the late 1980s the EIC had ceased to exist.

The most important event, however, was the creation in May 1960 of the Intelligence Policy Committee (IPC), chaired by Norman Robertson. I became involved in much of the preparatory work, particularly the drafting of proposals. The proposed membership included the deputy minister of defence, the chairman of the Chiefs of Staff, as well as the chief of each service, the deputy minister of finance, the commisssioner of the RCMP, and various senior officials, as well as the chairman of the JIC. At one of its first meetings Robertson suggested that its creation had been prompted in part by the aggressive espionage and subversive activities of the Soviets. He suggested that the IPC represented an attempt to strengthen Canada's intelligence-gathering capabilities in non-military fields.

The terms of reference required the IPC to 'maintain general control and policy direction over all aspects of the work of the JIC, determine what general intelligence objectives should be set for the JIC, recommend what financial and manpower priorities and resources it should be given in order to carry out its task, and to assess its performance in carrying out these tasks ... to maintain general policy control over all aspects of collection, processing and dissemination of signals intelligence (SIGINT) ... [and] maintain general policy control over all aspects of communications/electronic security.'

Some of the discussions in the IPC were useful and interesting. For the first time in Canada there was a forum at the most senior level to decide questions involving intelligence collection and dissemination of the products derived from it. The totality of Canada's intelligence effort, in terms of money and personnel, could be laid out and discussed. Though it was not comparable with what the British and the Americans were doing, it was respectable. I believe that the annual costs were estimated at between ten and twelve million dollars.

In March 1962, in a memorandum to Robertson, I referred to an earlier suggestion by Bob Bryce – that machinery be set up to enable certain ministers to take a direct and continuing interest in the work of the Security Panel and possibly also that of the IPC. I wrote that I thought it would be very useful indeed from the IPC's standpoint if those matters within its purview could be made known to ministers and discussed by them regularly. As usual, there was no immediate action, but the Cabinet Committee on Security and Intelligence was set up on 11 June

1963. By that time I had left Ottawa to become ambassador in Bonn, but I was delighted to hear of the committee's birth, since I believed that it gave meaning and substance to the work of the Canadian intelligence community.

In 1961 or 1962 Norman Robertson told me of a conversation that he had had with an American cabinet secretary during a meeting in Montebello, Quebec, of U.S. and Canadian ministers who met regularly to discuss a wide range of matters affecting U.S.–Canadian relations. To my surprise, he had committed the matter to paper – a rare occurrence. I have tried unsuccessfully to find the paper in the National Archives. His interlocutor did not have direct involvement with Defense or State Department matters, but he left Robertson with the impression that the U.S. government might be contemplating military action against Cuba.

Robertson asked me if there had been any hint through intelligence channels that the United States was contemplating anything of the kind. Discreet inquiries turned up nothing. However, as I was due later that week to travel to London on one of my regular visits and meet with the British JIC, I asked his authority to raise the matter with it. He agreed, and I broached the matter in a suitable forum, only to discover that it knew absolutely nothing about such a possibility and was shocked that it did not. After urgent inquiries in Whitehall it was discovered that the U.S. military authorities had made tentative inquiries through normal British military and JIB channels concerning Cuba (beach gradients, water depths and currents, and composition of soil inland from the beaches). Since the inquiries were not specific and had been made within the context of normal British–U.S. military exchanges of such topographical information, they aroused no suspicions.

Howard Green succeeded Sidney Smith as secretary of state at External Affairs following Smith's premature death in March 1959. I had occasion to see Green infrequently about intelligence or personnel security matters, but usually the latter. Though Robertson and Green saw eye to eye on a number of substantive matters such as disarmament and nuclear proliferation, and Green had known Robertson's father in Vancouver and respected him, Robertson dreaded having to deal with him on some matters, particularly personnel security cases, and tried to avoid having to do so.

Green viewed with palpable dislike anything that involved deviant human behaviour, which sometimes was the case with personnel security problems. There were occasions, for example, when Robertson felt that Green should be informed about some particular case. Almost invariably Green's reaction would be to get the person involved out of his department as quickly as possible, without much concern about how this might affect his or her future and that of the family involved. Robertson would always seek a solution that preserved as much as possible of the individual's self-respect and hold out some prospect of a useful future. Green could be very stubborn in such matters, and Robertson often would find himself frustrated and discouraged. In despair, occasionally he might ask me to try to deal with the minister.

Fortunately, a close family friend of ours in Montreal, Frank Raphael, who had served in the trenches with Howard Green during the First World War, spoke to him about me in very favourable terms, and thereafter Green appeared to trust me and would sometimes listen to me, depending on his mood and my ability to put the problem in a way he might understand and accept – not an easy task.

In this way I came to know and to like Green, as I think did all those foreign service officers who worked with him. We became friends, and after he left politics in 1963, Helen and I maintained contact with him and his wife, Donna. He was honest, very likeable, and of firm convictions. Most important, he had the complete trust of John Diefenbaker.

One of the worrying aspects about Green was his lack of knowledge of international relations, and in intelligence and security he lacked interest in and understanding of the complexities vis-à-vis both our allies and our enemies. Someone suggested that during a visit to Ottawa by Sir Dick White, head of MI 6, the two might meet. As I wrote in a review of Tom Bower's biography of White, *The Perfect English Spy*, 'Norman Robertson was unenthusiastic, in part because, while Green was familiar with the relationship and occasionally benefited from it, e.g. British intelligence material concerning nuclear proliferation, he was generally naïve and quite unsophisticated about this aspect of his responsibilities ... Robertson's misgivings proved to be well founded. In professional terms the meeting was a disaster. Green did not have any notion about much that White wanted to talk about and this became painfully apparent as the meeting progressed.' The meeting, however, discouraged MI 6 from suggesting ways in which Canada might assist its efforts, which obviously would have required Green's approval and support – for example, creation of a Canadian secret intelligence service modelled on MI 6.

In late 1961 or early 1962, I recall, Canadian military intelligence personnel, through their excellent U.S. connections, gained access to one of the most jealously guarded U.S. secrets – the quite extraordinary U.S. advances in extracting extremely valuable, accurate intelligence from photo-reconnaissance flights, including some over the Soviet Union and China. In February 1995 the U.S. government announced its intention to release more than 800,000 satellite photographs collected by the CIA between 1960 and 1972 and recorded on 2.1 million feet of film.

President Eisenhower in mid-August 1960 announced that an American flag carried in a capsule aboard the U.S. space vehicle *Discovery XIII* had been retrieved by a navy helicopter near Hawaii. He said that the experiment was part of a scientific exploration of environmental conditions in space. In fact, it was the beginning of a secret space reconnaissance program developed by the CIA and the U.S. Air Force to obtain photographs of the Soviet Union and China – a development described by a senior fellow at the (U.S.) National Security Archive as 'the biggest advance in the history of the intelligence world.'

The Americans had experimented with platforms, balloons capable of reaching altitudes of 90,000 feet equipped with specially designed cameras, and U-2 piloted aircraft able to fly at over 60,000 feet, beyond the range of Soviet missiles. Eventually the Soviet Union improved its SA-2 ground-to-air missiles and brought down a U-2, flown by CIA pilot Francis Gary Powers, near Sverdlovsk early in May 1960. Not long afterwards, the fourteenth *Corona* satellite flight produced photographs of 1.5 million square miles of the Soviet Union and eastern Europe. Experiments with different methods of film retrieval led to great improvements in this crucial aspect of the program.

I believe that the Canadian military intelligence personnel concerned deserve great credit for gaining access to this unique new source of reliable intelligence just when U.S. intelligence collection was becoming much more sophisticated. Some Canadian military personnel spent considerable time at U.S. intelligence-training establishments, forming valuable friendships and contacts. It is my recollection that this new source of intelligence material was not made known to the JIC members (other than the chairman) or to others in the intelligence community, no doubt because the Americans imposed strict limitations on dissemination.

When I told Norman Robertson about the development of this new source of intelligence, he suggested that, since this program was run by the CIA in collaboration with U.S. military authorities, Canada should negotiate access to the end-products under the long-standing umbrella arrangements for intelligence cooperation between External Affairs and the CIA. Accordingly, in due course I was invited to Washington by the CIA to be indoctrinated and given a briefing.

I recall being taken by a CIA officer to a rather run-down section of Washington, where we ended up in front of an apparently derelict building and were ushered into a ropey old freight elevator, which took us to an upper floor. There we entered a large, well-lit area filled with exotic-looking equipment of every imaginable shape and size and literally scores of staff running around. It was like a scene from *Star Trek*. I was introduced to the director, who, with other members of his staff, gave me a very thorough review of the history of *Corona* and an account of the astonishing results – images with a ground resolution of about 25–40 feet taken from heights in excess of 100 miles. Subsequently, with improved performance, cameras could distinguish and identify objects measuring as little as six feet in length. Heaven knows what further improvements have been made since then!

The most impressive results, however, were the new techniques for interpreting the myriad details contained in the photographs. The Americans were light years beyond where the British had been in the early 1940s.

Later in that visit we discussed ways in which such material might be made available to Canada and how to protect it in order to meet U.S. security standards. Eventually, for reasons of security, it was decided to use U.S. military channels to transport the material to Ottawa – an arrangement that worked well. I was told that each day the U.S. president received a dossier of photographic images, together with his regular intelligence digests, as did the secretaries of state and defence, selected members of Congress, and other key officials.

Subsequently, it was arranged for John Diefenbaker to be informed about this new source of intelligence. The preparations were made shortly before I left for Bonn, so I was not in Ottawa when they took full effect. However, I understand that they proved useful, particularly during the Cuban missile crisis, though I have no idea whether Diefenbaker thought so.

9

Intense Midday Heat

I thoroughly enjoyed my time as ambassador in the Federal Republic of Germany, which covered an intensely interesting period (1962–6), when the Germans were casting off the role of being 'occupied,' gradually assuming sovereignty, and becoming a potentially important member of the Western alliance. Our embassy's mission, moreover, had taken on a special flavour, owing to the presence on German soil of so many Canadian army and air force units and their families. The Canadian military units did their difficult jobs with great professionalism, thus earning the respect of the Germans and of the other Allied forces with whom they worked. But then the Canadian forces' role in Germany was quite unlike their difficult peacekeeping tasks now being carried out around the world.

We had endless, patient diplomatic negotiation with the West German authorities to obtain the kind of facilities and amenities (such as ice-hockey rinks) that Canadian troops and their dependants required. No sooner did one series of such negotiations end than another began.

I was able to pursue my interest in atomic energy matters. The London-based International Institute for Strategic Studies (IISS), which Bill Crean had helped me join, held a conference on the spread of nuclear weapons at Schloss Lenzburg in Aavbar, Switzerland, at the end of February 1965. With Norman Robertson's agreement, I was able to attend. The only other Canadian present was Omond Solandt, president, research and development, at de Havilland Company of Canada. He knew a great deal about atomic energy and had sat on the Atomic Energy Panel under Arnold Heeney when I was the secretary. Thirty-odd delegates attended from about twelve countries. I learned how advanced some countries were in their plans for the possible non-peaceful uses of atomic energy.

The IISS has appropriately strict rules about not making discussions public. Personal, informal talks during the two-day conference left me with the distinct impression that India and Israel already had decided to create their own nuclear weapons. Indeed I thought it probable that Israel already possessed such weapons, though not the means for delivering them by missile.

The Canadian embassy in Bonn was fortunate in having a first-class team of officers and administrative staff, who worked with energy, skill, and knowledge. We were able to call on experts from other missions in Europe if required.

Following my mother's death in Montreal in 1965, I brought my father back to live with us in Cologne. He was eighty-two. I recall on the flight from Montreal to Düsseldorf worrying about whether he would be able to make the considerable adjustments. On the flight we had a very pretty, attentive young stewardess looking after us. At some point she asked my father a question that he didn't hear. I told him what she had asked. When she was out of earshot he leaned across and said to me, 'Young man, I would appreciate it, if, when we are in the presence of a good-looking woman, you didn't call me Dad.' I stopped worrying! He very quickly adapted to life in Germany.

I was not enthusiastic, however, about my proposed posting in the spring of 1966 to Egypt (then part of the United Arab Republic, or UAR) and Sudan. There was political turmoil in the Middle East, and Canada had been acting since December 1966 as the protecting power for the British in the UAR, as relations had broken down between those contries. Moreover, our embassy had been without a head of mission for many months; Jean Chapdelaine, shortly after taking on the job, had left the foreign service to represent the Quebec government in Paris. In the interim, Canada was represented by a chargé d'affaires. When I arrived in Cairo the official was Arthur Broadbridge, who had uncomplainingly and ably carried on an increasingly difficult, sometimes unpleasant task.

Cairo was to be my base of operations; as ambassador to Sudan I would make occasional brief visits to that vast country, immediately south of Egypt. My introduction to its head of state proved both distinctive and memorable. As-Sadiq al-Mahdi was an impressive man, probably in his sixties or seventies. We chatted for some time, but I found it difficult to concentrate. The president sat with the light behind him, and as we spoke, I noticed with fascination that the top of one of his ears had a neat, round hole through it. The Khartoum sunlight was refracted through it at interesting angles and in different colours. Since the hole was nowhere near the lobe and quite regular, I assumed that it probably had been caused by a bullet.

Helen and I made the trip from Bonn to Cairo without my father, since we wanted to take our Ford car, and the long journey to the boot of Italy and thence by boat would have been difficult for him. We reached Alexandria on the morning of 27 April 1966. My father arrived a few weeks later on a Sabena flight from Düsseldorf, flushed with wine and excitement, having made friends with the Belgian stewardess who escorted him off the aircraft with a regal flourish.

I had not known my father very well. Egypt provided the opportunity. Though somewhat handicapped by physical ailments, he had all his mental faculties unimpaired and a lively, wicked sense of humour. He possessed a strong romantic streak, fed in part by his having at an early age read G.A. Henty's books of adventure for boys and the stories of Rudyard Kipling. Hence I think he actually looked forward to Egypt, the mysterious land of the Pharaohs and the Nile.

On one of our first Sundays in Cairo he came with us to the Anglican cathedral for the morning service. The provost, Donald Blackburn, was extremely pleasant. He and his rather saintly-looking wife, Mae, had found a place within the still relatively large British community and among Muslim Egyptians. After the service we assembled in the shade of a veranda, where Mae served us a cool, refreshing drink made of 'limoon juice' and water. When she got to my father I heard him ask in a loud, clear voice: 'And which are the martinis?'

Since the days were long and sometimes extremely hot, and there were not a great many things that my father could do, filling his time was a constant problem. It had become very difficult for him to walk. Helen dreamed up the bright idea of getting him to record his memories and reminiscences. She thought that this project might interest and amuse him and help him while away the time. While he thought it a splendid idea, he insisted that he dictate the memoir to her. We have retained the resulting document, parts of which have not lost a certain charm (Appendix B).

Given what I was able to learn of the political situation in the Middle

East, and particularly about relations between Egypt and Israel, I suggested that I be granted access to communications intelligence material. Though the embassy in Bonn had machine ciphers and the potential for receiving such top-secret intelligence reports, we received no such material, nor did we probably need it. Both the British and the U.S. intelligence representatives in Bonn kept us well informed in general terms. The Canadian embassy in Cairo also had machine ciphers (thank God) and could have become such a receiving point but lacked the means of protecting it adequately.

To my surprise and delight Ottawa informed me that it had been able to arrange with the Americans for me to be given access to such information through the CIA's head of station in Cairo. The arrangement enabled me to see the material in the 'safe speech' room in the U.S. embassy, which was reasonably close to our chancellery. I used the privilege sparingly because I did not want to attract undue attention by trotting around to the U.S. embasssy all the time. I believe that the military attaché, Bob Kingston, who was there when I arrived, had similar access through the U.S. military attaché's office. Kingston and I had been together at school in Montreal. I enjoyed working with him and his successor, Moe Smith (RCAF). I don't remember whether Smith had a similar arrangement with the American military attaché, but I don't think so. The access proved most useful to me in the days immediately before Israeli forces attacked in the Sinai and after the Six Day War when it was helpful to know what Egypt's Arab neighbours might be up to. Certainly, they communicated a good deal, but usually to no great effect. Lots of posturing but little real action!

My first concern in Cairo was to present my letters of credence to President Nasser. Until then, I was a 'non-person,' and any official contacts had to be carried out by Arthur Broadbridge. At least I was able to have meaningful discussions with the British officials in the British Interests Section of the Canadian embassy, who were members of my staff. Some of them were old Middle East hands and very knowledgeable about Egyptian affairs.

The Egyptians took their time in making the arrangements – forty days, to be exact. In the light of Egypt's subsequent unfriendly attitude to Canada I have wondered if the delay was not deliberate, indicating displeasure because Canada had left the post without a head of mission for so many months and persisted in playing up the value of the

United Nations Emergency Force (UNEF) and Canada's contribution to it.

I presented my letters of credence to Nasser on 6 June 1966, along with a number of other heads of missions-in-waiting. The setting was King Farouk's Abdeen Palace. On the avenues of approach the stately royal date palms were majestic, as was the Egyptian army's guard of honour. Given the intense midday heat I was relieved that I was not involved in an extensive review of the guard. My brief talk with Nasser was pleasant. I liked him and looked forward to talking with him less formally.

I soon began trying to get a further interview, even though my diplomatic colleagues and Egyptian ministers and officials claimed that Nasser seldom gave such private interviews. I met Miles Copeland, an American living in Cairo, through U.S. Ambassador Luke Battle. Copeland was a freelance writer, generally thought to be a CIA agent, who, through his friendship with Heikal, editor of the influential Cairo newspaper *al-Ahram*, had access to Nasser. Copeland knew of my interest in meeting Nasser and may well have tried to help – it was the kind of thing that he would do. With hindsight it seems likely that the CIA only used him occasionally, since every intelligence agency makes use of friendly journalists and others. I had no evidence that he was a full-time employee.

Several years ago the Department of External Affairs declassified the telegrams reporting on my private conversations with Nasser and subsequently with senior members of his government. I found Nasser's home comfortable but not ostentatious. Beyond the discreet presence of armed bodyguards and of his family on the upper floors, we were alone. He was relaxed and courteous, almost jovial at times. I appreciated his quick wit and mind, his sense of humour, and his unexpected frankness, which he had obviously perfected over time. I wished that I could have talked to him in his own language.

We spoke about U.S.–UAR relations. He referred to the U.S. Sixth Fleet, saying that he had ceased to worry about it in making his appraisals of situations in the Middle East. If he were to worry about U.S. policies in the area he would get no sleep – he would be sleeping under his bed rather than on it. At one time he had worried about numerous unfriendly comments about his regime in the U.S. press (which he said he read every night). He referred to an article in a U.S. publication, which he did not name, to the effect that the Soviets were establishing bases in the UAR. He assured me that such reports were absolute nonsense. If he were to allow foreign bases in the UAR, he would prefer them to be American, since U.S. forces have far more money to spend than anyone else.

We had a brief discussion concerning the UAR's indebtedness to the USSR. I said that I understood from talking recently to the Soviet ambassador that the Soviet Union had made available credit of between seven and eight hundred million Egyptian pounds. Nasser said that he did not remember the precise figure but that his country owed the USSR less than six hundred million pounds. During his last visit to the Soviet Union, its leaders had agreed to reduce the debt by two hundred million pounds – an outright gift.

Concerning the UNEF, I referred to a statement reported in the Cairo press from the Jordanian foreign minister, made at a meeting of the Arab Defence Council. I had taken the Egyptian foreign minister's comment on the statement to mean that the UAR still regarded UNEF as capable of making a contribution to peace. Nasser replied that his foreign minister's response had been correct. UNEF was nothing more than an observation force, which could have no role in a UAR–Israeli military conflict. As far as he was concerned, the force had value in terms of the foreign currencies its members introduced into the UAR and the additional business it stimulated in the Gaza area! He sounded contemptuous, and I believe he meant to, as later events proved.

Cairo was a fascinating city, unlike any I had lived in. I only wished that we had been posted there in different circumstances and had been able to explore more fully its many, peculiar delights. Lawrence Durrell's *Alexandria Quartet* and Olivia Manning's *The Levant Trilogy* certainly bring alive the sultry decadence, the smells, sounds, sights, and 'feel' of Egypt, and especially of Alexandria. But I think that Nobel laureate Naguib Mahfouz, in his *Cairo Trilogy*, has captured the special flavours of the capital and its millions of inhabitants. Artemis Cooper, wife of the author Anthony Beevor and granddaughter of former British ambassador to France Sir Alfred Duff-Cooper and his wife, Diana, has written another such book – *Cairo in the War* – capturing the essence of Egypt.

Our comfortable house in Zamalek, though in an up-scale residential district, was surrounded by many of the elements that these authors so skillfully conjure up. Darkness, which falls with astonishing suddenness in Egypt, assails all the senses at the same time – the cloying, unforgettable smell of sweet night-jasmine; the pungent, earthy smells of dung; the braying of tethered donkeys; the calls to prayer (now broadcast by electronic means) from nearby mosques; the smells from hundreds of charcoal braziers used for cooking and warmth throughout the city; and the annoying sounds of wild dogs, which at nightfall move into the city from the surrounding desert to hunt in packs for food. Their night-long fighting, eating, copulating, and howling seemed to reach a crescendo about two o'clock every morning.

After one particularly noisy such night, as I was leaving the residence to go to work early, before the heat set in, I made some scathing comments about the 'bloody dogs' and 'Why the hell can't they get rid of them?' I spoke in English, and so the only people who could have understood me were my driver, Gaber, the senior servant, Abdul, a delightful, most competent Nubian, and one of the armed guards posted outside our front door twenty-four hours a day.

Returning at day's end I learned that not long after I had left a couple of military vehicles, filled with armed police or soldiers, had appeared and proceeded to shoot every dog in sight and remove the carcasses! The next few nights were blissfully quiet, except for the donkey's braying and the crowing of the cocks, which some neighbours kept on their rooftop.

We were fortunate in having hard-working, skilled, and loyal members of the household staff, one or two of them Nubian. I believe that Theresa Ford recruited them while Robert Ford was the head of mission (1961–3). She managed as well to have a magnificent grand piano included on the inventory of the residence, much to the irritation of the bureaucrats in Ottawa.

In the immediate aftermath of the Six Day War the unsettled, sometimes chaotic conditions in Cairo were difficult for all those Egyptians employed by foreign missions, and especially by those such as ours, which had been publicly branded as pro-Israeli by Cairo's state-controlled press, TV, and radio stations.

I was particularly dependent on Gaber, my driver. The car, a Canadian-built Buick, was supposed to be equipped with air conditioning. It was impossible, however, to have the car in motion and the air conditioner working at the same time. To get anywhere quickly meant opening all the windows and letting the ambient temperatures in the high 90s (Fahrenheit) sweep through the car. Even when the car could be coaxed to speeds of thirty to forty miles an hour, the resulting flow of air brought no relief; it seemed merely to intensify the heat, operating rather like a modern convection oven. And when, as occasionally happened, the hot, dry, dust-laden winds from the desert blew across the city, the lack of air conditioning became a serious liability.

Gaber, whose name I'm told means 'healer of bones,' was a very good driver. Having served as a sergeant with the British Eighth Army, he was a good mechanic and an accomplished 'scrounger.' He had a vivacious girlfriend (in the Arab world she could have been a wife) who was a professional belly-dancer. At one of the embassy's staff parties she tried to teach me how to belly-dance. She was able to rotate the muscles around her navel in a clock-wise direction while the rest of the muscles on her abdomen appeared to move counter-clockwise. I was too distracted to be a good pupil.

Several days after the Six Day War ended and Israeli forces had stopped their advance at the Suez Canal the Egyptian government still maintained blackout regulations and imposed a curfew, largely as a necessary and effective means of controlling the population. One morning I received word that Canadian members of the embassy staff living in Maahdi, a relatively good residential area about ten miles outside the city, were being held up at gunpoint by 'vigilantes' and prevented from crossing the railway line on the road to Cairo. It appeared, moreover, that members of some diplomatic missions (including ours) were being singled out because of their alledgedly pro-Israeli attitudes.

I was angry as hell and decided to drive there to see if I could not stop this quite unacceptable behaviour. The 'vigilantes' had no apparent authority, though clearly they could not have operated at all, let alone have been well armed, if the police and the army had not turned a blind eye to their activities. Certainly they had no right to restrict the movement of members of the diplomatic corps, whatever country they represented or whatever their attitude towards the Israelis.

I was very reluctant to involve Gaber, but delighted to discover that he seemed more than willing to make the journey. When we arrived, the 'vigilantes' turned out to be a motley crew of 'citizen volunteers' (shades of Paris in the 1790s) armed with Soviet-made automatic rifles and sporting makeshift, dirty, white cotton armbands. The safety catches appeared to be in the 'off' position on some rifles. There seemed to be nobody in charge, but after repeated inquiries we were able to pin down an older man (most seemed to be in their teens), and with Gaber translating (Allah knows what he said) we seemed to be making headway. I discoverd that Gaber actually was enjoying himself, speaking with authority, apparent eloquence, and even vehemence.

Eventually, led by the Buick with the Canadian flag on the hood, the small cavalcade made its way across the tracks. I was reminded of a mother loon, dutifully followed by her brood, on some calm, cool Canadian lake. By this time it was as hot as hell, and I wished that the air conditioning and the car had been able to work simultaneously.

When it was all over I lodged a formal complaint with the Egyptian authorities, but I might as well have saved my breath. I'm sure the official to whom I spoke was being insincere, as well as shamelessly insolent, in saying that he knew absolutely nothing of the incident and regretted that 'concerned Egyptian citizens' had felt impelled to take such action. He hoped that no Canadian diplomatic personnel had been maltreated!

On 27 May 1967 UAR Foreign Minister Riad asked the secretary-general of the UN for the complete withdrawal and departure of Canadian forces 'immediately and not later than 48 hours from the time my cable reaches you.' Below in this chapter I deal with some aspects of the mystery of the Egyptians' sudden unfriendliness towards us. I hope that in due course historians will examine UNEF and Canada's part in it. Much, if not all, of the relevant documentation now is in the public domain, and the story is worth proper analysis and comment. There are lessons to be learned from it.

Riad's message to U Thant alleged that from the beginning the Canadian government had persistently resolved to procrastinate and delay the departure of UNEF. On 16 May 1967 the UAR's chief of staff had demanded withdrawal of UNEF troops from forward positions at El Sabha and Kuntilla. Riad accused Canada of 'certain military measures on which we have already received definite information that some Canadian destroyers have already sailed towards the Mediterranean.'

I was not as surprised as the authorities in Ottawa, though just as dismayed. Almost a year earlier, on 6 July 1966, I reported by telegram a conversation with Ismail Fahmy, head of the Department of Conferences and International Organizations of the Egyptian Foreign Office. Fahmy had made it quite clear that UNEF's continued existence or otherwise made no difference to the UAR, from either a political or a military standpoint. I reported that I found it difficult to judge what weight to attach to his rather unexpected, gratuitous comments. I said that they could denote a shift in the UAR's attitude to UNEF. My discussions with ministers and officials, or rather what was left unsaid, suggested to me that, contrary to perhaps what we believed, our participation in UNEF was an irritant in UAR–Canadian relations. I added that if this interpretation was correct, it perhaps should be taken into account in any review of UNEF's future, its financing, and Canada's continued participation in it.

Given the historical background of UNEF and Canada's prominent part in its creation, I did not expect that my report would be immediately welcomed either by officials or by Prime Minister Lester Pearson. I was surprised and a bit irritated, however, to receive a telegram in mid-August, thanking me for the report but saying that, given 'other available evidence,' the department did not believe that Fahmy's comments necessarily signified any significant change in the UAR's policy towards UNEF.

The last aircraft carrying the Canadian contingent to UNEF left the UAR at 3.45 p.m. on 31 May 1967. It just barely escaped the fate of other national contingents that were in the path of attacking Israeli forces early in June. There were a number of casualties, with the Indian contingent in particular suffering some wounded and killed.

By the end of May the general situation in Cairo quickly worsened and became potentially dangerous to our staff and their dependants. For example, a member of the diplomatic staff of the Brazilian embassy had gone into the streets to observe some demonstration and had been attacked and stoned to death by the xenophobic crowd. I proposed that all members of Canadian staff who were not absolutely essential to the running of the embassy should be evacuated with their families. This suggestion was accepted, and the evacuation proceeded without any major hitches.

Remaining behind were political officers Ken Merklinger and Louis Delvoie, military attaché Moe Smith and his staff, the communications operators, security guards, and enough secretaries to do the necessary work. The wives and children of all those remaining in Cairo were evacuated, except for Helen and my father. My father was not well, and we were reluctant to put him through the stress of a hasty return to Canada via Europe, unless it was obviously necessary.

At the chancellery we started the laborious business of destroying any classified documents that we did not need and retaining those required for day-to-day business. Needless to say, there had been an accumulation of papers over the years, and a great many files had to be hastily examined and stripped. Destroying documents sounds simple, but it took several days, with all of us pitching in, to destroy literally hundreds of such papers. Even with the aid of chemicals to promote combustion, which most of our embassies had for just such an emergency, it took us hours to destroy the documents thoroughly. Eventually, we rigged up a kind of incinerator on the roof. Our immediate neighbours in the Zamalek district must have felt like the inhabitants of Herculaneum and Pompeii in AD 79.

The Cairo sun, combined with the heat given off by our makeshift barbecue, made it hot work, but eventually we got the job done. We then had to worry whether, in our zeal and haste, we might have inadvertently destroyed some essential documents. I learned something from all this – most government departments squirrel away far too much paper! It was a lesson I attempted to apply later in 1967, with limited success, when, as assistant deputy minister in charge of administration in Ottawa, I had responsibility for the files and filing registries at External Affairs.

On 8 June 1967, without warning, our communications link with Canada was interrupted and eventually completely severed. We were obliged to use a commercial wireless link maintained by the UAR authorities between Cairo and Rome. This development followed hard on a decision by the British and the Americans, as a security measure, to destroy all their communications equipment, though the British maintained their capacity to send and receive messages *en clair* through their wireless link with London. After repeated requests to the Egyptian authorities, the Cairo–Rome wireless service was restored at noon on 12 June, after 116 hours of interruption. The speed with which 'repairs' were carried out and the link restored strongly suggested that the interruption was deliberate. Moreover, the interruption coincided with the break in diplomatic relations between the United States and the UAR and, even more ominous, with arrangements by the British Interests Section of the Canadian embassy for the immediate evacuation from Egypt of all British subjects (literally hundreds, since these included many Pakistanis, Indians, and others), which was ordered by the UAR government on short notice.

A few days prior to the Israeli attacks, we were awakened at the residence about 4 a.m. by the arrival of Moe Smith, the military attaché. He had received reliable information that the Cairo airport was about to be closed to all commercial flights, and he strongly advised that Helen and my father should leave that morning. We wakened my father and began hasty arrangements to get them out. We managed to get seats on the last commercial aircraft out of Cairo – an Alitalia flight. Helen and my father were met and very kindly looked after in Rome for a few days by Bill and Lib Crean (Bill was ambassador to Italy) and safely sent on their way to Montreal, where Helen had to find a suitable place for my father. It was with a heavy heart that I saw them off, but if they had had to remain there was no way of knowing what unpleasantness they might have experienced.

During the evening of 9 June 1967 Nasser made an address to the nation announcing his decision to resign from office. His mood was sombre, and his style muted. There was none of the sparkle, effervescence, and fanfare usually associated with his public appearances. He did accuse the United States and Britain of intervening on behalf of Israel, but he did so without conviction, and his comments were not particularly vituperative. His account of events was poignant, if not strictly truthful. I dearly wished that I had understood Arabic, since it was clear that in that language his speech was a tear-jerker. He was frank without being humble. He accepted full responsibility for what had happened, and he resigned, appointing Zakaria Mohieddin as his successor. He did not say that he was stepping down conditionally, nor did he offer excuses. His performance was superb, especially since it had about it an air of sincerity. It also hauntingly resembled Queen Hatshepsut's memorial inscribed on her obelisk at Karnak, 'Then my soul stirred, wondering what men would say who saw this monument after many years and spoke of what I had done.' Like so many of Nasser's moves it was shrewd and cunning and quite as likely to result in a massive popular demand for him to remain as in Mohieddin's confirmation in office.

That Nasser's resignation and the manner of his making it were a smart move was quickly evident. With all the blackout curtains drawn (on a particularly hot, humid night) I listened to his speech in the residence, a stone's throw from one of Cairo's main thoroughfares. Almost immediately huge crowds surged through the streets shouting, 'Abdul Nasser, Abdul Nasser.' They swept through the blacked-out streets like the incoming tide in the Bay of Fundy. The feral sounds were frightening. Luckily, the main body of demonstrators stayed on the large boulevards and streets, and only small parties appeared around the residence. I had taken the precaution of ordering all the household staff out of the house so that, even if some demonstrators had attempted to enter the premises, no one would have been harmed.

It was a strange experience to be listening to the magisterial proceedings of the Security Council in New York on Voice of America broadcasts, while the street mobs outside chanted for Nasser's return and anti-aircraft guns fired nearby against non-existent Israeli aircraft. Quite cleverly, the Egyptian authorities, to keep control of the population and some semblance of public order, pretended that Cairo still was in danger of attack from Israeli warplanes and maintained black-out restrictions and other war measures – anti-aircraft batteries and sand-bagged machine-gun emplacements at strategic crossroads throughout the city.

The demonstrations continued throughout the night and the next morning, when Nasser expressed himself as 'deeply moved by these popular manifestations in his favour' and said that he would 'reconsider his decision in the national assembly and before our people.' As I put it in my report to Ottawa, 'It will be intriguing to see what happens. However, whether or not Nasser eventually holds on to power it seems certain that his "Ka" will live on and his Aswan pyramid [dam] will endure.'

About this time, and after the UAR broke off diplomatic relations with the Americans, I had another early-morning caller at the residence. The head of the CIA station in Egypt turned up carrying a canvas bag. He said that he had destroyed his communications equipment and asked if he could give me for safekeeping the rotors for the cipher machines, which, if they got into the wrong hands, could seriously damage U.S. interests. I agreed to accept them and duly reported the incident to Ottawa. I was taken aback to receive a rebuke. Some nervous Nellie in Ottawa, presumably unaware that I was receiving communications intelligence material through the good offices of the CIA's head of station, obviously thought that Canada's fragile virginity might be compromised in some way by my decision. In the end it all worked out – the rotors were kept in our safe and, in due course, returned to their rightful owners, *virginitas intacta.*

The Suez Canal is quite a distance from Canada, and normally it is not something we think about. When it closed because of military action and remained shut down for many weeks, fifteen ships were trapped. Four were of British registry. Since Canada was protecting British interests in the UAR, the embassy became embroiled in the effort to get the ships freed and to ensure the welfare of their crews. It took so long to arrange clearance operations in the canal that eventually the ships were 'written off.'

We sought permission to send a consular officer to visit the ships to obtain information about the welfare and needs of the British seamen and a number of passengers on board. Two of the ships contained passengers from Australia as well as 'the annual fruit crop' from Tasmania. On 14 June I was summoned at midnight to the Egyptian Foreign Office by el-Feki, the permanent under-secretary, to discuss the problem, along with diplomats from all nine countries with shipping trapped in the canal. The communist-bloc representatives made life as difficult as possible for us in our role of protecting British interests. I was not amused by the sanctimonious ganging up that ensued.

At one point, in response to a question from me, el-Feki finally said that the canal was blocked and that it would not be reopened until the Israelis withdrew from the east bank of the canal. The meeting turned out to be a waste of time, called for no apparent purpose.

We persisted, however, and about ten days later we received permission to visit the four British ships. Ken Merklinger carried out the difficult and dangerous task. Israeli and Egyptian machine-gun positions were fully manned on both banks, with their weapons trained on anything that moved on the water, including the small Egyptian boat carrying Merklinger and the Bulgarian chargé d'affaires. Merkingler completed the task at high noon, in the blazing sun. Soon we were able to report that the British crews and their mainly Australian passengers were in relatively good health and had sufficient supplies.

I found el-Feki's strongly anti-British stance at the 'emergency' meeting somewhat hypocritical, knowing that he had recently arranged to have a prostate condition treated in London, rather than in Cairo.

Several years after leaving Egypt I came upon a curious story that concerns Egypt and its sudden hostility to the continued presence of the Canadian contingent to UNEF. The tale concerned the kind of military planning that goes on continuously in every military establishment around the world. In this case, planners dreamed up various military situations in which Canadian soldiers might be used in the Middle East and drew up detailed plans for their possible involvement in different situations. This type of activity is normal and very necessary for any military establishment worth its salt. Canadians are very good at it, having had years of military experience around the world, where meticulous planning has been the key to success.

I talked to a number of the officers, or former officers, who had been involved in this exercise. At first I got nowhere. When I began to learn more about the nature of the planning and the unusual precautions taken to keep knowledge of it confined within the Department of National Defence (DND), I understood why those who knew about it were reticent. However, despite their reluctance to discuss the matter, preliminary inquiries satisfied me that it was a story worth pursuing.

It could, among other things, explain some aspects of events surrounding the Six Day War in Egypt that had puzzled and worried me. For example, our relations with the Egyptians, while they had never been close, were reasonably good. However, for no apparent reason in 1967, almost overnight, Egyptian ministers and officials became distinctly unfriendly, even accusing Canada of helping the Israelis. Thereafter the relationship deteriorated rapidly. 'Spontaneous public protests' were staged against us. Indeed, on the morning of Saturday, 10 June 1967, it appeared as if the Canadian chancellery building was about to be assaulted by 'an angry crowd.'

That morning TV cameras, power generators, and sound equipment were being set up at the back of the embassy building. I immediately telephoned el-Feki to ask that the activity be stopped immediately, since I knew, as did he, that it was a prelude to an assault on the mission. He was in no doubt that I was angry. I didn't think that the *démarche* would have any effect, but to my surprise and relief it did. Those preparing the assault soon began dismantling the equipment, and the 'angry crowds' dispersed.

From my inquiries in 1976 it appeared that Jean Allard while chief of the defence staff had requested planning of scenarios involving possible use of Canadian forces in the Middle East for different purposes, which was carried out under the code name *Exercise Lazarus*. Similar, but not necessarily related, planning also took place under the code name *Phoenix*.

Allard and I had known one another for a number of years, but it was not until he commanded the Fourth British Division, British Army of the Rhine, while I was Canadian ambassador in West Germany, that we got to know one another better. Indeed, he and his wife, Simone, came to stay with us in Cologne for a weekend. Their arrival by army helicopter, in a field near our house, caused quite a stir in the quiet, residential neighbourhood.

On 16 October 1976 I asked Allard to have lunch with me in Ottawa to see if he could take the story a bit further. I made a very careful note of the conversation the same day, while it was fresh in my mind. Subsequently, at its request, I gave a copy of the memorandum to the Directorate of History at DND. Allard spoke at length about the events that led to the Egyptian request for the withdrawal, 'within 48 hours,' of the Canadian contingent to UNEF and the plans that had been initiated for its evacuation.

None of these comments, however, seemed to touch directly on any of the more interesting aspects of *Exercise Lazarus*. Therefore I backtracked while we were having lunch to a comment that he had made at the beginning of our conversation dealing with his evident lack of sympathy for Canada's passive role in UNEF and 'peacekeeping' generally. He had said that while planning for possible evacuation he also began to think about the possibility of Canadian forces' being used in some other, presumably less passive role in the area. Without denying knowledge of *Exercise Lazarus* as such, he flatly denied that there had been any plan to interpose Canadian troops between the Israelis and the Egyptians.

Late in the conversation, however, he said that there might have been such plans, about which he knew very little. He added that a series of scenarios had been drawn up, about eight or ten, 'from feathers to guns.' Some had found their way into a memorandum for cabinet, which had rejected any idea of a fighting role for Canadian forces. Allard was vague about when such a document might have been prepared and submitted to ministers, but he agreed that it probably had been about the time of the withdrawal of the Canadian contingent to UNEF.

Military communications relating to evacuation of the Canadian contingent, and plans for possible further use of Canadian forces in the area, must have passed between Canada and overseas points such as Cyprus, Gaza, and Italy. As our conversation drew to an end, I asked Allard if he thought it possible that they could have been intercepted and decrypted by the Soviets and passed on to the Egyptians by the KGB resident in Cairo. He agreed that it was possible that communications among Air Transport Command in Canada, naval headquarters in Halifax, and points overseas, such as Cyprus and HMCS *Provider* at sea, could have been intercepted and their ciphers broken. He acknowledged that because of difficulties with the government of Cyprus, the Canadian forces there did not have secure communications with Canada. Moreover, the ciphers used at the time by DND might not have been secure from Soviet cipher-breaking techniques.

Following my talk with Allard I got in touch with the Directorate of

History at DND headquarters in an attempt to obtain any documentary evidence of the planning for *Exercise Lazarus*, which, it seemed clear, had taken place. W.A.B. Douglas, the director, was extremely helpful, and eventually, through the Access to Information Section of National Archives, I obtained a document, dated 14 July 1967, which includes 'Annex A,' dated 27 June 1967 and entitled 'Planning Assumptions' (see Appendix C). It is quite clear from the rest of the document that the planning for at least the air element – CF-100 aircraft from Canadian bases in Europe (assigned to NATO) – was carried out in response to a ministerial directive of 5 June 1967.

I then initiated further inquiries, in particular to find out if there had been any cabinet involvement. I spoke to Paul Martin in March 1988. He had never heard of *Exercise Lazarus* or of the idea that a Canadian military force be interposed between the Israelis and the Egyptians. He suggested that I get in touch with Paul Hellyer. I wrote to Hellyer explaining my interest, and he telephoned me on 7 July 1988. He said that he had no recollection of *Exercise Lazarus*, though the documents I had sent him rang a faint bell.

He suggested that I get in touch with Robert McNamara, the former U.S. secretary of defence; McNamara and/or some NATO military planning group might have prompted the study. He recalled that after the Six Day War, U.S. military authorities had expressed concern about possible adverse effects of Middle East hostilities on NATO's southern flank. Hellyer suggested that the Americans may have proposed that Canadian and other military authorities do some contingency planning. It is a reasonable explanation.

I did not contact McNamara, but I did make inquiries among Americans, mainly those who had worked for the U.S. Department of Defense on intelligence matters. I drew a blank there. Others to whom I talked included Geoffrey Pearson, as custodian of the Pearson Papers in the National Archives, and Gordon Robertson, as secretary to the cabinet at the time. Neither had heard of *Exercise Lazarus*. I was unable to confirm in particular that the subject had ever been raised at the cabinet level. I could find absolutely nothing to support the idea that Pearson or his colleagues, other than Hellyer, might have known of the planning and given it their blessing. In 1987 I obtained from the Privy Council Office a copy of the minutes of a cabinet discussion on the 'mid-east crisis' on 6 June 1967, the day following the successful Israeli attack on Egypt. There is no mention therein of reintroducing a Canadian military presence into the area, and the general tone suggests that the idea would not have had much support in cabinet.

My inquiries also uncovered hints that extraordinary measures were taken to confine knowledge of the military planning to a handful of officers and officials within DND. All copies were numbered, and no distribution appears to have taken place outside DND. I have spoken to the senior officers in External Affairs who normally might have known of such planning. None of them had heard of the idea, and all seemed very surprised when the relevant documentation was shown to them.

There is a considerable difference between routine military planning for every conceivable contigency and the extensive, specific planning involved in *Exercise Lazarus*, much of it fraught with domestic and international political overtones. During the course of my inquiries I received various soothing assurances that 'nothing had ever come of the planning.' However, that particular argument misses the point – whether or not such plans ever were translated into action, the planning itself could have been exploited by those with an interest in disturbing Arab–Canadian relations – a dimension that the planners seem not to have considered.

My hypothesis about how information concerning *Exercise Lazarus* might have got into Soviet hands, and eventually to the Egyptians, is no more than that – a theory. However, the KGB had a particularly strong and well-staffed station in Cairo. Its members were into everything and had very close ties with Egyptian security and intelligence agencies. The Soviets might have been able to produce decrypts of parts of the messages exchanged by the Canadian military authorities in planning *Exercise Lazarus*, sufficient to convince the Egyptians that Canada intended to intervene in some unfriendly, unspecified way.

Given the shocked state of Egyptian ministers and officials following the Six Day War, the Soviets would have had little difficulty in deliberately obscuring the difference between Canadian military planning and military action if they had wished to do so.

10

Winds of Change

I was not sorry when word came in the spring of 1967 from Marcel Cadieux that I was to return to Ottawa as assistant under-secretary of state for External Affairs, in charge of administration and personnel. Certainly, my time in Egypt and Sudan had been stimulating, challenging, and exciting, not least because of the fracas over the enforced withdrawal of the Canadian contingent to UNEF. While we were in London, en route to Ottawa, David Owen, secretary of state for foreign and commonwealth affairs, asked me to see him so that he could express his government's appreciation of the way in which we had been acting as protecting power.

After Helen and I got back to Ottawa we had to make a number of decisions concerning where to live and a place for my father, who was in frail health and could not be left on his own. In 1962, before leaving Canada for Germany, we had built a Norwegian-style log cabin on some land that we had bought in Chelsea, Quebec, in the 1950s. It was the only real estate we owned. On our return in 1967 we used it only occasionally, mostly as a ski cabin, while living in a rented apartment in Ottawa. It had no basement, one bathroom, and one small spare bedroom. In winter, though we had a space heater continuously lit, we sometimes were faced with solidly frozen water pipes. Eventually we found a place for my father in a nursing home in the Eastern Townships not far from Knowlton, Quebec, where he and my mother had lived for several years. There were a number of of his friends in the nursing home and in the area.

Not long after we returned to Ottawa Lester Pearson asked me to have lunch with him at the prime minister's residence on Sussex Drive. He went out of his way to say some nice things about the work done by the Canadian embassy in Egypt. We had a most pleasant lunch and gossiped about many things. I remember being taken aback, however, when he asked me, in that deliberately casual way he had, if I had ever thought of going into politics. Clearly, he meant as a Liberal candidate. I knew him well enough to know that he was being far from casual. I gave more or less the answer I had given to Lionel Chevrier ten years earlier – that the idea of a political career did not attract me. He accepted my reply without comment and never raised the matter with me again. I remember thinking that it was no wonder that the Liberal party had been in power for so many years; it worked tirelessly at recruiting whenever it had the opportunity!

Several months later another such suggestion came from Jeanne Sauvé, Speaker of the House of Commons, when we met at a diplomatic reception given by one of the Latin American heads of mission. She asked me if I had ever given thought to becoming a member of Parliament. Given her own political affiliations, clearly she meant as a member of the Liberal party. I gave the same answer that I had given Chevrier and Pearson. It was my impression that Sauvé's query was not in any way premeditated, but something said on the spur of the moment.

My only experience with political activity came in 1968–9, when I was persuaded to run for office as a councillor in West Hull. Since I was a federal public servant, Treasury Board rules required me to obtain the permission of the minister (Mitchell Sharp) to accept the candidacy. Sharp gave his consent, and in due course I was elected. Later events, including my joining the RCMP, obliged me to resign.

Being assistant deputy minister in charge of the department's administration kept me busy. It was a job that earned the incumbent few friends and a number of enemies, since not everyone could be promoted or transferred to postings of their choice. However, I was very happy to be working closely with Marcel Cadieux again. There were many changes in the wind, some of which arose from the work of the Glassco Commission or had been in the works for some time. The most discouraging was the evident desire of Pierre Trudeau to whittle down External Affairs. His method was to make an arbitrary percentage cut to our budget and to tell us to get on with the job. Mitchell Sharp seemed unwilling to make an issue of the matter with his colleagues, particularly Trudeau. Ministers were not happy, however, when we responded by proposing that some of our missions be closed. Since a considerable percentage of our annual budget was given over to salaries and allowances, closing a few missions and reallocating the personnel affected appeared preferable to widespread layoffs, with all the personal and other problems attendant on such action. Hanley Bennett, whom I had recruited from the Treasury Board, proved very helpful in the ensuing negotiations. He knew the ropes from the Treasury standpoint and how to get things done and, equally important, undone.

I managed to persuade Larry O'Toole to join External Affairs. He had headed the team from Woods Gordon & Co. of Toronto that designed a detailed financial management plan for the department. When the report was finished and accepted, I suggested that we attempt to hire O'Toole to implement the plan. Cadieux agreed, and O'Toole accepted. I gained much from his professional advice and experience and from our friendship.

I have often wondered whether, if Pierre Trudeau and Norman Robertson had been closer in age and had worked together, Canada's foreign policies might not have benefited. The combination could have been quite extraordinary. Trudeau would have found his intellectual match in Robertson, and vice versa, and each would have found satisfaction in the unusual imagination and mental agility of the other. If the human chemistry had been right, it could have been a partnership arranged in heaven. Some of the futile initiatives launched by Trudeau and Ivan Head in the 1970s might have been averted or modified, to Canada's advantage.

One project that I pursued with enthusiasm about 1968 was a departmental 'operations room' that would have integrated, displayed, and updated information from all sources, including that derived from communications intelligence and other sensitive intelligence material, with our normal political and economic reporting. In part, I was inspired by the kind of operations rooms set up by the NATO military in Europe. There were problems of funding, of satisfying various security restrictions, particularly those involving communications intelligence, and of staffing the centre during a crisis. It was eventually set up and, I believe, subsequently proved useful. After I joined the RCMP in 1970, I was able to have a somewhat similar facility set up in the Security Service. It was a useful place in which to attempt to brief solicitors general on what the Security Service did and exactly how, though I don't think that it was an unqualified success in this regard.

Not long after I became director-general of the RCMP Security Service, Dick Helms, director of the CIA, paid an official visit to Ottawa and to External Affairs in particular, where he was shown its newly installed operations room. By this time (probably late autumn 1970) almost all the officials he saw were obsessed with Quebec's problems. Unfortunately, his only apparent interest – and presumably the principal reason for his visit – appeared to be to impress on the Canadians the threat to North America posed by Eastern-bloc espionage and other clandestine activities. The United States wanted Canada to do much more to help counter these activities. His rather aggressive line merely irritated Canadian officials, though I don't think that he noticed. Those in Washington who had briefed him obviously had not been following political events in Canada very closely.

Part Three:
Rethinking Security
1970–1994

11

Compromise Candidate

Out of the blue, on 23 September 1969, I received a telephone call from Gordon Robertson, secretary to the cabinet, asking me to meet him for lunch that day at the Rideau Club to discuss a 'matter of some urgency.' I can outline the event by referring to a slightly expurgated and declassified version of a fifty-seven-page written submission that I made to the McDonald Commission on 16 December 1977, which has been made public (excluding the appendices) and describes the meeting. I quote from it at several places below.

When we met, Robertson quickly came to the point. The prime minister wondered if I would be willing to present myself as a candidate for appointment as commissioner of the RCMP. I need hardly say that I was taken aback. I said that it was not a position to which I ever had aspired, and I would like time to reflect on the idea and its implications for my future. Robertson explained that this might not be possible, since ministers planned to interview candidates that same afternoon. He mentioned Len Higgitt and a more junior member of the RCMP who had some university education. I agreed to appear, though reluctantly, and with serious misgivings, since I disliked making such a decision in haste.

I never discovered why I was considered a likely candidate. Apart from having a relative, Cortland Starnes, who had been commissioner of the RCMP in the 1920s, I had had nothing to do with the force except on the intelligence and security side, though I had been a friend of several commissioners – Leonard 'Nick' Nicholson, Clifford 'Slim' Harvison, George McClelland, and Charles Rivett-Carnac. Of these I knew McClelland best, since he was one of Bill Crean's close friends. McClelland was a marvellous character, full of fun and a gifted ranconteur. Some of his stories about the RCMP and their counter-intelligence activities were hilarious, if unprintable.

A couple of hours after our lunch I was asked to go to Gordon Robertson's office, adjacent to the room in which the cabinet usually met in the East Block. In due course, I was led into the cabinet room through a connecting door to find myself placed at the end of a large, green baize table, facing the prime minister and a gaggle of ministers, including Leo Cadieux, Bud Drury, George McIlraith, Gérard Pelletier, Mitchel Sharp, and John Turner. The atmosphere reminded me a bit of the Rhodes Scholarship board in Montreal, chaired by Sir Edward Beatty.

One minister asked me my view about members of the force wearing turbans as headgear, instead of the traditional 'Smokey the Bear' hat. I replied that I could see no reason why turbans should not be worn, which seemed to evoke a favourable reaction. I was taken aback, however, by the final question put to me by the prime minister – why was I interested in becoming the commissioner of the RCMP? I replied that I was not at all sure that I was interested, having first heard of the idea only a few hours earlier!

That evening I received a telephone call from Bud Drury, a friend of many years' standing, asking me if I could come to his office the following morning. The next morning's discussion was lengthy and rambling. He told me that ministers had concluded that it might be premature to appoint a civilian to head the RCMP, a view with which I agreed. Eventually, he came to the point. The prime minister wondered if I would be interested in becoming the first civilian to head the security and intelligence activities of the RCMP. I said that I knew something about the work involved, and it was not a job that I coveted. It was a tough, thankless task and, in hierarchical and other terms, less important than that of the commissioner. Apart from all this, I said that I was not especially attracted to the idea of leaving the foreign service, in which I had spent twenty-six years. After some further, desultory discussion, I told Bud that I was not enthusiastic. It was left that I would reflect on the matter and get in touch with him.

Drury, in his inimitable manner, argued that if I were to take the job there was no reason why I should continue to receive the same salary I was getting as an assistant deputy minister in External Affairs! I knew him well enough to know that he was simply teasing me, and I tried to keep my temper. However, I wondered if he remembered the occasion when we were at the same school in Montreal in the late 1920s and, for whatever reason, he and his younger brother Chipman (Chip) decided that I needed a beating. I very probably had been sassy. It was arranged that we would meet after school in the small cobble-stoned courtyard behind the church on the corner of Sherbrooke and Simpson streets, not far from the school. I was horrified to learn that my mother in some way had learned of the assignation and announced that she intended to be present. My heart sank. I could just hear the catcalls – 'mother's boy, sissy, sissy.' All the actors duly turned up. My mother, who was well known to the Drurys, stood in the middle of the scene. To my utter surprise and delight she spoke only one terse phrase: 'Fight fair. One at a time.' The Drurys were as surprised as I was. As we stood gawking at one another her only other comment was: 'Well, what are you waiting for?'

After discussions with Marcel Cadieux and a good deal of soul-searching, I telephoned Drury to tell him that I would accept the job. At the same time I asked Gordon Robertson if I would still be considered a candidate for the commissioner's job at some future date. I received such an assurance in a confidential letter from the prime minister dated 20 November 1969, a copy of which I attached to my above-mentioned fifty-seven-page statement to the McDonald Commission. As I told the commission on 16 December 1977, my principal motivation in accepting the job was a belief that I might be able to contribute something.

In retrospect, however, I believe that I was overconfident and naïve. I thought that I knew enough about the intelligence and security problems facing the RCMP Security Service to be able to manage that side of the job, but there was a good deal that I did not know and which I had to learn the hard way. More important, what I had not reckoned on was the quite different culture of the RCMP and the mistrust that had grown up between the Liberal government and the force. I now believe that both the force and the government were to blame, though the latter's rather unsophisticated and dilatory treatment of the rec-ommendations of the Royal Commission on Security (1966–8) headed by Max Mackenzie certainly worsened the unsatisfactory relationship.

As I expressed it in my written submission to the McDonald Commission on 16 December 1977:

I was shocked, however, shortly after taking over the job by an incident which demonstrated the extent of the distrust of the RCMP on the part of ministers and senior officials and their apparent ignorance of security operations.

In March 1970 I was approached on behalf of the Prime Minister by an Assistant Secretary to the Cabinet to ask if I could ascertain if the RCMP had 'bugged' the telephones of ministers and senior officials and the cabinet offices during the period when the [Mackenzie] report was being debated by them behind closed doors. Evidently the Prime Minister and his officials had felt that the RCMP were uncommonly well prepared for the questions and propositions put to them by ministers. They appeared to be so well briefed, indeed, that it was suspected they might have used their arcane skills to eavesdrop on the Prime Minister and his advisors.

I expressed my surprise at the suggestion that the Directorate of Security and Intelligence would attempt to use its capabilities in such an improper manner. I undertook to make discreet enquiries and to report back. This I was able to do in due course. I reported that I had discovered absolutely nothing which would support such an allegation. Moreoever, I had satisfied myself that it would have been virtually impossible technically for anything of that kind to have been undertaken and sustained. A telephone tap would have had to be carried out with the co-operation of Bell Canada in accordance with long-standing, precise legal agreements between Bell and the government. The telephone company would have refused to act without a warrant personally signed by the appropriate Minister – in this case the Solicitor General.

To introduce microphones into the Cabinet Offices clandestinely would entail a major operation involving numerous persons and substantial technical support.

Apart from the fact that the building was under twenty-four hour guard there existed in the East Block facilities maintained by External Affairs which were devoted exclusively to the detection of eavesdropping devices. These facilities were maintained in Room 77 in the basement of the East Block and used principally by External Affairs as a sophisicated research and training centre in counter-intrusion methods. Detection tests were constantly being run and the risks would have been very high that wireless transmissions only a few metres distant would have been detected immediately. Microphones depending upon a wired connection to some point outside the building would have been quite impossible to install without detection.

My explanation appeared to have satisfied my interlocutor since I heard no more about the matter. However, it left me with a profound uneasiness and an early appreciation of the apparent depth of distrust and sheer ignorance about the technical capablilities of the Security Service on the part of ministers and their senior advisors. The latter point is not without relevance to the task which has been given this commission.

Had I been aware of this deep distrust, I would have been a good deal more cautious and might even have turned down the job. I proba-bly should have attached more significance than I did to the failure (inability) of the government to tackle Mackenzie's recommendations and to have drawn the approprate lessons.

I now feel that a number of others and I paid far too little attention to the work of the Mackenzie Commission. For example, Kevin O'Neill (secretary) and Jack Trotman (research director) did most of the draft-ing of the report and were constantly advising the commissioners (Max Mackenzie, James Coldwell, and Yves Pratte). Both O'Neill and Trot-man were very experienced, capable, and knowledgeable members of the intelligence community. O'Neill was for years deeply involved in communications intelligence and communications security and was from 1971 to 1980 director of the Communications Branch of the National Research Council (CBNRC) – now Communications Security Establishment (CSE) in the Department of National Defence. Trotman was a most active, intelligent member of the Joint Intelligence Staff (JIS), very ably serving the Joint Intelligence Committee (JIC) for sev-eral years. Both men were very literate and experienced in drafting documents and proposals. Moreover, because of their background, they knew a good deal about the operations of the RCMP Directorate of Security and Intelligence, not in detail, but much more thoroughly than most others outside the RCMP. By contrast, the McDonald Com-mission had no such in-house, detailed, expert security and intelli-gence experience on which to draw and thus remained largely unaware of the activities of a significant proportion of the intelligence community and of its valuable connections with the RCMP.

In my view, the recommendations of the Mackenzie Commission should have received much more attention. The government should have been much firmer in dealing with the RCMP's largely emotional and sometimes unrealistic objections to the idea of a security service divorced from the RCMP. It should have paid far more attention to Mackenzie's detailed proposals and to their effective implementation. I should have been quicker to note the warning flags and to have insisted on receiving direction when none existed. I was a compromise candidate and, as it turned out, not a very propitious one – a stop-gap, not a lasting solution.

Following my acceptance of the job, I met with Solicitor General George McIlraith in October 1969 to work out the details of the appointment – my title and status, preparation of a public statement about the appointment, and the precise nature of my relationship with the minister, the prime minister, and the commissioner.

As I wrote to the McDonald Commission in 1977: 'I should like to turn now to the complicated and important question of the relationship between the Security Service and the Prime Minister and the Security Service and the Minister responsible to Parliament for its activities, including those of a clandestine nature. In many ways, the problem is central to this Commission's work and no doubt it deserves the most careful attention.' I explained further:

At the outset it was made quite clear to me by the Prime Minister that there were certain matters on which he wished me to deal directly with him. These included any information about his Ministers which might cause him difficulties and information of a similar character concerning members of his family and personal entourage, Liberal Members of Parliament and persons holding senior government appointments which were within his power to make, e.g., Deputy Ministers and heads of government agencies. He also made it clear that I should not hesitate to deal with him directly on any other matter on which I felt it important for him to be informed or which might require his decision.

... I should add here that 99.9% of the time the Security Service was unable to provide anything more than a 'negative' report on the kinds of persons he had mentioned.

Usually there was nothing on the files about such persons, for the simple reason that the service investigated individuals only at the specific request of departments or agencies seeking security clearances for their employees. On rare occasions an investigation of some suspected espionage or subversive activity might appear to involve persons subsequently selected for appointment by the prime minister – for example, people who, by some unwise activity, might have attracted the attention of the KGB. So long as the person in question was a private individual, the matter would be of little interest from a national security standpoint. However, if the prime minister wished to appoint such a person to a senior position of trust, obviously the situation would be changed.

I found the arrangement useful and, for the most part, satisfactory. The Prime Minister was a pleasure to do business with. He was quick, perceptive and decisive and inevitably patient and courteous. I would not have had occasion to see him in this way more than half a dozen times a year and I was very careful to avoid taking advantage of the privilege.

... As I mentioned earlier George McIlraith encouraged me to see the Prime Minister and certainly he was aware of the P.M.'s wish to have me deal directly with him on certain matters. Unfortunately, his successors, Jean-Pierre Goyer and Warren Allmand, were not made aware of the arrangement before their appointment.

... In the case of Jean-Pierre Goyer this led to some awkwardness. I cannot now remember how the matter arose but it became necessary for me, shortly after Jean-Pierre Goyer's appointment as Solicitor General, to inform him about the arrangement, a chore I would have preferred to have avoided. The Minister reacted badly and the Commissioner and I had an unpleasant argument with him. Goyer felt that he ought to be the intermediary through whom any information about his Cabinet colleagues, Liberal members of Parliament, members of the Prime Minister's family or personal entourage or senior officials should be transmitted to the P.M. Indeed, he also insisted that he should be informed about personnel security problems in any department of government.

... The Commissioner and I urged him to consider carefully the position he was taking. We pointed out that for him to be informed about his Cabinet colleagues could be embarrassing and certainly inappropriate since all ministers held their portfolio at the Prime Minister's pleasure, as did senior officials. We said we assumed, moreover, that the Minister would not wish to be privy to information about the Prime Minister's family and personal entourage or Liberal Members of Parliament. Insofar as security information about public servants was concerned, there existed a very clear Cabinet Directive (No. 35) which required information of this kind to be communicated directly by the Security Service to the deputy head of the department concerned. It was then the deputy's responsibility, together with his Minister, to decide how each case should be handled. To follow any other procedure would require an amendment to that Cabinet directive.

... Eventually, no agreement was reached and the matter was left on a very sour note. We pointed out that if the Minister felt the matter was unsatisfactory he should raise it with the Prime Minister ... I was worried that the affair could adversely affect the whole tenor of my relationship with the Minister and I subsequently mentioned the problem to the Prime Minister on a suitable occasion. I assume the Prime Minister dealt with it in some way since Jean-Pierre Goyer never raised the matter again and certainly Goyer's successor, Warren Allmand, never questioned the arrangement.

This unpleasantness could easily have been avoided if the prime minister or the secretary to the cabinet met with each newly appointed solicitor general and the head of the Security Service – a suggestion that I advanced on various occasions. I urged also that each new member of the cabinet be briefed in general terms by the Security Service when he or she took office, as was the practice in Britain. Nothing was ever done on either score. These practices could have been useful to ministers and to officials and would have avoided the occasional misunderstanding.

I recall in early October 1970 having had to inform the prime minister that through Robert Ford, Canadian ambassador in Moscow, we had learned that a man calling himself Professor Nikitin of the Institute of History in Moscow was directly involved in Soviet preparations for a visit to the Soviet Union that Trudeau wished to make. With the agreement of Gordon Robertson, I told Trudeau what we knew about Nikitin's real identity, so that he might be on his guard. Nikitin was actually Anatoli Borisovich Gorsky, an old-time KGB officer who sometimes also used the name Anatoli Gromov and, from 1936 to 1944, had operated out of the KGB residency at the Soviet embassy in London. Among other things he had helped run high-level espionage and agent-of-influence operations against the United States and, using the codename 'Henry,' had handled Soviet agents Guy Burgess, Donald Maclean, and Kim Philby. Gorsky was known to the RCMP Security Service, as he had also been involved in attempts to recruit Canadians, including John Watkins, while he was ambassador in Moscow.

It was difficult to believe that the Soviet Union would be bold enough to mount an operation against the prime minister of Canada, but, given its record, we could rule out nothing and felt that he should be warned. I believe that Trudeau was grateful to have been informed about Nikitin and as puzzled as we were to know what the KGB expected that it might gain from such crude, unfriendly behaviour.

I know now that I should have obtained a clear written statement from the government as to precisely what it wished me to do. Indeed, it gradually became clear that it really didn't know what it expected me to do, other than to be a visible sign that it was getting a firm grip on the RCMP and its security and intelligence activities in particular.

This lack of clear direction reminded me of a characteristic of many regimes in the Middle East – the assumption that simply because something is announced (in this case, making the RCMP Security Service 'more civilian and separate in character') it will happen without any further action being taken by ministers or interest shown. This attitude became a characteristic of Trudeau's governments, especially in their handling of security and intelligence.

At a chance meeting with Chief Justice Antonio Lamer I recently learned that Trudeau had asked him in 1969 to consider whether it was appropriate for a national police force also to be engaged in counter-espionage. Lamer was permitted to consult two colleagues and old friends, Jean Beetz and Julien Chouinard, both later members of the Supreme Court. Their unanimous view was that such activity was inappropriate, for it clearly conflicted with the force's police functions. Thus Trudeau was already concerned about 'the inherent contradiction' in having a police force involved in activities that could be illegal, such as surreptitious entries to premises in order to install microphones or video equipment for surveillance. I assume that he may have been influenced by the Mackenzie Commission, which recommended separation of the RCMP's police functions from those carried out by its Directorate of Security and Intelligence. Even it, however, would have permitted the opening of first-class mail in certain, carefully controlled circumstances. The only outcome of those lengthy discussions was a compromise – my appointment as the first civilian to head the RCMP Security Service.

My mission was never spelled out except in the very general terms of the prime minister's statement to the House of Commons on 26 June 1969. George McIlraith encouraged me to deal directly with the prime minister whenever I thought this desirable or necessary. My title of 'director-general' was one widely used in the public service and abroad and thus would be recognized. McIlraith suggested that I should also have the personal rank of deputy commissioner, to reinforce my position within the RCMP. Detailed arrangements about salary, pension rights, and method of appointment were left for me to work out with the deputy minister at External Affairs, the secretary to the Treasury Board, and the commissioner.

At some point following my appointment, Mike Pearson and Arnold Heeney invited me to lunch with them at the Rideau Club. This thoughtful and generous gesture of support was not lost on the denizens of the club. I greatly appreciated it, since it was clear that I would need all the support I could get. They also intended the lunch to mark their having successfully proposed me for membership. At the time Pearson was president, and Heeney a long-time member. I recall that during the lunch Pearson wore a black patch over one of his eyes, which had had to be removed. He was remarkably cheerful for someone who had undergone such a serious operation and full of good advice, tactfully disguised in the form of good-natured banter.

Some time in October 1969, when I was still in External Affairs, I had been approached by representatives of the RCMP Security Service who informed me about CAZAB. This organization, made up of senior officers from the intelligence communities of Canada, Australia, New Zealand, 'America' (the United States), and Britain, exchanged top-secret information on counter-intelligence, particularly the espionage activities of the KGB and its allies. Meetings took place about every eighteen months, the first having been held in Melbourne in November 1967.

I learned that Mike Pearson, as prime minister, had given his approval to the RCMP's joining this unique 'club.' To maintain the extreme secrecy of the venture, the participants had agreed to limit knowledge about CAZAB in each country to as few persons as possible. Pearson decided that at the ministerial level in Canada only the prime minister would know about CAZAB. Among officials, nobody outside the RCMP Security Service was to be informed.

Later I discovered that Pearson, who had become seriously ill in 1968, never was able to pass on the knowledge to his successor, Pierre Trudeau, which complicated my job and the McDonald Commission's. To have indoctrinated Trudeau would have involved reopening the whole question of Canada's membership – something that the commisioner was reluctant to do.

A second surprise in October 1969 was to be told that CAZAB was meeting shortly, in New York City, and that the 'club' had agreed for me to be there. I was relieved that the commissioner, W.L. (Len) Higgitt, would be able to accompany me, since he already was fully indoctrinated into CAZAB and was very knowledgeable about espionage matters. I regarded it as a good opportunity to meet my opposite numbers in the club – the directors of MI 5, MI 6, the CIA, and the Australian and New Zealand secret services. It then remained to find a believable reason for the two of us to be absent from Ottawa for a couple of days. However, since we were able to use an RCMP aircraft for the occasion our absence was hardly noticed.

As a prelude to my attendance at the CAZAB meeting, the Security

Service informed me that it would like me to meet Anatoly Golitsin, a high-ranking KGB officer who had worked inside the First Chief Directorate of the KGB, responsible for espionage operations against Britain and the United States (including Canada). Golitsin defected to the Americans in Helsinki, subsequently providing a good deal of information about KGB espionage operations, leading, among other things, to British re-examination of those suspected of being among the 'Cambridge Five.' Golitsin had been made available to the RCMP Security Service for 'consultations' by Jim Angleton of the CIA, whose protégé he was.

Shortly thereafter it was arranged for me to meet Golitsin, in suitably secure circumstances, in a suite in Ottawa's Château Laurier Hotel. I found it a curious experience. He put me off by his unctuous manner and by his pressing his arguments too strongly, including the theory that the rumoured dispute between the Soviet Union and China was an elaborate piece of communist disinformation. Most of his arguments on this score were far too convoluted and byzantine for me to follow intelligently. If he had a sense of humour, it was well disguised. I was glad of the chance to meet him, however, since there was a good deal of controversy over him, especially between the British and the Amercans. I was not particularly impressed by the man. Indeed, I felt rather sorry for him. Perhaps if I had been able to speak Russian I might have felt differently.

The CAZAB meeting in New York at the end of 1969 has been amusingly described by Peter Wright in *Spy Catcher*. Some of the participants were more interested in betting on the horse races than the top-secret matters that we gathered to discuss. Wright's rather scurrilous account is particularly interesting because of its shrewd, unkind, and sometimes accurate picture of James Jesus Angleton, head of the CIA's counter-espionage activities, without whom CAZAB would not have been established. Angleton pushed the sensible idea of pooling all available information on KGB espionage and tradecraft activities thoughout the world. Since this kind of information inevitably concerned citizens of participating countries, it was particularly sensitive in terms of protecting the rights of citizens. Unfortunately, Angleton tended also to use CAZAB to pursue his own pet theories and prejudices, sometimes to the detriment of the national interests of other members. This did not make for harmonious relations.

I found that I could get along with Angleton, which was fortunate, given his key position in the CIA. However, we did not always agree, as is clear from a review of a book about Angleton by Tom Mangold that I wrote for *bout de papier* in 1992:

Jim Angleton is a biographer's nightmare. An attractive, complex, eccentric, interesting and contradictory character whom, so far as I'm concerned, Mangold has almost but not quite captured ... On occasion I disagreed with Angleton, sometimes sharply. For example, when I was his guest at a late night dinner, given at la Nicoise restaurant in Georgetown about 1972, he casually trotted out the idea that Mike Pearson, when he was Prime Minister, had been a KGB agent. To my utter astonishment, Angleton appeared to be deadly serious ... In my view any suggestion that Mike could be disloyal to Canada was preposterous. I angrily rejected Angleton's charges, which were based upon the flimsiest of circumstantial evidence ... Angleton and I remained on reasonably good terms, although I confess that had I known some of the matters revealed in Mangold's book I would have been even more distrustful than I was of his personal judgements.

Among the courtesy calls that Len Higgitt and I made together was to meet FBI director J. Edgar Hoover, in March 1970 – Higgitt as the new commissioner, and I as the new head of security and intelligence. The RCMP's relations with the FBI were long-standing and close, particularly on the police side of the FBI's work. The relationship seemed to work reasonably well, even though the United States, because of its sheer size, wealth, and influence, was the senior partner. The security and intelligence side of the FBI's work sometimes seemed to be in conflict with the CIA's role both at home and abroad, which occasionaly made life difficult for third parties such as Canada.

The senior FBI officer in charge of security and intelligence was Chief Inspector William C. Sullivan, whom I came to know and like. Indeed, he kindly gave me a copy of *The FBI in Our Open Society*, which he inscribed: 'To Director General J.K. Starnes – All of us welcome you aboard the RCMP-FBI Team with much enthusiasm – Bill Sullivan and staff.' It was a friendly gesture, which I appreciated. I was sorry when Sullivan died a few years later. He had his problems working for Hoover, but then he was not alone in that respect.

When Higgitt and I were received by Hoover, it was quite a performance, one that obviously had taken place many times before. Hoover dominated the conversation, discussing only things that interested him. It seemed to me that the room was filled with American flags and the walls were covered with memorabilia. We sat opposite Hoover at an enormous, relatively uncluttered desk, with the light behind him. I recall being fascinated by his ears, which, with the light behind them, seemed quite prominent, reminiscent of cauliflowers.

In 1969 I was fully occupied with winding up my duties at External Affairs and handing them over to Bill Barton. However, George McIlraith suggested that I accompany him to a meeting of the Cabinet Committee on Security and Intelligence on Friday, 19 December. Pierre Trudeau agreed to my being there as an observer.

The meeting, chaired by the prime minister, proved important in terms of future events. The centre-piece of the discussion was a paper that had been circulated earlier to ministers (see Appendix D) and was signed by the prime minister – 'Current Threats to National Order and Unity – Quebec Separatism' (S&I-10, 17 December 1969) (Appendix E). Copies were handed to the dozen or so officials present at the beginning of the meeting (see minutes, Appendix F). Dissemination was limited to twenty copies, and each copy was numbered, with recipients being required to return them to the committee secretary after the meeting. It is difficult to tell who might have written the paper. Though in Trudeau's name, it was unlikely to have been drafted by him. The paper was probably descended directly from a similar paper prepared in the Privy Council Office (PCO) for Pearson and first discussed at a 'special committee' of the Security Panel on 14 August 1967. It is quite clear from the documents in Appendices D–F (despite many deletions made under the provisions of the Access to Information Act) that ministers were discussing the collection of information not merely about the Front de libération du Québec (FLQ) and other extremist groups in the separatist camp, but about Quebec separatists as such!

My lawyers and the lawyers of others subpoenaed on various occasions to appear before the McDonald Commission (1978–81) attempted to get these and other such relevant documents released to them to assist the defence of their clients but were refused access on the grounds of cabinet confidentiality. The commission itself made a similar request but also was refused access on the same grounds, though I believe that Commissioner David McDonald was permitted to see, but not retain, some of these documents. For the Liberal government, pleading cabinet confidentiality was a convenient way of not having to make public documents that could be embarrassing, since they would show clearly, contrary to what was argued before the

McDonald Commission and subsequently, that as early as 1967 the Liberal government was actively involved in countering Quebec separatist political movements as such, and not just the more extreme elements.

At the time, I did not object to the argument that if Canada's parliamentary system is to work, discussions in cabinet must remain confidential. I was surprised therefore in the 1980s to receive copies of almost all the minutes that I had sought, in some cases without any excisions, and with statements attributed to ministers by name. The minutes are models of clarity and precision, a number having been written by Marshal Crowe, then deputy secretary to the cabinet. In former times, when Arnold Heeney was secretary to the cabinet, ministers were seldom identified by name. Though some passages in the minutes have been excised, enough of the text remains to indicate the role that the RCMP Security Service was expected to play. The commissioner of the RCMP emphasized

that he would require clear direction from the government before embarking on the same investigative activities against separatists as he now conducted against communists, because of the extreme sensitivity of the problem ... The RCMP could produce documents on separatist organizations, despite the lack of government direction in this area, and suggested that the problem was not so much that of obtaining information but of putting to use information already available. [Some words have been excised.] ... that such information was readily available. As to taking further action to gather information by clandestine means, this was, of course, possible but he would feel obliged to point out the risks involved.

It was during the McDonald Commission's hearings that I first learned that in August 1967 Mike Pearson, incensed by Charles de Gaulle's infamous intervention in Canadian affairs ('Vive le Québec libre'), had ordered, in great secrecy, the creation of a hand-picked group of senior officials to meet as a 'special committee' of the Security Panel to consider the threats posed by Quebec separatism and to devise ways of countering them. I knew nothing of these secret meetings, because it was not my business at External Affairs to know. The group held two meetings in 1967, on 14 August and 29 September, chaired by Secretary to the Cabinet Gordon Robertson. Eventually, in the 1980s, I was able to get some of the relevant documents released; much of the released material has been censored, with entire pages being blank.

By mid-1972 I had come reluctantly to the conclusion that I had failed to make any real progress in changing the Security Service. Because of a personal commitment I had made to the commissioner at the outset and because he had become part of the problem I took particular care not to let him realize how discouraged I had become. I phrased the problem in the following terms in my lengthy statement to the McDonald Commission on 16 December 1977: 'I do not know and, indeed, I do not know to this day whether Len Higgitt was aware that I was a rival, albeit an unenthusiastic one, for the job of Commissioner. I suspected he was but I was careful to give him no hint of the fact. I was particularly careful also to do the same with every other member of the Force and those outside it. In the circumstances to have done other than to have accepted to serve the Commissioner loyally would have made a difficult relationship even more difficult, and, more important, would have made it impossible to obtain his support without which the extensive reforms apparently contemplated by the government could not have been accomplished.' I had made it quite clear to Higgitt that he could count on my loyalty and that I had no intention of going behind his back to achieve my goals, which would not have been difficult to do, had I chosen that path. I think that he was surprised and genuinely grateful for my declaration. It certainly helped the relationship but did little to help me get the job of 'civilianization' of the Security Service accomplished. Accordingly, I decided to seek early retirement from public service. I put the wheels in motion to obtain my early release by informing the secretary to the cabinet, the commissioner of the RCMP, and the solicitor general of my intentions.

In my statement of 16 December 1977 I explained my decision to resign and my method of doing so:

My failure to make the Security Service more separate and civilian in nature, continual uninformed criticism of its work in Parliament and in the news media, coupled with the never-ending bureaucratic squabbles and indifference to Security Service concerns on the part of senior officials and Ministers led me to conclude my usefulness probably had ended ... I was, however, so discouraged and fed up I decided my resignation probably was in my own best interests and in the interests of the Security Service. I hoped a fresh mind and a different approach might succeed where I had failed ... I was very careful in giving effect to this decision not to reveal my reasons for wanting to resign since I felt to have done so would have made my successor's task unnecessarily difficult and it could harm the continuing work of the Security Service.

With such thoughts in mind I wrote to Gordon Robertson, the secretary to the cabinet, to see if the prime minister would convene a meeting of the minister, the commissioner, Michael Dare (designated as my successor), Robertson, and me to enable the prime minister to emphasize the importance that he attached to having the Security Service develop along the lines that he had set out in his speech to the House of Commons on 26 June 1969. Attached at Appendix G is a copy of my letter to Gordon Robertson (21 February 1973) and a memorandum that I made on 20 March 1973 (also censored under terms of the Access to Information Act) of what transpired at the meeting convened by the prime minister on 16 March 1973.

The compromise candidate may not have succeeded in his appointed goals, but the times in which he served were, as the next two chapters show, fraught and fascinating.

12

Tough Cases

Preliminary briefings of all kinds had been completed by the time I took over as director-general of the RCMP Security Service on 1 January 1970. In fact, however, my position and rank as a public servant meant that I was subject to the same rules and regulations and code of discipline as 'regular members' of the RCMP, except that I lacked certain of their powers. For example, I was not a 'peace officer' or a 'justice of the peace' under the terms of the RCMP act and thus was unable to sign warrants for submission to the minister – for instance, for the interception of telephone conversations. Similarly, I was not able to take disciplinary action against any member of the service; only the commissioner and senior regular members could do that. Given the government's desire to appoint a civilian and to emphasize the fact, it is difficult to see how the matter could have been handled otherwise without changing the RCMP act.

I concluded that, given my background and experience, I probably could be most useful in areas in which I was knowledgeable and already had some useful contacts. For example, I knew senior officials in other government departments, the Privy Council Office, and Treasury Board and a number of ministers. I also had a number of such personal contacts with senior members of the security and intelligence agencies of a number of countries with which the RCMP Security Service regularly did business.

I had little or no practical, technical experience of running such Security Service operations as counter-intelligence and counter-espionage operations. Therefore, with the commissioner's agreement, I left this side of my responsibilities to the many able and experienced staff members in the Security Service. I left it to them to tell me of specific cases, particularly if they involved something on which I might have to make decisions. The weakness in this arrangement was that in some cases I lacked the background knowledge necessary to a proper understanding of them. Attempting to read the relevant files – perhaps many volumes – against the possibility that the case might become active again proved impractical. Given many other responsibilities that took me away from headquarters for long periods, it became almost impossible.

I was pleased to discover that I already knew quite a number of the people in the RCMP's Directorate of Security and Intelligence, including Leslie James Bennett, head of counter-espionage activities, whom I had known at the Department of External Affairs.

During the war Bennett spent six years in the British army, much of it in intelligence (communications intelligence work). A good part of this service was in the Middle East, in Malta, and with the British Eighth Army. Given his excellent credentials and wartime service it is not surprising that he was able to join the British Government Communications Headquarters (GCHQ) in July 1946. In October 1947 Bennett was sent to the British consulate-general in Istanbul to help expand the capabilities of the small intercept station established there during the war. By this time, however, GCHQ's primary targets had become Soviet espionage agents. It happened that the MI 6 station chief in Turkey was Kim Philby. Bennett met Philby during this time, largely to obtain promise of MI 6's help, should he need it. He never needed Philby's help and, like almost everyone else in the British intelligence community, including MI 6, was quite unaware of Philby's treachery.

His job in Istanbul well done, Bennett returned to Britain some months later to work in GCHQ. In 1950 he was posted to Australia as a liaison officer, and then he was sent to Hong Kong, continuing his intelligence work. He returned to GCHQ, where he continued to work on identifying Soviet espionage agents and pinpointing their communications. In 1958, through a friendship with Joe Gibson, then liaison officer for the Communications Branch, National Research Council (CBNRC), at GCHQ, Bennett came to Canada with a possibility of employment with CBNRC.

Unfortunately, as proved to be the case far too often in Canada's intelligence community at that time, Brits were unwelcome. Mary Oliver, Norman Robertson's sister, then in charge of personnel in CBNRC, was unhappy about the treatment given Bennett and did what she could to have him hired. Her efforts were unsuccessful, but she was able to have him considered for employment with the RCMP by Don Wall (an assistant secretary to the cabinet in the 1970s) and Mark McClung. Both men then worked in the RCMP. Eventually, thanks largely to Terry Guernsey of the RCMP, Bennett was hired as a research analyst grade 3 at RCMP headquarters.

When I joined the Security Service of the RCMP Bennett already had established a name for himself in the intelligence community. I recall that one of the problems with which the Security Service was grappling arose from its belief that the KGB, operating from the Soviet embassy building on Charlotte Street in Ottawa, was intercepting telephone conversations then being carried on Bell's microwave circuits. From normal surveillance it had been noted that unusually large numbers of heavy diplomatic bags were being sent to Moscow every week, presumably stuffed with reels of tape. Since the telephone communications took a path only a few degrees off the Soviet embassy building, it was theoretically possible for it to intercept the conversations involved. What was not known then was whether in fact it could be done.

Shortly after taking up my appointment, and with Higgitt's support, I encouraged Bennett to carry out an experiment to see if, using suitably powerful equipment, such conversations could indeed be intercepted by the Soviets. Since RCMP headquarters and the Soviet embassy were relatively close to one another, we reckoned that if we could intercept intelligible conversations, so could the KGB. Bennett got the job done in jig time and with professional skill. The results were astonishing and disquieting. Not only were we able to intercept conversations, but the reception was exceptionally clear, enabling us to hear both sides of conversations. In some instances it even proved possible to identify some of the interlocutors.

Most of the interesting intercepted conversations were those of senior public servants and members of the armed forces, freely talking about a wide range of subjects, some of them highly classified, certainly matters that never should have been discussed on an open, unprotected telephone line. Some conversations dealt not only with top-secret subjects but also with senior officials and ministers. In due course, the resulting transcripts were destroyed, and steps were taken to try to warn the departments involved that there was evidence that some of their senior employees were not observing the rules about telephone security and of the need to do so. Far more important, we had established that the Soviets could intercept such conversations, and, given what we had discovered in a couple of days of experimentation, it was very likely that the KGB had found such eavesdropping well worthwhile.

Doubts about Bennett's loyalty appear to have gathered momentum in the late 1960s and to have been given added impetus by similar concerns expressed by the CIA and particularly by Angleton. I cannot recall exactly when I was first informed of the suspicions about Bennett's being a KGB mole, but it was probably about the time when the situation in Quebec also became critical. I was shocked and upset, finding it difficult to believe that he could be a traitor. I was being asked to approve a clandestine surveillance of his activities. Such action could hardly be defined as disciplinary in nature, and so outside my authority, but I chose to consider it as such. Therefore I informed Higgitt of the allegations and sought his agreement to having surveillance commence immediately. Higgitt agreed, and then there began the bizarre, unpleasant business of keeping the former head of counterespionage under investigation without his knowledge.

During nearly two years of intensive investigation, secrecy was increasingly compromised by members of the service unable to keep their mouths shut. In my 1977 statement to the McDonald Commission I wrote, 'It is now painfully evident that several members or former members of the Security Service have systematically provided information to journalists and others about specific Security Service operations and in more general terms about the methodology and techniques used. The net effect of these disclosures, apart from their political impact, has been a disruption and discrediting of the Security Service in ways at least as damaging as if it had been successfully infiltrated by a foreign intelligence service.

I decided that the surveillance of Bennett must come to an end. Its continuation was sapping the energies of the service, and it had been unable to help us decide if there was any substance to the allegations about him. Higgitt agreed, and those carrrying out the investigation then proposed that Bennett should be confronted and interrogated. Again I consulted Higgitt, and, with his agreement, I undertook to see Bennett as soon as possible. It was not a duty I liked having to perform, particularly as it involved someone whose work I admired.

Howard Draper, my deputy, brought Bennett to my office, and I told him of the suspicions and that in the circumstances I was lifting his security clearance. To avoid making the task of his interrogators more difficult by perhaps revealing such details of the case as I knew, I said no more than was necessary and kept the discussion short. Bennett was remarkably composed. Though clearly shocked, he offered to cooperate fully in order to satisfy whatever doubts about his loyalty there might be. I admired the way he handled himself and wondered how I might have reacted in a similar situation. He conducted himself with great dignity and strength of character.

The ensuing, exhaustive investigation led to the conclusion that there existed not a shred of evidence that Bennett had ever been a KGB agent. One of the experienced interrogators, Murray Sexsmith, was quite adamant on that point. A remaining, serious problem was whether Bennett, though innocent of the charges, should remain a member of the Security Service. Given the extent of the rumours then circulating within the service and within the RCMP generally, which were being reported to me almost daily, I concluded that his continued usefulness seemed doubtful. Under the CAZAB agreement, we had kept our allies fully informed. It had been Canada's turn to hold the next meeting, after Melbourne (1967) and New York (1969), and as host I had chaired the meeting, some part of which was given over to discussion of Bennett's case. Views were divided, with some firmly believing Bennett a KGB agent and others just as firmly convinced of his innocence. Moreover, if we decided to keep him, it seemed likely that there always would be doubters among our allies, on whom we relied for all kinds of assistance.

For example, a couple of years after retiring in 1973 I attended a meeting in London of the Council of the International Institute for Strategic Studies (IISS). Maurice Oldfield, then head of MI 6, invited me to have dinner with him at his club, the Athenaeum. To my surprise he raised the Bennett case, saying something to the effect that he still believed that Bennett was 'a bad un.' We argued for some time. I pointed out that there was not a shred of evidence to support his belief, but I was unable to convince him.

In 1971 I did not see how Bennett could continue with the Security Service, but such a decision could be taken only by the commissioner. I consulted Higgitt, who accepted my conclusion. I then had the unpleasant duty of telling Bennett that while, as a result of the investigation, I had no doubts of his loyalty, it would be impossible for him to remain in the service.

I was shocked to discover about the same time that his wife of twenty years had announced that she wished to leave him and return to Australia (her native land). I was quite unaware of this most unfortunate situation. Apart from that, I was very concerned that the normal pension he would be entitled to receive after only eighteen years of service would be small. Bennett decided to apply for a medical pension and eventually was discharged on medical grounds, with a slightly better annuity than he otherwise would have received.

At the time I offered to speak to John Carson, head of the Public Service Commission, to see if suitable employment could be obtained for him at roughly the same salary. In due course Murray Sexsmith and I went together to see Carson to explain the complicated background and to seek his assistance. Carson was most sympathetic and helpful, holding out the possibility of useful employment. However, in the meantime, Bennett's application for a medical pension was accepted, and he decided to accept it and to go to live in Australia.

My recollection of my conversations with Bennett appears to differ in important respects from the account of them given in John Sawatsky's book about Bennett, *For Services Rendered.* I would like to add that my memory is supported by the careful notes I made on 9 December 1978 of a private meeting that I had with David McDonald and his colleagues on 8 December, at which we discussed, among other things, the Bennett case. An expurgated version of notes of that meeting made by the commission's secretary has been made public under the Access to Information Act. Any mention of Bennett was expurgated from the version made public, presumably to meet the privacy requirements of the law. I believe, however, that all my conversations with Bennett on this score were recorded on tape at the time we met and duly transcribed. Presumably these records are still held in the archives of the Security Service and would be irrefutable in terms of their accuracy.

The investigation of Bennett had been long and drawn-out, disrupting and quite unsatisfactory for Bennett and the Security Service. Unfortunately, several more years were to pass before Bennett could get his name publicly cleared and to receive at least some compensation for the serious disruptions to his life caused by the false allegations made against him.

Establishing Bennett's innocence had been an accomplishment, achieved at great cost to Bennett and, though perhaps not immediately evident or acknowledged, to the Security Service. Most important, it created the reluctant realization that a KGB mole probably still existed in the service and remained unidentified.

I learned only recently that investigation of the matter continued, resulting eventually in identification of the mole, a former member of the RCMP Security Service who worked in counter-intelligence in Ottawa until late 1968 and then was transferred to similar duties in Montreal.

Since these events occurred long after I had retired from the public service, I have no first-hand knowledge of them. The authorities have not made the mole's identity public, but Radio Canada, in a broadcast made by Normand Lester from Montreal on 29 May 1991, identified him as Gilles Brunet, a former member of the Security Service.

I understand that it is now believed that Brunet continued as an active KGB agent-in-place for about five years (1968–73) before being obliged, as a disciplinary matter, to leave the RCMP and that thereafter he continued as a KGB agent until 1978. Brunet died in April 1984 in Montreal, apparently of a heart attack, before investigators were able to interview him. He was identified partly by a Soviet defector, Vitaly Yurchenko, who, after providing the CIA with information about KGB espionage operations (including Canada), decided to return to the Soviet Union. I never met Gilles Brunet, but I knew his father, a former deputy commissioner of the RCMP, when he was assigned to carry out security work at NATO headquarters in Paris at the time I was there, in the 1960s.

Gilles Brunet was instrumental in providing documentary and other evidence of RCMP wrongdoing, sufficient to confirm the belief of officials and ministers that a commission of inquiry was needed to look into the allegations. Transcripts of the testimony that he gave to government officials in June 1977 is available in the National Archives under the provisions of the Access to Information Act. At the time, of course, neither the officials and ministers concerned nor the Security Service were aware of the man's secret role as a KGB agent.

The KGB, of course, would have known that its agent was providing evidence of RCMP wrongdoing, which could lead to public inquiries. It may even have – though I think it unlikely – proposed his actions on the grounds that this might lead to a serious disruption of the Security Service's counter-espionage work, always one of the KGB's principal goals. I understand that Oleg Kalugin, former chief of counter-intelligence in the KGB, has claimed that the mole was acting under instructions from his KGB handler.

If Brunet was indeed acting on KGB instructions, it is ironic that the creation of the McDonald Commission may have been the result, in part at least, of the persistent efforts of a disaffected member of the RCMP Security Service who was acting as a KGB double agent. One wonders what the commissioners would have thought had they been aware of the facts and how this might have affected their findings.

Urged on by me and others, the McDonald Commission eventually went to great lengths to ensure that its in camera discussions could not become known to the KGB and others. The electronic security measures taken seem to have been effective. As far as I know, no classified information leaked in this manner to the press, the Soviets, or anyone else.

There were during the late 1970s a number of cases of Soviet espionage in which I was not directly involved. They had their origins before I became director-general or came to fruition after I retired. Among these was the strange case involving Hugh Hambleton.

Hambleton, a Canadian economist, while working in NATO headquarters in Paris handed over to the Soviets so many classified documents that the head of the KGB Station in Paris had to establish a special unit to cope with them. It appears that the KGB began its cultivation of Hambleton in 1951 and that between 1957 and 1961 he was so valuable a source that it was arranged for him to be invited some years later to a private dinner in Moscow with the KGB chairman, Yuri Andropov.

I appear to have been at NATO headquarters while Hambleton was there, but I have no recollection of having met him, though when I worked in Mike Pearson's office in the late 1950s I had known his father, George Hambleton, a member of the parliamentary press gallery. Hugh Hambleton's motives for his treachery appear to have been to satisfy his self-importance and a craving for excitement, rather than any ideological belief.

Hugh Hambleton returned to Canada and the Université Laval in Quebec City after receiving a PhD at the London School of Economics in 1964. Apparently in 1967 he was reactivated as a spy by Colonel Rudolph A. Herrmann, a Czech-born KGB officer acting as an 'illegal' KGB agent in the United States. In 1977 the FBI discovered Herrmann's true role, and eventually it persuaded him to act for it as a double agent. In the course of his debriefing, Herrmann named Hambleton as a valuable KGB agent. The RCMP Security Service was informed of this, and the FBI and the Security Service ran a joint operation, code named

'Red Pepper,' to place Hambleton under surveillance. He was filmed while in contact with Soviet-bloc espionage agents, leading to the discovery in his mother's house of a radio transmitter and other espionage equipment and his admission that he had assisted the KGB's efforts. He was never prosecuted, presumably because Canadian legal authorities did not think that they would be able successfully to do so under Canada's Official Secrets Act.

In due course he made his way to England, where he was arrested and, after admitting his guilt, was sentenced to ten years in prison. At the time of his arrest he had British and Canadian citizenship, which made his arrest and subsequent sentencing possible. The charges against him related to the period between 1956 and 1961. The affair proved to be an embarrassment to the Canadian government, which had been unable or unwilling to prosecute him, despite clear evidence of his espionage activities.

The question of whether Canada should have an espionage capability to serve its interests abroad is not restricted to any particular period of time. I have chosen to discuss it in this chapter, which deals with espionage in general, though not espionage carried out by Canada.

In the recent past I have expressed some views on the matter, which have beeen published. My opposition to the notion appears to have been interpreted in some quarters as being too dismissive. The criticism may be valid, part of the price of my trying to inject a note of realism (hard-headedness) into a debate that in recent years appears to me to have lacked realism and proper appreciation of what an espionage service is and what it can and cannot accomplish.

In 1994 the House of Commons Special Committee looking into such questions invited me to give my views on a proposal made by the Security Intelligence Review Committee (SIRC) to amend the CSIS act to allow that agency to conduct espionage abroad. I made it quite clear that I was not opposed in principle to the creation of a Canadian espionage service – that I had qualms not on moral grounds but rather on practical grounds. I said that I was unsure that Canada needs an espionage service, as I did not possess the knowledge to make such a judgment. I do not know whether the information we are receiving from our present intelligence-gathering activities is adequate for our needs.

It is becoming increasingly obvious, however, that we are passing through a period of tremendous change in the world that could bring with it new and quite unpredictable threats to Canada's well-being, such as an independent Quebec's becoming a hostile neighbour. There may well be discernible threats that will justify the need for Espionage Canada. At the moment they don't seem very obvious.

I haven't seen or heard convincing arguments of a present and urgent need for an espionage service. Certainly the argument that we should have one simply because other countries have one is not very convincing, and I have reservations about our ability to operate and to control such an unusual asset. The 1994 study done by SIRC suggested that establishment of such a spy agency could be 'incremental and secretive' and that 'given the importance of a foreign-intelligence service it is more likely to be under the authority of the Privy Council Office or External Affairs than to be an extension of CSIS. The result would be an organization which like the Communications Security Establishment would probably fall outside the review mandate of SIRC.'

I don't have difficulty accepting the suggestion that such a service would have to be 'secretive' or that it might be under the authority of Foreign Affairs. Almost any activities carried out by such an agency must remain secret if it is to succeed and will have some foreign policy implications, whether the actions involve clandestine efforts to destabilize some foreign government or to obtain military, trade, or technological secrets from some state. As I see it, these are more important, unmentioned questions. What should be the targets of such an agency? Who makes decisions about targets? What role if any should Parliament play in its activities? How should the agency be funded?

Logically, our prime target should be the United States, since so many of its actions vitally affect our economic and cultural well-being. However, I cannot imagine any foreseeable Canadian government agreeing to carrying out full-scale espionage of some kind or another against the United States, which has been a staunch ally for so many years and our principal military bulwark. If we were to decide to carry out such espionage, certainly it would have to be done in such a way that it could not be detected – not a goal easily or quickly achieved. At the moment we have neither the professional ability nor, I suspect, the political will that would be required.

There are of course a number of other legitimate targets, such as all countries contributing to the proliferation of weapons of mass destruction and actively encouraging international terrorism, and countries actively attempting to achieve trading and commercial advantages by covert means, in defiance of international and bilateral agreements. There is also the possibility of having an espionage agency actively supporting Canadian soldiers in carrying out difficult peace-keeping missions, as in Somalia. However, I doubt that any of these possible developments warrant creation of an espionage agency at this time.

13

October 1970

Much has been written about Canada's October Crisis of 1970. Without doubt it was the most momentous event that occurred during my career with the RCMP, but I was unable to be an active player, for the simple reason that I was struck down with a severe bout of pneumonia on 8 October and remained out of the picture until 23 November, when my doctor pronounced me sufficiently recovered to return to work.

Apart from the illness itself, which turned out to be an unpleasant form of lumbar pneumonia, I found the unfortunate circumstances very frustrating. It was rather like looking through the wrong end of a telescope at the unfolding events, which I could only watch on television from bed or read about in the newspapers – an unsatisfactory, myopic view for the director-general of the RCMP Security Service.

I recall that I saw the prime minister on the evening of Wednesday, 7 October, in his office in the Parliament Buildings, principally to discuss some security aspect of a trip to the Soviet Union he was planning to make. By that time British trade commissioner James Cross had been abducted by the Front de libération du Québec (FLQ), but beyond a brief discussion of the abduction I do not believe that we mentioned the situation in Montreal. Certainly there was no mention of a possible 'apprehended insurrection.' Remarkable events had been occurring in Quebec with alarming rapidity, and I recall that I had been unusually busy, but not to the point that I was obviously exhausted. However, an appointments book that we used at the time has a notation on 7 October by Helen – 'John tight chest' – presumably the beginning of the infection that manifested itself with a 103-degree Fahrenheit temperature on the night of 8 October, when we were having a dinner party at our home in Chelsea. By the ninth, the trouble was diagnosed and I was ordered to bed. I have little recollection of the following week or ten days, except of having to swallow massive doses of antibiotics and to force myself to cough and spit a great deal.

Friends and colleagues came to see me during this period and later during the lengthy, exasperating period of recuperation. Visitors came not, as David McDonald later attempted to suggest, on Security Service business and for the taking of day-to-day decisions! They dropped by simply to find out how I was faring and to tell me about what they believed was happening. I was in no shape to transact business and had little interest in doing so.

About this time, and after Pierre Laporte had been found murdered, the government decided to take steps to protect various ministers and senior officials who might be possible targets of the FLQ. Bodyguards were provided for quite a number of ministers and officials, and a series of security measures were put in place to protect such persons and certain institutions.

The commissioner of the RCMP decided that since Helen and I were living in Quebec in a relatively remote location similar arrangements should be made to protect us. Accordingly, a team of armed members of the RCMP Security Service was dispatched to act, around the clock (three shifts), to guard us and our property in Chelsea. I believe that many of them were drawn from the Watcher Service. They must have been bored stiff, but they never made us feel that they resented the duty. Helen, of course, saw far more of them than I did. Indeed, on occasion they insisted that when she had to leave the house for any length of time she should be accompanied. Long after they had 'stood down,' I discovered that at night they set up a lookout point in the garage, where they had cover from the weather and a reasonably good field of view up the road. As it happened, the garage backed onto our bedroom, separated only by well-insulated but flimsy dry-wall. It was just as well that I did not know about this arrangement; throughout the night a loaded, double-barrelled shotgun was always but a few feet from the head of our bed.

I note from Helen's appointments book that among my visitors were Jim Bennett and Howie Jones from the Security Service, Don Wall from the Privy Council Office, Len Higgitt and his wife, and Ernest Côté, deputy solicitor general. None of them sought to transact serious business. Among my foreign visitors was Peter Wright (MI 5), the author of *Spy Catcher*, and Sir Martin Furnival-Jones (director of MI 5), then travelling as Mr Edward Jones. Furnival-Jones was anxious to know about poor James Cross. I wasn't able to tell him much, since anything I had learned was at second or third hand. We managed to have a good talk, however, about a number of matters, especially about dealing with the KGB and its unflagging espionage efforts against Canada.

Towards mid-November the siege mentality had begun to lift. It was decided that our guards could be withdrawn. I received in their place a powerful, battery-operated wireless transmitter and receiver and detailed instructions concerning their use. I never quite mastered the instructions. It was thought that should our telephone and power lines be cut, or some such emergency arise, we could use the equipment to seek immediate help. We set up a routine to test the system from time to time. I believe that I was assigned the code name 'Blue Spruce One.' I had the equipment for some time, but I never had to use it for an emergency.

I was upset to learn from some of my visitors that during the earliest days of the crisis the Security Service had been sharply criticized for 'quite ineffectual briefings of ministers.' I found it very frustrating to hear of such serious criticisms and be unable to do anything about the situation. Even after returning to work late in November I had great difficulty in piecing together the story. It was only years later that I obtained access to the minutes of the discussions about the 'crisis' in cabinet and cabinet committees. I realized with surprise that Len Higgitt had taken a very forthright, albeit low-key approach, not at all in accord with accounts of these events that had found their way into print and were being widely circulated by word of mouth.

Cabinet documents normally were not circulated to the commissioner of the RCMP, even when he might have participated in some cabinet committee discussions. The solicitor general normally would receive such cabinet papers, but George McIlraith was not noted for sharing ministerial secrets with officials. In any event, it was only rarely that some cabinet paper found its way into RCMP files. Thus no amount of searching of Security Service files in November 1970 revealed what had transpired at the cabinet level during the crisis, and those in the RCMP who might know were not particularly forthcoming.

I discovered from the minutes of morning and evening meetings of the Cabinet Committee on Security and Intelligence on 14 October that Higgitt had opposed special legislation to deal with the crisis and had expressed doubts about estimates by the Quebec authorities of the number of persons who should be arrested.

I have found it puzzling that Higgitt's views were not given more weight. I guess that it had partly to do with how he was regarded by ministers. His low-key style was not such as to attract their interest and admiration. He was uncomfortable with the abstract concepts then much in vogue in the Prime Minister's Office and made no attempt to present his ideas in 'trendy' terms. He was no intellectual, but he was bright and had years of experience in police work and in intelligence work in particular. Perhaps these characteristics led ministers and others to dismiss what he had to say. But what he said was clearly recorded, and his comments seem wiser than those that were offered by many others.

When I was beginning to feel a bit better, I believe that Don Wall, on one of his visits, said that the secretary to the cabinet, Gordon Robertson, would appreciate it if I could put down on paper any thoughts I might have about the situation in Quebec and recommendations for improving the machinery of government to deal with similar problems in future. I said that I would have a crack at it.

I found that I was handicapped without files, but I was able to respond with two memoranda – 'The FLQ and Quebec,' dated 22 October 1970, and 'Pro Memoria – Revolution in Canada,' on 12 November 1970. The two documents were released to me a number of years ago under the Access to Information legislation, with only a few passages expurgated. I attach the first one, as Appendix H, and it may be the document given to members of the Cabinet Committee on Priorities and Planning at their meeting on 24 November 1970 (see Appendix I, below, p. 227: mention of 'Mr Starnes' paper'). I wrote both memoranda in pencil on foolscap. Presumably I had them sent into the office to be typed. In due course I must have given them to Wall to transmit to Robertson, since I remember being told that they were used in discussions with the prime minister. Indeed, I think that Trudeau said some kind words about them to me after I got back to work. Some of the recommendations were acted on. For example, the Security Panel was replaced by a more suitable, interdepartmental Security Advisory Committee.

The government's efforts to recover control of the situation in Quebec led to a proliferation of 'crisis centres' and interdepartmental task forces. Some of these were necessary to a coordinated approach to a complex problem, but the existence of so many centres did little to help the kind of unspectacular, patient investigative work that the RCMP had set in motion to try to discover James Cross and to obtain his safe release. The irony, of course, was that to be able to operate properly these centres depended heavily on RCMP information. The success of this kind of work depended on absolute secrecy and the use of all the investigative aids and techniques available, such as Watcher Service, microphones, telephone taps, and informers. The well-meaning involvement of so many persons not directly responsible for the investigations made it very difficult to keep day-to-day progress from being splashed across the headlines of some newspaper or broadcast by some radio station.

External Affairs and National Defence had a legitimate interest in the matter, but it seems to me that quite a number of individuals simply wanted to be part of the action. To have kept them in the know would have interfered with the investigation.

Unknown to me at the time, the government was moving to create one centre for conducting operations for dealing with the FLQ. At a meeting of cabinet on 19 October 1970 the prime minister introduced a paper entitled, 'A Strategy for Dealing with the FLQ.' As the accompanying memorandum for the cabinet expressed it, 'This memorandum and its Annex have been prepared by my staff to place the events of recent days in the context of what appears to be either an explicit or at least an implicit FLQ strategy. The government not only needs to understand the nature of the strategy being used against it, but, and this is much more important in the long run, it must have its own strategy which contains and quickly pre-empts the FLQ strategy. The outline of a possible government strategy is included in the Annex.' I believe that the principal author was Jim Davey in the Prime Minister's Office. The clear thinking and the prose in the paper could be only his.

The prime minister informed his colleagues on 22 October that he was setting up a 'Special Operations Centre' for the Quebec situation. 'He read to ministers the decision of the Cabinet Committee on Priorities and Planning, relating to the Special Operations Centre, Can. Doc. 1221-70, and explained the terms of reference. He said that it would be a one-to-two-month operation and that [Jim] Davey of his office would be in charge. This was an attempt to remove from ministers the need to be concerned daily about overall strategy. He said that he would report back to Cabinet on how the Special Operations Centre was working.'

Out of the discussion came agreement that

III. (a) a Special Operations Centre for the Quebec Situation be established under the direction of the Secretary to the Cabinet and of the principal Secretary to the prime minister [Marc Lalonde], to implement the strategy and with the following terms of reference:

(i) political direction was *NOT* delegated to the chief of operations;

(ii) the chief of operations was to act in accordance with the directions of the Prime Minister and the Cabinet in implementing and conforming to the strategy and plan approved by Cabinet;

(iii) the chief of operations was to direct all information for action by departments and agencies through the responsible minister.

(iv) the chief of operations should have access to the Prime Minister, the Secretary to the Cabinet and the Principal Secretary to the Prime Minister, to inform them of developments, to get instructions for actions and reactions and to receive directions;

(b) that the provincial and municipal levels of government should be informed of the establishment of the Special Operations Centre and of the assistance available to them; and that their co-operation and support should be encouraged.

14

McDonald, Keable, CSIS

Between 1977 and 1984 Canada thoroughly examined and carefully reconstructed its security and intelligence system. Two investigative efforts – the Commission of Inquiry into Certain Activities of the Royal Canadian Mounted Police (McDonald Commission, 1977–81) and the Commission of Inquiry into Police Operations on Quebec Territory (Keable Commission, 1977–81) – helped lay the groundwork for the Canadian Security Intelligence Service, established in 1984.

I would be a hypocrite if I pretended that what I write about the McDonald Commission is without bias. In all I spent about one hundred and twenty hours under oath as a witness before the Keable and McDonald commissions, most of that time before the McDonald Commission, and much of that in camera. I have tried to be impartial in my comments, but clearly the adversarial atmosphere of the McDonald Commission's hearings makes this difficult. I soon discovered that I did not admire Mr Justice David McDonald as an individual. He was intelligent and quick but had very little knowledge of security or intelligence matters. He was a very active supporter of the Liberal party, with apparent ambitions to be a Supreme Court judge. He had no discernible sense of humour and a well-developed sense of his own importance.

On some occasions David McDonald would be downright hostile, even rude. For example, at one point he was examining me about the invocation of the War Measures Act and the October Crisis of 1970. I carefully explained, as I already had done in writing to the commission in 1977, that I had been completely out of action with a serious bout of pneumonia from 9 October until 23 November and thus had had no first-hand knowledge of events.

To my astonishment and irritation, McDonald asked me a number of questions which seemed to imply that my illness was some ploy (to what purpose was never made clear) and that, in reality, I had continued to run the Security Service from my sickbed! I pointed out that all he had to do to establish the truth was to get in touch with the doctor who looked after me for several weeks and that for most of the period my temperature had hovered about 103 degrees Fahrenheit. I was angry as hell at his questioning on this score, and disgusted.

At other times McDonald would be almost obsequious in his treatment of me. His behaviour towards me was in marked contrast to that of the other two commissioners, and especially Don Rickert, who made a conscious effort to be impartial and to approach his task in a non-partisan manner and with an open mind.

When public attention reached a crescendo in 1977–8 concerning the allegations that the Security Service of the RCMP had engaged in illegal activities in pursuit of its mandate, Governor General Jules Léger, a friend of many years, asked me to come to see him in Rideau Hall. When we met he asked about the allegations, concerned that they would harm the good reputation of the RCMP and adversely affect me.

I told him what I then knew about the various allegations and thanked him for his concerns. As deputy minister at External Affairs Léger also had been chairman of the Intelligence Policy Committee and was very knowledgeable about the activities of the Canadian intelligence community, including the RCMP. I said that I had no idea how the inquiry would unfold, but I believed that it would be lengthy and complicated. Because of the office he held and the state of his health I urged him not to involve himself in any way, a view that he accepted. Because of the nature of our conversation I made no record of it, but I was most grateful for his kind gesture and his solicitude.

The Inquiries Act, the framework for the McDonald Commission, makes it difficult, if not impossible, to avoid an adversarial atmosphere, something which has become evident from other recent inquiries – for instance, the Krever Commission, about the blood supply system, and the inquiry into events in Somalia. The act may be suitable for inquiries involving clearly criminal activities and acts of misfeasance or malfeasance or political chicanery, but it has its limitations when used to assess the activities of an unusual government agency such as the RCMP Security Service, or the Canadian Security Establishment (CSE), or an espionage service, should one ever be created.

For the Keable Commission of Inquiry, the atmosphere was adversarial not only between the commission and those subpoenaed to appear before it, but also between the federal government and its officials and lawyers, on one hand, and the lawyers and provincial officials appointed by the Parti Québécois government, on the other hand. It represented a complex, delicately shaded political tussle between Quebec and Ottawa, with many witnesses caught in the middle.

The McDonald inquiry ran for four years and cost over $10 million. Whether it was worth it is difficult for me to judge. I thought that some of its activities were clumsily handled. For example, the commission chose to comment in some detail on whether Canada should have 'a foreign intelligence service' – something not required by its mandate. In my view the result was a hodge-podge of fact and fancy, and some of the comments were simply misleading, no doubt because of lack of understanding of some of the important activities carried out by Canadian intelligence and security agencies other than the RCMP Security Service – for example, CSE – and the complex relations among these quite different agencies within a national and an international framework.

On the whole, however, I think that the commission performed a useful function. It succeeded in bringing security and intelligence questions to the attention of the public, and it forced the government to face up to some of the difficult decisions it had sought to avoid – for instance, whether to create a separate agency to deal with internal security and the provision of a legal framework for all of its necessary clandestine activities, under appropriate safeguards.

In due course the difficulties that the government experienced in tackling the question of whether to create a separate agency led indirectly to the examination of some of the same problems in the Senate, resulting in the Canadian Security Intelligence Service Act (1984). I appeared on several occasions as a witness before the Senate committee, chaired by Michael Pitfield, who had been intimately involved in many of the events leading to the legislation.

I was pleased when Solicitor General Robert Kaplan sent me a red, leather-bound copy of Bill C-9 inscribed; 'To John Starnes, who knew the whole story, and worked to make CSIS happen. In appreciation.' Some months earlier Kaplan had approached me privately to ask if I would be willing to help him establish a new agency to replace the RCMP Security Service. I readily agreed. In the ensuing months I worked hard, behind the scenes, to do what he had asked. This effort entailed trying to get Liberals and Conservatives to agree on the need for legislation and to avoid the temptations to try to make political gains out of their narrow difference in strength in Parliament. Eventually common sense prevailed.

The act is far from perfect and contains some equivocal clauses, such as sections 16 (I), (2), and (3), the implications of which certainly are not fully understood by the public or, I suspect, even by some key ministers and officials. However, what exists now is much better than the earlier situation.

My first appearance as a witness was before the Keable Commission in 1977. It took place in the main-court house in Montreal. Until that time I had never appeared in any court, even for a traffic violation. I had had no legal training whatsoever. Moreover, I had never been under oath, and I certainly had never been exposed to the sometimes frenzied, unwelcome attentions of the media. The business of having to appear as a witness before commissions of inquiry was an interesting learning experience, but not one that I would have sought or would wish to repeat. The televising of such proceedings had not yet become an accepted and popular item on the public's television bill of fare. I was appalled by the amount of sloppy reporting on television and radio and by some of the books that came out purporting to reveal the 'true story' about the activities of the RCMP Security Service and some of its operations. Much of what was written was only partly correct, some of it apparently derived from relatively junior members of the RCMP, who had limited knowledge of some operations and little or none of the bigger picture. A number of authoritative books have since appeared on various aspects of Canadian intelligence and security matters, particularly with regard to international activities, written by former senior offices of the KGB and the GRU (the intelligence directorate of the Soviet General Staff). They have been able to cite official documentation.

Being under oath means that one tries, to the best of one's ability, to answer questions truthfully. That sounds simple but in reality telling the truth depends on one's ability to remember past events, some of which may have occured many years earlier. I had always prided myself on my ability to recall events with precision, something that a career in the foreign service required and fostered. I was therefore surprised to discover that it proved more difficult than I expected. Fortunately, there was a profusion of documentation on which to draw. The difficulty often lay, however, in not being able to remember specific documents and their context. This became especially complicated and frustrating when, as often happened, many of the documents were classified top secret or higher (communications intelligence data) and were withheld from the public by the government on grounds of national security, cabinet confidentiality, or objections to release by third parties, such as the United Kingdom and the United States.

My in camera testimony before the Keable Commission has been in the public domain for a number of years. One of its principal interests concerned 'Operation Ham' – the surreptitious entry by the RCMP Security Service in 1972 into the premises of 'Les Messageries Dynamiques,' a Montreal data-processing centre. The intention was to remove, copy, and return tapes bearing information concerning membership of the Parti Québécois. The commission wanted to determine whether and to what extent the federal government might have been involved. In my testimony I explained that in approving the operation I had done so without the knowledge of the commissioner of the RCMP or the government, since involving ministers might have given the operation an apparent political flavour it never was intended to have. Moreover, because of this concern, I had forbidden any dissemination of the material derived from the operation outside the Security Service. In fact, the deputy director (Operations) had approved the operation in principle three weeks before I first learned of it. My approval was sought on 8 December 1972. Certain crucial preliminary steps already had been taken.

In due course, the crown prosecutor in Montreal laid charges in connection with the operation. Eleven members of the service were charged. For some reason, which I never discovered, the Quebec authorities did not lay charges against me. In the circumstances I was very unhappy that these men were being charged, and when I was asked to be a witness for the defence I readily agreed, appearing before Mr Justice Maurice Rousseau of the Quebec Sessions Court in Montreal in November 1981. Since Bill Kelly (a former deputy commissioner of the RCMP), who also appeared as a witness for the defence, and I wished to give testimony about matters still deemed classified by the federal government, Judge Rousseau gave us the protection of the Canada Evidence Act. As a consequence our testimony was very frank, some of it being extensively reported in the French- and English-language press. Curiously, the story contained in our testimony never seems to have been followed up by the legions of 'researchers' and investigative reporters who delight in such matters. What we said, of course, is part of the court's records and is public knowledge.

I was very upset about the charges brought against my former colleagues concerning 'Operation Ham' and frustrated that I could do so little to help with their defence. On 24 April 1985 I wrote to my lawyer and friend Richard Mongeau, who had acted so ably for me on many occasions and who also was representing the accused. I expressed in writing my willingness to enter into a plea-bargaining arrangement with the crown prosecutor in Montreal. I set out my minimum conditions for entering into such an arrangement: '(a) That all the charges against the various members and former members of the RCMP involved would be dropped, (b) That I would be charged with an appropriate and lesser charge than those which have been laid, (c) That I would receive an unconditional discharge, (d) That the minimum time possible would elapse between the laying of the charge, my acceptance of guilt and the bringing down of a judgement.'

Mongeau put my proposition to the crown prosecutor, but the offer was turned down. Subsequently Mongeau reported to me that he had learned that my offer had been considered by Quebec's minister of justice, Marc-André Bédard, and rejected, for reasons unknown. Eventually, all the cases were disposed of in one way and another, with the majority being dismissed by the courts on the grounds that there had been unreasonable delays in bringing them forward.

By the time I had appeared under oath on numerous occasions, before the McDonald and Keable commissions, and in different courts, I was beginning to discover a bit about the law and more important, about criminal lawyers and their techniques. At first, I found myself upset by the tricks employed by some lawyers, but I came to realize that such tricks are but a part of the process of the criminal justice system, a game to be played. In addition, I came to understand that each lawyer has his or her individual style and a certain sense of *amour propre*.

In time I concluded that it was best to take these legal tactics with a grain of salt and to try to prepare my defences against them. For example, I found that if one wasn't paying close attention to questions being put in cross examination, lawyers would sometimes try to put into my mouth words purportedly uttered by me in previous testimony. The questioner then had to be challenged immediately, and a request made to the chairman to have the words in question checked against the verbatim record of the proceedings. If a challenge was supported by reference to the official record, there were grounds for requesting that the inaccuracies be corrected.

With regard to the McDonald Commission, I was delighted when virtually all the in camera records of its hearings were turned over to the National Archives and became available to researchers and others. In due course I sought and gained access to them. During my research I discovered that commission counsel had prepared a number of independent studies to assist the commission in making its determinations, including whether to issue notices to certain witnesses under section 13 of the Inquiries Act.

I found ten separate papers prepared by commission counsel, identified as papers no. 2 to 11 (no. 1 dealt with the scope of the submissions and general legal issues). All these documents were among those eventually released with the records of the in camera hearings. However, paper 11 – 'Government Knowledge of R.C.M.P. Activities not Authorized or Provided for by Law' – in which I had the greatest interest, did not appear along with the others. My curiosity was aroused.

I first made application on 14 December 1989 to the Privy Council Office (temporary custodians of all the commission's papers) for release of paper 11. After a delay of over a year, and only with the assistance of John Grace, the information commissioner, was I able to receive an expurgated copy of the paper, a ninety-two-page document, which had a handwritten note on its cover: 'This is not an official exhibit. Being processed as response to Accesss request 908123 [my request]. Disclosed version should be sent to the archives to complete the numbered set of submissions prepared by Commission Counsel.' In other words, if I had not spotted the absence of paper 11 among those released, it probably would not have become public. The document, dated 12 February 1981, was expurgated under the exemptions provided for in the Access to Information Act. The accompanying letter read, 'This information qualifies for exemption under sections 15(1) (international affairs and defence) and 23 (solicitor–client privilege) of the Act.'

The 'excluded material' included pages 87–9, which were entirely blank, with only the page numbers remaining. Pages 90–3 dealt with the sharp conflict between my evidence and that of George McIlraith concerning a meeting that we had on 24 November 1970 (the day following my return to work after pneumonia). I claimed that I had said to McIlraith that the RCMP had been breaking the law for twenty years and never been caught. McIlraith denied having been told this by me.

Very recently, and to my delight, I learned from an article in the *Globe and Mail* that a Montreal author, Pierre Godin, had marked the publication of his three-volume biography, *René Lévesque, héros malgré lui, 1960–1976,* by releasing a draft version, dated 12 February 1981, of a report prepared by McDonald Commission counsel, which included the missing pages. Godin told reporters that he had received it from an unidentified source who had worked inside the commission. I obtained a copy from a journalist friend in Montreal. It does indeed contain the text of the missing pages.

When I was able to read the material released by Godin I could understand why it had proved so difficuilt to obtain. Much of it dealt with my in camera testimony, some of which had been vigorously challenged during the hearings by lawyers representing various ministers.

McDonald Commission counsel made a detailed assessment to determine 'government knowledge of RCMP activities not authorized or provided by law,' their findings being contained in the above-mentioned paper 11.

The commission's legal counsel were satisfied that Mr Trudel, one of the assistant secretaries from the Privy Council Office attending the meeting of the Cabinet Committee on Priorities and Planning (CCPP) on 1 December 1970, had faithfully recorded, in his hand-written notes, words used by me to inform the prime minister, other ministers, and senior officials present that the RCMP had been breaking the law for twenty years without being caught. Commission counsel concluded that the justice minister, John Turner, and Prime Minister Trudeau understood the significance of what I had said and submitted that it was incumbent on them to inquire into the nature of the 'illegal things' I had referred to, their extent, and whether or not such activities were authorized or provided for by law.

Their report added that there was no evidence before the commission that any inquiry was made by or on the instructions of Trudeau or Turner at the meeting itself or later by a cabinet committee or other senior governmental committee and that the two men may be found to have breached a duty owed by them to direct the Security Service to discontinue such activities. Their report also inferred that the failure so to inquire and to direct the Security Service to cease its involvement in illegal activities constituted tacit assent by them to the continuance of such activities (see Appendix I, p. 227).

I referred above to my differences with George McIlraith. On this score commission counsel wrote:

Mr. Starnes' document of November 26, 1970 purports to record a meeting between John Starnes and Senator McIlraith, the then Solicitor General, on November 24, 1970. In his evidence, Mr. Starnes confirmed the fact and substance of this discussion with Senator McIlraith. Although he has no actual memory of the words used during that meeting he further testified that the document is a relatively contemporaneous one which sets out the substance of that discussion. Senator McIlraith denies the existence of the meeting of November 24, 1970 or that he had such a discussion with Mr. Starnes at any point in time.

This Commission is satisfied, upon examination of the relevant documents, that the two page list of questions accompanied the Maxwell Memorandum [prepared by an interdepartmental committee chaired by the deputy minister of justice, Don Maxwell] and accordingly, formed part of the Agenda of the meeting of the C.C.P.P. on November 24, 1970. The seventh question in that document, it will be remembered, reads: 'What should be done to eliminate inherent contradiction in existing Security Service which turns around the question of crime in the national interest?' Although he was in attendance at the meeeting of the C.C.P.P. on November 24, 1970, Senator McIlraith cannot recall whether the two page list of questions accompanied the Maxwell Memorandum at that time. As stated earlier this Commission is satisfied that the list did so accompany the Maxwewll memorandum.

The first paragraph of Mr. Starnes' document sets out the question posed to Mr. Starnes by Senator McIlraith in the following language; '... What should be done to eliminate inherent contradiction in the existing Security Service which centres around the question of the commission of crime in the national interest?'

The question as recorded is in a language dramatically similar to the language [of the] question numbered seven which was before the C.C.P.P. on November 24, 1970. The question recorded in Mr. Starnes' document purports to have been put by Mr. McIlraith on the same day, November 24, 1970.

In the opinion of this Commission the dramatic similarity in language and the fact that the two page list of questions was in existence and was before the C.C.P.P. on November 24, 1970, lends credence to the conclusion that Mr. Starnes' document was prepared at a time relatively contemporaneous to November 24, 1970. The Commission would also point out at this juncture that the question purportedly put by Mr. McIlraith to John Starnes on November 24, 1970 would be likely to be one to be asked by the Solicitor General of the day, of the Director-General of the Security Service given the substance of question number seven on the two page list of questions.

In the third paragraph of Mr. Starnes' document he records 'I mentioned to the Minister that the R.C.M.P. had in fact been carrying out illegal activities for two decades and that this point had been made in various discussions.'

In his handwritten notes of the discussion that occurred at the meeting of the C.C.P.P. of December 1, 1970, Mr. Trudel recorded the following statement by Mr. Starnes: 'Misunderstanding of, contradiction – has been doing S & I illegal thing for twenty years but never caught – no way of escaping these things.'

The thought so recorded as expressed by Mr. Starnes to the meeting on December 1, 1970 is, in substance, the same thought expressed in the third paragraph of Mr. Starnes' document referred to above. More importantly, it is expressed in all but identical language; in his document Mr. Starnes records that: 'The R.C.M.P. had in fact been carrying out illegal activities for two decades.'

In his notes Mr. Trudel records: 'Has been doing S & I illegal things for twenty years ...'

As stated earlier, the Commission accepts the evidence of Mr. Trudel that his notes record the words used by Mr. Starnes at the meeting of the C.C.P.P. on December 1, 1970. In fact there is no evidence to the contrary.

And the commission's third report (August 1981) documents my longstanding concerns and makes apparent a good deal of internal argument concerning the 'overview and conclusions of the Starnes–McIlraith conflict.' Two of the commissioners concluded: 'We believe that a conversation between Mr. McIlraith and Mr. Starnes did in fact take place as set out in that memorandum [mine of 26 November 1970]. Mr. McIlraith's firm denial of such an encounter that day on that subject is a result, we believe, of an inability to remember a brief event that took place a decade ago.' David McDonald, as chairman, prepared a minority report: 'I am not prepared to conclude, and I do not find, that Mr. Starnes, on or about November 24, 1970, told Mr. McIlraith that the R.C.M.P. had in fact been carrying out illegal activities for two decades.'

It can only be assumed that the commission also did not reach agreement on the conclusions contained in the missing pages of paper no. 11 recently leaked by Godin in Montreal, since the material never was published. On the contrary, commission documents classified top secret, which have been declassified and made public under the Access to Information Act, indicate clearly that McDonald as chairman made the extraordinary statement that paper 11 'never came into existence.' These documents are a verbatim account of discussions among the commission's members and lawyers and the lawyers representing various clients. They quote an unidentified lawyer (presumably representing members of the RCMP Security Service) as saying,

[Counsel] However, in the fulness of time, it developed that Paper No. 11 did not see the light of day.

THE CHAIRMAN: I should re-phrase that: it never came into existence.

[Counsel] Yes.

THE CHAIRMAN: It not only did not see the light of day, but it never came into existence.

I think it should be made clear ...

[Counsel] I believe you.

THE CHAIRMAN: ... for a variety of reasons.

[Counsel] Yes, of course, I accept that: that Paper No. 11 did not come into existence because it was never conceived.

So I believe – it is my submission that to a certain extent, not to say: to an extent that is certain, [those] whose conduct was the subject of inquiry by your Commission, were put at some disadvantage vis-a-vis others who have received Section 13 Notices and whose conduct was explicitly recited with references to boot, in the series of papers which originated from eminent and learned counsel for your commission.

I say this not to suggest that we were given less than total and complete cooperation by counsel for the Commission when, after receipt of the three Section 13 Notices, with which I will deal presently, we asked for particulars.

We were given enthusiatic and total cooperation by Mr. Goodwin [one of the commission's lawyers] and his colleagues.

But still, I believe the point should be made that we were lead [sic] to believe, in the course of this Inquiry, that at the conclusion of the public hearings, there would be a written submission by your counsel, which would deal specifically with ministerial responsibility.

That paper, for whatever reason, was not produced; it did not come into existence. And it is my submission that it has made our addressing of the issues mentioned in the three Section 13 Notices which ... [name apparently withheld] has received, that much more haphazard, if you wish, from our point of view.

And with that preliminary statement or with these two preliminary statements, I am now ready to deal specifically with the three Notices.

I find it very difficult to accept the grounds on which the crucial information contained in the pages in question was exempted and withheld – namely, international affairs and solicitor–client privilege. The first hardly seems to need comment. As for the second, the claim can scarcely be given any credit whatsoever, given that all the papers prepared for the commission by its counsel were released to the public, including all of paper 11 except the pages in question. Beyond this, however, from my standpoint and that of my former colleagues in the Security Service, it is a pity that the view of the commission's counsel concerning ministerial knowledge of and responsibility for security service activities has taken so long to reach the public record. *It need hardly be said that it is a matter of the first importance to all of us to have their views publicly known.*

In their assessment of the CCPP meeting of 1 December 1970, commission counsel relied in part on handwritten notes by Len Trudel, recording secretary for the meeting. The existence of his notes was unknown, at least to me, and I must say that it came as a very pleasant surprise when, while the commission's hearings were continuing, someone in the Privy Council Office serendipitously came across Trudel's notes stuffed into the back of some filing cabinet and brought them to the attention of the RCMP task force set up to assist the commission's work. The task force was led by Archie Barr, a dedicated and extremely able and knowledgeable member of the RCMP Security Service. I naïvely thought that the discovery would effectively vindicate my repeated contention that ministers were made aware that the Security Service had been obliged to carry out illegal activities in the performance of their mandate. Subsequently, however, I learned of suspicions in some quarters that the notes might have been planted!

For example, eventually, I was allowed to see Trudel's notes, but only under the most stringent conditions. Harry Johnson, secretary to the commission, under instructions from McDonald, showed them to me in an atmosphere of great secrecy, in one of the commission's offices. I was not permitted to have a copy nor to take notes, and when I said that I would like my lawyer also to see the notes, I was told that this would not be permitted. Indeed, I believe that there were even objections to the notes' being seen by RCMP Commissioner Higgitt, who also had been present at the 1 December 1970 meeting of the CCPP. Eventually the objection about Higgitt was withdrawn.

An interesting footnote to this chapter is to be found in the unexpurgated minutes of the discussions on 'Law and Order' in the Cabinet Committee on Priorities and Planning (in effect, the inner cabinet) held on 24 November 1970 and 1 December 1970, copies of which I obtained under the Access to Information Act and which are reproduced as Appendix I. On both occasions Michael Pitfield was secretary, with Michael Butler and Trudel assistant secretaries.

Why do the minutes of the meeting of 1 December 1970 make no mention whatsoever of the statement that I made about the RCMP's having carried out illegal activities for twenty years? That what I said was faithfully recorded by Trudel was quite clearly established by the legal counsel for the McDonald Commission. Why was such an unusual, even startling statement, made before twenty-six people in one of the country's most important cabinet committees, simply omitted from the official record?

15

Spy Novelist

After retiring in April 1973, I began tentatively to write my first novel, but I was soon asked to take on a number of quite different jobs, some involving personal service contracts with government departments or agencies and some in the private sector. Between June 1973 and March 1977 I received about thirty-five such approaches. The majority I refused. Some I was quite unsuited to perform – such as managing a well-known linen specialty shop in Montreal. I accepted a personal service contract with the Department of Justice, at the behest of Mr Justice Gerard La Forest, to prepare a study on 'Freedom within the Law.' Somewhat later Allan Gotlieb, deputy minister at Citizenship and Immigration, asked me to study the national security aspects of immigration policy. External Affairs signed me on to examine its records to determine if sufficient material existed to warrant commissioning a historian to write a biography of Norman Robertson. I found that there was sufficient material, and in due course Jack Granatstein was commissioned to write the book. I turned down a request to study the structure of Saudi Arabia's foreign service and to make recommendations for its improvement.

The most time-consuming and frustrating job turned out to be a study for the Treasury Board on compensation in the public service. It lasted from July 1974 until March 1975 and eventually involved about thirty people, some of them talented and very dedicated. I never felt that I was able to come to grips with the complex problems involved or to offer my employers practical proposals for dealing with them. However, I came across a curious story concerning *Exercise Lazarus*, described above, in chapter 9.

During the seemingly interminable hearings and inquiries that went on for the better part of four years, from 1977 to 1981, I decided, largely out of a sense of frustration, to try my hand at writing a spy novel. By chance my path crossed that of Alex Inglis, who was editing *International Perspectives* in the Department of External Affairs. Inglis, a Glaswegian, and I had the same sort of sense of humour and enjoyed many of the same things in life. He had been chosen to be one of the editors of Mike Pearson's memoirs. He was a skilled writer and a good editor, apart from being a delightful companion.

When he learned that I had started to think about writing a spy novel, he offered to help. We discussed the ideas that I had about plot, characters, and how they might be developed. I found his suggestions most helpful, particularly concerning matters about which I had little knowledge – style, syntax, editing, printing, and what was likely to appeal to the reading public.

Eventually a rough manuscript appeared. Inglis offered to accept it for publication by Balmuir Book Publishing Ltd., the small Ottawa company he was in the process of establishing. We came to a written agreeement, and my first spy novel, *Deep Sleepers*, appeared from Balmuir in 1981.

I found fiction of this kind fun and challenging to write – hard work, but not as difficult as non-fiction. Contrary to what I expected, I have found that non-fiction is far more demanding to write than fiction. One can portray a fictional character in any way one wishes and decide his or her fate, but it is quite another matter to write about King, St Laurent, Pearson, or Diefenbaker and numerous others who come into the story. They are anything but fictional characters and have to be portrayed as accurately and fairly as possible.

It was bold of Alex Inglis to take on a totally unknown writer who had never been published before. *Deep Sleepers* received a reasonably good reception from various reviewers. Then I wrote three more spy novels in quick succession and had them published by Balmuir – *Scarab* (1982), *Orion's Belt* (1983), and *The Cornish Hug* (1985). The first three books formed a trilogy and were marketed as such. *The Cornish Hug* was also a spy novel but was set in North America in the 1770s.

About mid-1982, while I was writing *Orion's Belt*, Pied Piper Films Ltd of Toronto and Robert Anderson Associates Ltd of Ottawa made an offer to buy the television and motion picture rights to the first three books – an offer that I accepted. In 1989 the Canadian Broadcasting Corporation (CBC) approached me about a two-hour radio adaptation of the three books. I agreed, and the project went ahead, with the adaptations being done by a renowned and skilled script writer.

Shortly thereafter the editor of a book about spy fiction to be published by Frank Cass & Co. Ltd in London, England, invited me to write a contribution entitled 'Why I Write Spy Fiction.'

Born in 1918, I was brought up, like many of my generation, on thrillers by authors such as John Buchan, Erskine Childers, Joseph Conrad, Compton Mackenzie, Herman C. McNeile, Somerset Maughan, E. Phillips Oppenheim, Baroness Orczy, and Edgar Wallace. Being an only child, I had the run of the small but well-stocked library in my parent's house. I learned to appreciate spy fiction from an early age, and an urge to write seems to have been with me for many years. I began to turn over in my mind the idea of writing a novel about espionage that could deal with some of the unpleasant realities that lead to the existence of an organization such as the RCMP Security Service. The idea for *Deep Sleepers* began to take shape. I have been asked whether the book had a didactic purpose. I believe that it did, in that the dispiriting discussions that I heard about the work of a security service during the McDonald Commission's hearings convinced me that Canadians generally were uninfomed, uninterested, and hypocritical about security and intelligence matters. Using the novel form I hoped, perhaps naïvely, to change Canadian attitudes in some slight measure.

Deep Sleepers does illustrate some of the unpleasant realities of espionage and counter-intelligence, but it was not long before I began to forget my didactic purpose and found telling the story a worthwhile and satisfying end in itself. The story became, among other things, a Soviet–Canadian love story. The characters took over and became real people with whom I lived each day, and sometimes part of the night and early morning as well. I began to forget my frustrations about the McDonald Commission and to enjoy the sheer pleasure of creating something.

After finishing *The Cornish Hug* in 1985 I made a start on a fifth spy novel, to be entitled *Albric's Cloak*. Eventually the story became the victim of glasnost. Given the unexpected speed with which the Soviet Union began to fall apart, it became clear that I would have to rewrite the book, which I proceeded to do. The first revision I entitled *The Wages of Glasnost*, but, unsatisfied with some parts of the story, I revised it extensively again. In due course a completely new manuscript emerged. I gave it the title *Latonya* – I liked the cadence of the name, which, though not Russian, sounded as if it might be. I then began looking for an agent/publisher. By sheer chance I was able to get assistance from an unexpected source, John Le Carré. He was writing a new book, to be set partly in Canada, and his literary agents put me in touch with him with the thought that I might be able to assist his arrangements in Canada. Not only did I admire his writings, but it happened that we had been in Bonn at the same time – when I was Canadian ambassador and he was a member of the MI 6 station in Bonn, using his real name, David Cornwell.

When David Cornwell arrived in Ottawa, I took him to lunch at the Rideau Club, where we recalled at leisure some of the more humorous events of earlier days in Bonn. I found that I enjoyed him, his sense of the ridiculous, his quick wit, and his views about the literary world and life as a spy in the British foreign service. He offered to help me in my quest for a publisher and put me in touch with people in the Canadian book world. Eventually the volume was published in New York in 1994 by Vantage Press.

When I started writing spy fiction I was careful to avoid plots or characters based on real people and specific operations of which, as director-general of the RCMP Security Service, I had knowledge. As my novel writing progressed, it became clear to me that this precaution was no longer necessary or practicable, since so much of what, only a short time earlier, had been treated with the greatest secrecy now was public.

There is no question that some of my plots and characters, while not based on real situations of which I had knowledge, were nevertheless an amalgam of some of them. It also became clear to me that fact is often more exciting and amusing than fiction – even that created by the most imaginative and gifted authors of spy fiction, such as John Le Carré.

For example, while no particular character in any of my spy novels is a portrait of James Jesus Angleton, the former head of the CIA's counter-espionage activities, about whom I have written above, his extraordinary personality certainly informed some of my creations, though I am hard put to say exactly which. Angleton was a remarkable man, blessed with a touch of genius, eccentric to the point of being outlandish, irascible, unpredictable, highly intelligent, and possessed of views about communism at least as fanatical as those of many of his real-life KGB enemies. Though not gifted with much of a sense of humour, he could be very witty. In short, in real life he was a character – ideal material for any spy novelist.

No shortage exists of plots that one could draw on from actual espionage cases. While I avoided using specific cases to create plots, some plots and situations in my spy novels do represent a composite of such cases, and some of my Canadian, French, German, Israeli, American, and English characters are caricatures of people with whom I have done business, though I was always careful to avoid identifying them in any way.

Epilogue:
Security and Democracy

This memoir is a very personal commentary principally concerning my experience of security and intelligence work as functions of the military, foreign affairs, and diplomacy during a period of more than fifty-five years. I have found writing it demanding, but the task has enabled me to look back on my life in all its facets, private and professional, and it has taught me something about myself, about others, and about our country. It also has served to remind me of the extraordinary men and women with whom I have worked, who have added so much to my life.

In retrospect, I believe that the two decades following the outbreak of the Second World War may have been the 'golden years' of the Canadian security and intelligence community – the phrase so often used by historians to describe approximately the same period in the Department of External Affairs. With any luck, the years to come may prove to be equally rewarding to the Canadian intelligence community.

The concatenation of events and people in these two decades was a lucky coincidence, leading to a singular role for Canada in a worldwide security and intelligence web. This network originally was built up to deal with threats to the Western alliance posed by the hostile activities of the Axis Powers and later the Soviet Union and its allies. It now provides Canada with a good intelligence and security base from which to try to cope with the ever-changing threats posed by the unstable, unpredictable world in which we live as we approach a new millennium.

People such as Doug Abbott, Bob Bryce, Bill Crean, George Glazebrook, Arnold Heeney, C.D. Howe, C.J. (Jack) Mackenzie, Mike Pearson, Norman Robertson, Louis St Laurent, and Tommy Stone were interested in and knowledgeable about many different aspects of security and intelligence work. They used the power of their personalities and their various appointments to ensure that Canada benefited to the fullest extent possible from its participation in these secret activities. I think on balance that they were very successful, despite some mistakes and errors of judgment. It is only surprising that mistakes did not occur more frequently.

Over several decades, for valid security reasons, it was not possible to provide Canadians with details about Canada's role in security and intelligence matters as functions of government, making it difficult for ministers, members of Parliament, and many officials to be informed. Fortunately, this situation is changing, and the public may come to be much better informed. However, there always will be matters that cannot be disclosed until a number of years have passed.

Within this broad context I would like to pay tribute to the men and women, but especially the women,who have played such an important, unsung part in Canada's security and intelligence activities. From the outset scores of women, serving as secretaries, archivists, undercover agents, translators, transcribers, librarians, executive assistants, and in many other capacities, have carried out important and highly sensitive tasks in security and intelligence. I have in mind, for example, those who served Bryce, Heeney, Pearson, and Robertson in such capacities and were privy to virtually all the information that these men had, including sensitive details about intelligence and personnel security. They acted as custodians of such information and were indoctrinated and cleared to handle it.

This was particularly the case in specialized government agencies such as the Communications Branch of the National Research Council (CBNRC, now CSE), the Intelligence Policy Committee (IPC), the Joint Intelligence Committee, (JIC), the Privy Council Office (PCO), the RCMP Security Service, the Security Panel, and their subcommittees and secretariats. In the RCMP Security Service, women performed such duties as being members of the Watcher Service (physical surveillance), translating and transcribing audio-tapes involving intercepted telephone communications (in many different languages and dialects), and conducting clandestine microphone operations. Much of this sensitive, difficult work was performed by women who were dedicated, completely trustworthy professionals. They also performed essential jobs in connection with Canada's participation in CAZAB.

It would be inappropriate for me to identify those I have in mind. It would unecessarily attract publicity to them and would result in an unintended invasion of their privacy. All those involved, however, deserve praise for the manner in which they carried out sometimes thankless jobs with discretion, skill, intelligence, and loyalty. Many of these public servants are the reason why John Bryden, MP, in his recent book about Canada's work in communications intelligence, was able to characterize those activities as Canada's 'Best-Kept Secret.'

Many of the women of whom I am thinking were relatively young when they assumed positions of great trust, but age was not a major factor in their successes. Far more important, they possessed a high degree of intelligence and a willingness to work tirelessly, to be unfazed by the nature of the work, and to keep their mouths shut.

I would like to end with some observations that will, I hope, provide context to certain events which caused controversy in Canada, and in which I was involved. It is not my intention to attempt a revision of recent history of the Canadian security service; Canadians now are able to make their own judgments. Wherever possible, I have let such official records as are available tell the story, since most of the relevant documents now have been made public under the Access to Information Act. For example, in chapter 14, above, the clear, authoritative language used by the McDonald Commission's legal counsel speaks for itself.

The ever-evolving arrangements for governing Canada are a reflection of the very concept of Canada as a nation. My professional career in the armed forces, in the diplomatic service, and in the development of national security arrangements mirrors that process of change. The Canada of my youth was relatively uncomplicated. There were levels of internal coherence that are almost unimaginable today. Hugh Mac-Lennan's 'two solitudes' and the potential that they created for internal division were facts of life, but the political and constitutional framework then in place minimized the extent and the degree of this dysfunction. This is not the case in the Canada of today.

Canadians have committed themselves to a multicultural and multiracial society. The legal and constitutional framework that gives substance to this concept, maximizes the political and personal rights and entitlements of the individual. This vision of Canada, which I support, creates a threshold for individual freedom that has few if any equals elsewhere in the world. In fact it is arguable that there is no precedent for the extraordinary future that Canadians are trying to create for themselves.

When I first entered public service, the concepts of national interest and national security were largely unarticulated. Without exception, threats to the internal security of Canada were externally based or driven. The RCMP – the agency responsible for internal security – investigated such threats according to policies and procedures that remained little changed from the period of the First World War. The force carried out those responsibilities in a tough-minded way, with virtually no direct involvement from the government, well beyond the end of the Second World War. Essentially these were the same operational approaches and the same investigative policies and procedures on which the RCMP found itself relying in dealing with outbreaks of politically inspired violence in Quebec in the 1960s and 1970s.

During the time I was the first civilian director-general of the RCMP Security Service, there were many politically motivated acts of violence. The violence that took place was criminal and wrong. Use of the unselective instruments of containment then available to the RCMP also was wrong. The whole point of the McDonald Commission that followed was *not* that effective internal security arrangements were unnecessary, but quite the opposite.

The commission said two very important things. First, it was wrong to have used the unchanged and unacceptable procedures then in place. And second, Canada needed new procedures, within an agreed legal framework, to be able to tackle the potential for politically motivated violence not just in Quebec, but also in the other provinces and regions of Canada and as problems endemic to one area or segment of the population might arise.

As I see it, there is, in security and intelligence terms, no 'Quebec problem' but rather a 'Canada problem.' In the context of the societal and constitutional framework to which I have referred above, I do not believe that there is a 'root source' for subversion in Canada. Rather the multicultural and multiracial, 'mosaic' approach to nation-building creates the potential for tensions (domestic as well as imported), which require modern arrangements for internal security. Such arrangements we now have in the Canadian Security Intelligence Service (CSIS) and the act on which it is based.

The legacy of the McDonald Commission was the creation of new legislation defining for citizens and governments the extent of tolerance for political expression and of intervention by the state. The CSIS act gives the solicitor-general the power in extreme and well-defined situations to authorize use of the most intrusive investigative methods available to the CSIS – in effect, to suspend the constitutional protections and guarantees otherwise provided for in the Constitution Act and other statutes. That is quite an improvement over the arrangements in place at the time of the so-called October Crisis of 1970.

It is clear to me that Canadian history as it relates to the events that occurred in the 1970s would have been quite different had the current internal security laws been in place at that time. I wish that they had been, but they were not, and as Canadians we can be reassured by the fact that we face the future with these new arrangements in place.

There are additional points I would like to make about the historical legacy of the internal security crises in Canada in the 1960s and thereafter. I was personally affected by some aspects of the McDonald Commission's deliberations and by the conclusions that some observers reached on what, it now is quite clear, was an incomplete public record. I regard it not as a matter of ascribing blame, but simply as a statement of fact, that all those who needed to know of what were in effect insensitive, inappropriate, and in some cases unlawful investigative practices and procedures *did in fact know*. No one took comfort from these facts, but Canadians can be confident in the knowledge that those who did know subsequently designed and built a modern, effective, contemporary, internal security system.

Last, but not least, recognition and credit must be given to the democratic nature of the process by which Canada developed its modern internal security infrastructure, with its careful checks and balances, including the involvement of the Federal Court. The process was intensely debated in public. To my knowledge, only one other country, Australia, has followed a similar process. We should understand just how unique our experience is in this regard. To have defined 'threats to the security of Canada' for statutory purposes also has been to define the extent of political tolerance, and the limits on deviance, in Canadian society. In the never-ending attempt to define and redefine ourselves, such statutory definitions are bound to fail in the absence of a complementary, fully accountable process of wise and sensitive interpretation. I believe that this is in fact happening and that the Canadian Security Intelligence Service has been supporting, and is being required to support to the fullest extent possible, the levels of political tolerance envisaged in the constitution, even as the service carries on its duty to ensure Canada's internal security in the future.

Documents re Wartime Military Intelligence

While doing research recently in the archives of the Department of National Defence I was surprised to come across four top-secret memoranda written in mid-December 1945 – 'MI 6,' 'MI 5,' 'MI 8,' and 'Sigs Int.' The original documents offer no indication as to who may have written them, or for whom, and nothing on the file helped to resolve the mystery. It would have been unusual for some of the subjects to have been dealt with by any department other than External Affairs.

The phrasing suggests that the author probably was a senior military officer, knowledgeable about at least some of the complicated subjects discussed. The documents released to me have been declassified, except for half of the third paragraph of the earliest one, presumably withheld on grounds of national security. The documents throw light on the close relationships concerning intelligence developed by 1945 between the British and the Canadian military.

'MI 6' (11 December 1945)

I had a 50 minute conversation with 'C' [head of MI 6 – Stewart Menzies] in which both SI and Sig Int problems were passed in review.

2. Concerning the former, we discussed the proposed allocation of an area of Intelligence interest to Canada and whether or not this should extend beyond the normal bounds of overt Intelligence. MI 6 is particularly interested in Mexico because of evidence to show that it is being used as a penetration base for the whole of North and South America [presumably by Soviet intelligence agents]. 'C' was of the opinion that although ISTD [British interdepartmental

topographical intelligence service] and similar agencies might be more interested in the West Coast, the country as a whole was of more interest to him and to us. We reviewed the possible methods of establishing an organization.

[Several sentences have been deleted at the beginning of paragraph 3, the remaining undeleted portion reads] ... These discussions centred round the new set-up which will not conform to the original British plans for a London directed network, but, because of the terms of the North American security pact, will be tripartite with joint Anglo-Canadian-American control. He agreed that a conversation with Capt. Hastings was desirable to get full information on the new stations.

5. He informed me of the existence of two MI 6 set-ups in Canada. One is a Signals Passing Station with Canadian personnel in Toronto. The other is a Cipher Research project ['Camp X'] which has been going on during the war in Washington, but which will be transferred to Toronto, and is operating under the direction of Professor Bailey [*sic*]. The terms of reference and activities of both organizations are known to Mr. Robertson. It is likely that the former will shortly be transferred to Foreign Office control.

6. Other matters reviewed were current American indiscretions regarding Sig Int matters, difficulties in the way of securing Australian co-operation, rate of recovery for Germany and Japan and the taking over of SOE, which 'C' confirmed is slated for 15 Jan 46.

'MI 5' (14 December 1945)

I spent an hour and three quarters at MI 5, mainly occupied in a review of the situation with Capt. Liddel who heads the Counter Espionage Section and has done a great deal of liaison with Canada and the U.S.

2. I first exchanged politenesses with Brigadier Allen, who had not got much to say for himself. He took me down to see Capt. Liddel and left after about half an hour.

3. We first discussed the question of the proper scope of the RCMP. It was apparent that both Brigadier Allen and Capt. Liddel and, presumably, MI 5, felt that whatever the ideal limits to the functions of the RCMP may be, they have, in fact, taken over the donkey work of Counter Espionage and Counter Sabotage in Canada and, in the course of the recent war, have acquired a good deal of experience. Both spoke particularly of Superintendent Carnac, Senior Officer of the RCMP Intelligence Section. Factors which have made their work effective are their ability to work in close contact with their own network of operatives spread throughout the country and possessed of detailed local information. Also they are on excellent terms with the FBI and, to use Capt.

Liddel's phrase, 'sit in one anothers's pockets.' Their relations with MI 5 have, I gather, been uniformly good.

4. On the other hand, the weaknesses of RCMP work have been dictated in the main by nervousness, particularly the fear that they will be rapped over the knuckles by External Affairs. The best illustration of this was afforded in the earlier part of the war when it became necessary to supervise discreetly the activities of Spanish Consuls and Consulates in Canada, which were passing information to the Japanese. The RCMP, though in full possession of the facts, were most reluctant to do anything. This has been corrected, in part, by approaching External Affairs direct. Capt. Liddel had conversations with Norman Robertson on the occasion of his recent visit.

5. Capt. Liddel felt that should a JIB be set up in Canada, somewhat similar to the projected British one, it would be necessary to include the RCMP, though in such a case they would act on direction from above and the whole would be meshed in with Service Counter Intelligence [presumably Canadian armed forces' activities].

6. There was a fairly frank discussion of the relationship with MI 6, which, I gather, is now under review. Work in the field together during operations undoubtedly brought the two departments closely together, but I gather there is friction every now and then due to fundamental differences in method and small arguments over de-limitation of activities and zones.

7. Capt. Liddel described the integrated workings with MI 6, Deuxieme Bureau and OSS X 2. In the preparation for North Africa, Sicily and D-Day they meshed together in a common War Room at MI 5. Relations with the Americans continue to be good, particularly with FBI, though there are occasionally ominous signs on the horizon. FBI keep a representative at MI 5 but MI 5 are not allowed to reciprocate because of the tangle with MI 6 over jurisdiction in Washington.

8. Capt Liddel discussed very interestingly the struggle just before and during the war. His view is that German Intelligence failed because of over-confidence and the employment of second-rate personnel. Their main effort from 1938 on was concentrated in two fields;- (a) Propaganda [and] (b) War Potential Intelligence. Both were too easy. As a result, when the break came and they no longer had wide open barn doors to every British arms factory through their machine tool agencies, they were completely lost. All subsequent attempts to regain lost ground were comparatively easily checkmated.

9. I asked Capt Liddel if there was any intention of putting out a restricted circulation Post Mortem on German Espionage and he said that the matter was in hand. Both he and Brigadier Allen deplored the tendency in the press to publicize matters of this sort and to depict British Intelligence as either intelli-

gent or effective. It would be much preferred if the contrary assumption were widely held.

'MI 8' (18 December 1945)

I had a talk with Lt-Col. S.V. Bone, G1 of MI 8. He will be remaining for some months but will not be the permanent G1 as he is 'I' Corps and not a Regular. This decision to continue the 'I' Corps as part of the British Army is proving a great embarrassment, particularly to 'Y' Services, as all the technical Intelligence personnel are affected. Even on the Sigs side officers who have been engaged for any length of time in 'Y' grow away from regular Sigs procedure and fall out of favour in their own Corps. Many are therefore having to return to normal Corps duties in order to get promotion. I explained to Col. Bone that we had not been quite so silly in the Canadian Army.

2. Bone was very frank in giving me the full details on the disposition of 'Y' units in the proposed peace-time set-up, all of which is gravely dependant on the U.S. loan because of the great expenditure involved. The plan is for Station 'X' [Camp X and Hydra] to have a peace-time establishment of some 1000 personnel, all under Foreign Office control. The station itself will move around 1 Apr 46 to the neighbourhood of Pinner. In addition, each of the three Services and PID [Political Intelligence Department] will maintain some 200 out stations scattered over the world.

3. The 200 Army stations will be distributed as follows. 50 in the Mediterranean, based on Gibraltar, Malta, Cyprus and Palestine. Because of the uncertainty regarding the future of Palestine, all arrangement are being made to transfer a station there to an augmented Cyprus station. There will be 30 stations in the Far East. The remaining 120 stations will be distributed in the U.K. In the U.K. the plan is to have two large fixed Army stations, one of which will be manned by Regular Army personnel, the other by civilians who will be ex-'I' Corps types demobilised and re-employed outside the Army but under Army control.

4. Bone knew nothing regarding proposed arrangements for Canada although he was aware that conversations had been in progress. The Australian and South African picture is also obscure. It is clear that within the Sigs Int set-up there is a great deal of compartmentalization which can only be broken down by going to see a great many people. I gather that there is to be a Commonwealth Conference on Sigs Int matters meeting in London in the early spring.

'Sigs Int' (20 December 1945)

I had a fruitful talk with Capt. Hastings at the Berkeley Street Headquarters and shortly after the conversation began he brought in Kendrick, who returned in April after being stationed for three years in Ottawa as the Head of the Examination Unit.

2. Hastings thought it appropriate to give me the whole inside story regarding the origin of Sigs Int work in Canada dating back to the original employment of the notorious Yardley, at that time masquerading as Professor Osborne. This individual was apparently foisted upon Ottawa by Washington who wanted to get rid of him. The result, for some time in 1940 and 1941, was that neither London nor Washington would trust Ottawa with any of the results of their cipher activities. Eventually a rapprochement was effected between External Affairs and Sig Int Great Britain, with Mike Pearson and Norman Robertson as the prime movers on the Canadian side. Relations are now good and Hastings and Company continue to be very well satisfied with the work done by Drake, who they hope will continue to remain in charge of his present set-up.

3. A man by the name of Evans is going out shortly from here to take over the Examination Unit.

4. Hastings gave me a little additional information on the post-war set-up in the U.K. What he did tell me I had got already from MI 8. The bulk of information regarding future plans will undoubtedly be discussed in detail at the February Commonwealth Conference on Sigs Int to be held here and which I or some representative of DMI should attend.

5. One useful suggestion was that Canada appoint a trustworthy and intelligent official to sit in at the Sigs Int Headquarters here [presumably Government Communications Headquarters, or GCHQ]. Such an official would have full access to all material and would be treated as one of the family. His main function would be to earmark material which he thought would be of interest to Canada. Under present arrangements this decision is taken by the British. Such an arrangement would not be an innovation as there has been for some time an American officer accredited under similar conditions and the plan has been found to work very well in his case.

6. Most of the interesting Army traffic for the present comes from BOAR [British Army of the Rhine] and the British Zone in Austria. From Austria there is a wide coverage of the whole Balkan area. The senior 'Y' officer in BOAR is Col. Walter Scott, who on 31 Dec 45 will be taking over from Brigadier Vernham as DD'Y'. He came into the office and I made an appointment to see him at 1100 hours on 1 Jan 46. Vernham, not being a Regular, has to go. Also co-operating in BOAR at this time is the small RSS Section which gets its directives from MI 5 and MI 6.

7. I discussed the JIB situation and was told that a small part of MI 8, dealing with Telecommunications, is likely to split off and come under JIB.

8. Col. Bone felt that it would be highly desirable that I should get in touch with Capt. Hastings and probably go and have another look at Station 'X', which has now shrunk to almost peace-time proportions.

The authorship of the above documents is uncertain. My guess is that Felix Walter probably wrote them about the time he was sent to England in 1945 by the chief of the Canadian General Staff, Charles Foulkes. In England he was to write a report on the wartime activities of MI Section at CMHQ and particularly Canadian participation in the secret activities of SF, MO1 (SP), MI 6, MI 9, and so on. The prose style and language are very similar to those used by Walter in his report of 27 December 1945 to Foulkes. Another possible writer was Colonel Jock Murray, director of Military Intelligence (DMI) based in Ottawa, but I rather doubt it. Norman Robertson, had he known of these contacts, especially those involving the head of MI 6, might not have been entirely happy, since he probably would have considered it an inappropriate invasion of matters within his purview.

My Father's Memoir (Excerpt)

I was always spoiled and pampered by my grandmother and grandfather, but principally by my grandfather [Henry Starnes, a Tory 'bagman' who raised my father]. I remember him taking me many a time to Freeman's restaurant. A Major Freeman, ex-American army, was the proprietor. It was on Nôtre Dame Street [in Montreal] and you could get to it by walking through from St. James. There were many tables and a very long bar. Oysters and seafood were the speciality from October through the winter months. I was allowed to order whatever I wanted and I distinctly remember starting with oysters on the half-shell, then oyster soup, then scalloped oysters and finishing up with a 1/2 dozen fried oysters. They were delicious.

... I can also remember the old Victoria rink of 75 years ago. The headquarters of the Victoria Hockey Club were there, and they had some wonderful hockey games. The rink was on Drummond Street just north of Dorchester and, therefore, just above our house. Behind the house were our stables. We had two horses and a carriage and I remember the coachman catching a rat and the rat's skin coming off in his hand. The coachman would stand by the rat's hole and, as it appeared, he would pounce on it and grab it...

... About the year 1880 my grandfather was President [Speaker] of the Quebec Legislative Assembly and, in accordance with his duties went to Quebec frequently and remained sometimes for long periods.

... He had permanent quarters in the Quebec parliament buildings, which was situated near the Grande Allée. His quarters were on the first floor up. The provincial police force guarded the building and their guard room was in the basement of the building. I got to know these policemen very well. My grandfather had a butler-valet who served all our meals in these rooms, which were large enough to give soirées.

... In the summertime we travelled to Quebec by steamer, which we called the 'Quebec boat.' It would leave Montreal about 7 p.m. and arrive in Quebec about 7 the next morning. The ship belonged to a company called the Richelieu and Ontario Navigation Company, which is now the Canada Steamship Lines. The ships were fairly large and painted white. They served excellent meals and had a very good assortment of wines in the bar.

... Coming and going there were always a number of prominent politicians on board, who frequently gathered in my grandfather's stateroom for refreshments both before and after dinner.

... William Fitzsimmons of Brockville, Ontario, was my grandfather on my mother's side. My grandfather William lived in Brockville all his life and, when he died, he was the postmaster. He had a large family, several daughters and sons. He was married twice ... He lived to be about 75 years old and was a very good Conservative.

... This chronicle would not be complete if I did not mention something about Sherbrooke [Quebec]. I married a Sherbrooke lady 54 years ago and got to know the Eastern Townships very well. It was a very large family I married into. My wife was the second eldest of a family of nine ... They lived in a very large house on Melbourne Street ... They had a large garden and stables and kept a cow, and there was an ice-house where they would store vegetables and sides of meat. We met at Kennebunk Beach, Maine, where we became engaged and we were married in Sherbrooke 13 months later, on September 13th, 1911. Frankly, I was superstitious about the 13th and wasn't very happy about that date ... After the wedding there was a reception at the house and we took the 8 o'clock train to Boston where we started our honeymoon.

... Neither of us knew Boston and we were standing on a street corner when we decided to go back to the hotel. We called a taxi and he drove us around the block and delivered us at the hotel front door, which had only been a few steps away! We went to a Big League baseball game which I enjoyed very much but, as my bride did not know anything about the game, she was not very interested. We stayed in Boston 4 or 5 days and then took the boat from Boston to Yarmouth. It was an overnight trip and was exceedingly rough. After such a trip none of the passengers had their sea-legs, and in disembarking we all took steps 4 feet high. From Yarmouth we took the train to Halifax, stayed there a day or so, and took a small ocean steamer up the St. Lawrence to Montreal.

APPENDIX C

Planning Assumptions for *Exercise Lazarus* (1967)

ANNEX A
TO: V3289-2 (DLFORT)
DATED: 27 JUNE, 1967

PLANNING ASSUMPTIONS

Mission

1. To constitute *an autonomous Canadian presence in the Eastern Mediterranean region, which is capable of functioning semi-independently under the aegis of an international force having as its mission the enforcement and maintenance of peace in the area.*

General

2. The Canadian Force would be of the size and type shown at Annex B.
3. The Force would receive 14 days warning and seven days notice to move.
4. *It is envisaged that the host nation would not be friendly but that the landing and build-up would not be actively opposed.*
5. *The Canadian Force must be so organized and maintained that it is not dependent upon other nations for communications, supplies, services or facilities which are essential to the existence of the Force or attainment of the mission.*
6. That portion of the Force shown at Annex C must be deployed in the operational area by D+14. The remainder of the Force must be landed by D+60 at the latest but preferably by D+45.
7. RCAF, RCN and commercial means of transportation will be utilized to effect the build up within the timings stipulated above.

Operational Capability

8. *The Force must be capable of conducting land operations of a conventional nature by day and night. This implies the ability to engage in offensive action of a sporadic nature against indigenous hostile elements of up to battalion size.*
9. Notwithstanding the above it is envisaged that operations will for the most part consist of long range patrolling, the manning of outpost and observation lines, local protection, and occasionally intervention in localized conflicts and / or pre and post-conflict situations.
10. The Force must be capable of joint and combined operations – though *it is envisaged that the Force would normally operate independently within an assigned operational sector.*
11. The Force must be airtransportable.

Functional Capability

12. The Canadian Force will consist of:
    a. A National Headquarters (Task Force Headquarters).
    b. A Forward Base (in theatre).
    c. A field formation.
The Task Force Headquarters will be separate and distinct from the headquarters of the field formation. Similarly the Forward Base would be separate and distinct from the service support elements of the field formation.
13. The Commander Task Force Headquarters will be the senior national representative in the area *and as such will be accredited to the headquarters of any international agency and to the host country.*
14. Should circumstances so require the field formation could be placed under operational control of an international commander and may be embodied into *a multi national force provided that such an arrangement would not be prejudicial to Canadian identity and autonomy.*
15. Canada will be the main base. Circumstances may require the use of advanced base facilities in Europe for some types of support and services.
16. Reserves are to be held in theatre as follows:
    a. Ammunition — 18 standard days
    b. POL   — 300 miles per vehicle
    c. Rations   — 14 days
17. Resupply will begin on D+3. Theatre Reserves are to be built up at the following rates:
    First third   — by D+14
    Second third   — by D+28

Final third   — by D+45

18. Local contracts for the provision of POL and fresh rations must be negotiated as soon as possible following the decision to commit the Force. A fuel supply point system would be required. MT, AVGAS, JP4 and unleaded gasoline natures would be required.

19. Supply arrangements should be based upon a battalion group and subsequently a brigade group ration break.

20. Air support elements assigned to the Force would be placed under command. A Movements Control Group would be organized to coordinate all movement into and out of the Theatre of Operations.

21. *Heavy reliance would be placed upon indigenous labour.* Negotiations, contractual arrangements and payment could be under Canadian arrangements. It is envisaged that the establishment of Task Force Headquarters would include a Civil Affairs Officer who would perform these duties.

22. Required within the organization of the Forward Base would be:

a. A Guard Company.

b. A Construction Engineer element.

c. A 100 bed hospital with associated laundry facilities and fresh water supply.

d. An airfield control and forward maintenance organization.

APPENDIX D

Memoranda re Security and Intelligence (1969)

MEMORANDUM FOR THE PRIME MINISTER

[Re] Meeting of the Cabinet Committee on Security and Intelligence – Friday, December 19, 1969

I attach in draft form a possible memorandum for the Cabinet Committee on Security and Intelligence to be considered at the meeting to be held this Friday. As it has been drafted for your signature, you will wish to ensure that it accurately reflects your own views. You will recall agreeing that you as Prime Minister should take the initiative in this matter in order to ensure that the problems requiring attention were brought forward in proper context and within a more manageable structure than was evident at the last 'briefing' meeting of the Committee.

If the attached paper or some modification of it is acceptable to you, I would suggest that it be sent to the Ministers concerned a day or two prior to the meeting (possibly on Wednesday) to provide them time to study it.

As to the attendance at the meeting on Friday, I think it is desirable that, owing to the nature of the problem for discussion, the following officials be invited by their Ministers:

[Deleted words]

Mr. Wall and I will attend from this Office. If you agree to this roster of attendance, we will suggest to Ministers that they invite their Deputy Ministers to attend.

Privy Council Office.

MEMORANDUM FOR THE PRIME MINISTER

December 17, 1969.

Meeting of the Cabinet Committee on Security and Intelligence – Friday, December 19, 1969

I attach Copy No. 1 of the Top Secret Memorandum for the Cabinet Committee on Security and Intelligence entitled 'Current Threats to National Order and Unity – Quebec Separatism,' which will be considered at the meeting on Friday next at 2:00 p.m. in 340-S. It has been sent only to Ministers, but they have been asked to discuss the paper with their Deputy Ministers, and to invite them to the meeting [deleted words] If you agree, I will collect all copies of the document at the end of the meeting.

The purpose of the paper is to set out the problem in general, to identify certain of the areas in which control and corrective action might be taken, and to propose a number of specific actions which might be taken in the immediate future. I think it is important to establish at the outset that the problems discussed in the paper must be dealt with in the larger context of the priority problem of National Unity (Mr. Sharp) and its subsidiary problem of Law and Order (Mr. Turner), in order to preserve the logical integrity of the [deleted words]. There is no question that the problems discussed in this paper are multi-departmental in scope, and that solutions will require extensive consultation and a joint effort by the departments concerned.

[deleted words] to provide a cohesive information base for decisions as to policies and programmes.' It seems to us desirable that any such organization should be under the control and direction of the Prime Minister, and that it should be located in your Office or in the Privy Council Office. If the other Ministers agree to this, we might then proceed to devise the kind of mechanism required. If there are strong arguments against it, they should emerge in discussion.

The other possibly contentious recommendation [deleted words]

Should there be other matters in the Memorandum which you wish to discuss prior to the meeting, I will be happy to do so at any time.

D.F.W.

Privy Council Office

MEMORANDUM FOR MR. WALL:

December 22nd, 1969.

National unity; Quebec separatism, etc.

Pursuant to the meeting of the Cabinet Committee on Security and Intelligence on Friday, I suppose that what is now wanted is a revision of the document – or is it sufficient to have the conventional type of Secretary's report in forwarding the document on to the Cabinet? The reason I am inclined to favour a revision is because in this particular subject area [missing words]

Perhaps you could give this some thought and then we can discuss where we should go from here.

I am returning herewith the Prime Minister's copy of the memorandum that was discussed on Friday, together with the covering memorandum to him of December 16th.

R.G.R.

'Current Threats to National Order and Unity – Quebec Separatism' (1969)

Memorandum for the Cabinet Committee on Security and Intelligence,
[Document S8I-10, 17 December 1969]

I. *Purpose*

To consider such further action as might reasonably be taken by the federal government to understand and deal effectively with the disruptive forces at play in Canada, and particularly in Quebec, which threaten the order and integrity of Canada.

II. *The Problem*

The Cabinet recently agreed, on the recommendation of the Cabinet Committee on Priorities and Planning, that National Unity and Law and Order constitute the third highest priority problem facing the government at present.

The most pressing and immediate aspects of the joint problem of national unity and law and order are related to [missing words]

Numerous indicators point to the seriousness of the situation, with the following being only a few of the more significant:

- A high degree of labour unrest, especially in the essential services of the public sector.
- A high unemployment rate which may become higher and more serious owing to the low level of investment on the one hand and –
- Large numbers of students coming into the market next June, both as graduates without permanent job prospects and as student workers without jobs to absorb their energies and provide financing for further studies.
- Political difficulties of the Provincial Government: bare majority, internal

splits, serious financial problems, widespread criticism of the Language Bill and a forthcoming election, probably in June.

- More 'open' conversions to the Parti Québécois on the part of 'respectable' middle class people, e.g., [deleted words]
- Continued influence of outside mass demonstrations on Quebec groups' imitations, e.g., U.S. Moratoria, and possibly further university disruptions [deleted words].
- Continued financial strains in the community generally.

A few hopeful signs have appeared, such as Premier Bertrand's firm stand on Bill 63, a couple of labour agreements in the public sector, the arrangement reached at the Education Conference in Paris, and the absence of serious violence during Grey Cup weekend. Despite these rare positive signs, however, the number and seriousness of the negative ones would appear to command that immediate attention be given to the Quebec situation.

In light of these factors, it is clear that the problem cannot be dealt with entirely within the 'security' context as it is usually understood. It is therefore my intention to have the whole matter brought before the Cabinet Committee on Priorities and Planning in the near future, in order to determine how the various aspects of the problem can be dealt with in an integrated and coordinated manner. In the meantime, however, it is essential that action be taken to improve the quantity and quality of information necessary as the basis on which the government might

(a) anticipate serious difficulties;

(b) plan and execute preventive and control measures; and

(c) plan and execute long-term curative measures.

III. *General Principles*

In addition to the obvious necessity to gather more and better information and to coordinate it, analyse it and put it to effective use, it is desirable that certain general principles in relation to the larger problem be adopted and made known to those concerned, as a base for policy direction and for controlling and curative action. The two basic principles would appear to be these:

(a) The thrust as well as the substance of policies and programmes intended to preserve the order, unity and integrity of the nation must be such as to command a widespread consensus in all parts of the country and must be in full accord with our legacy of freedom and responsibility within a Parliamentary democracy.

(b) There must be full agreement at all levels among the governments concerned as to the basic objectives, and complete understanding that they can only be fulfilled in a spirit of cooperation, not competition.

IV. *Federal Policy in Relation to Separatism*

The Royal Commission on Security, on the basis of its study of Quebec separatism, recommended as follows:

Security policy concerning separatism should be made clear; the federal government should take (and be seen to take) steps to prevent its infiltration by persons who are clearly committed to the dissolution of Canada, or who are involved with elements of the separatist movement in which seditious activity or foreign involvement are factors; information concerning membership in or associations with extreme separatist groups should be reported on the same basis as information concerning other allegedly subversive movements, and the departmental decision process should be similar.

In order that a policy may be established and announced on this subject, it will be necessary to determine the public and private position which the government should adopt in relation to separatism, and questions such as the following will require to be answered: [deleted words]

V. *Information*

(a) *Present Sources*

The major current source of federal intelligence concerning the separatist and other dissident groups and individuals in Quebec is the R.C.M.P. While the Force has devoted a good deal of attention and effort to the intelligence-gathering task, and has produced [deleted words] their efforts have been hampered by a number of factors. Jurisdictional arrangements necessitate their depending for much of their intelligence.

Although there are undoubtedly other actions which the Force could take to obtain more intelligence, particularly [deleted words] the risks are such that they would require specific governmental instructions to proceed along these lines. There is the further difficulty of [deleted words] in a situation in which political loyalties are often uncertain and divided. In any event, even if those difficulties were met, it is probably beyond the capacity or functions of any security service to provide all of the information necessary for federal planning and action to deal with this problem in the larger context of National Unity and Order.

The other main sources of information are the mass media, 'political intelligence' (that is, unpublished information available to the government through Members of Parliament and such mechanisms as party organizations, Regional Desks in the Prime Minister's Office, the Federal–Provincial Relations

Secretariat, and our diplomatic posts abroad), and published literature based on research into some of the broad and basic problems.

(b) *Need for Coordination and Analysis*
Although it is probable that each of these sources of information could be considerably improved, the most immediate need is for the coordination and analysis of the information they currently provide, both in order to determine where the gaps are and how best to fill them, and also to form an integrated basis of information upon which initial control and long-term curative action might be taken

(c) *Need for Particular Kinds of Information*
Some of the larger gaps referred to above are, of course, already apparent. For example, [deleted words]

Minutes of Cabinet Meeting
(19 December 1969)

January 5, 1970

A meeting of the **Cabinet Committee on Security and Intelligence** was held on Friday, December 19, 1969, at 2:30 p.m., in Room 340-S.

Present:

The Prime Minister (Mr. Trudeau) in the Chair
The Secretary of State for External Affairs (Mr. Sharp)
The Solicitor General (Mr. McIlraith)
The President of the Treasury Board (Mr. Drury)
The Minister of National Defence (Mr. Cadieux)
The Minister of Justice (Mr. Turner)
The Secretary of State (Mr. Pelletier)

Also Present:

The Secretary to the Cabinet (Mr. R.G. Robertson)
Mr. M. Cadieux (Under-Secretary of State for External Affairs)
Mr. J.K. Starnes (Assistant Under-Secretary of State)
Mr. E.A. Côté (Deputy Solicitor General)
Mr. E.B. Armstrong (Deputy Minister of National Defence)
Major General M.R. Dare (Department of National Defence)
Mr. D.S. Maxwell (Deputy Minister of Justice)
Mr. D.H. Christie (Assistant Deputy Attorney General)
Mr. J. Leger (Under-Secretary of State)
Commissioner W.L. Higgitt

Assistant Commissioner J.E.M. Barrette (Royal Canadian Mounted Police)
Mr. M. Lalonde (Principal Secretary to the Prime Minister)
Mr. D.F. Wall (Secretary) (Privy Council Office)

Current Threats to National Order and Unity –
Quebec Separatism

The Cabinet Committee had for consideration a Memorandum of the Prime Minister entitled 'Current Threats to National Order and Unity – Quebec Separatism' (S&I-10, December 17, 1969). The Document had been circulated earlier to the Ministers of the Committee, and copies were handed to officials at the beginning of the meeting.

The Prime Minister, in introducing the Document, said that the Cabinet had recently agreed that the problem of national unity be regarded as a priority problem to be dealt with on a multi-departmental basis, and had further agreed that it be considered together with the related priority problem of law and order. In light of the current situation in Quebec, the Memorandum before the Committee had been drafted in such a way as to take into account the two priority problems, with particular emphasis on the problem of Separatism in Quebec. It was desirable that great priority be allocated this aspect of the problem, bearing in mind that no modern state would allow a threat of this magnitude to its unity and integrity without mounting a consistent and coordinated defence against it.

The Prime Minister then summarized the various sections of the Memorandum including the conclusions and recommendations. He stressed the urgency of the problem and the need to cooperate with the other governments concerned, preserving the right of the Federal Government to establish and maintain its own policies. It would be necessary to establish a clear policy on Separatism and to provide clear directives to the departments and agencies primarily concerned with Separatism. The danger of back-lash inherent in these policies and the procedures flowing from them would need to be carefully assessed. The need for coordinated information and action was paramount, and sources of information other than the R.C.M. Police would have to be developed. Contingency plans and long-term counter-action would have to be considered by the Cabinet Committee on Priorities and Planning and in due course by the Cabinet in the general context of national unity. There appeared to be a requirement for an overall planning unit in order that Ministers would have an effective tool to sift information and to coordinate *all* policies towards Quebec.

The Minister of Justice said that the Memorandum reflected two separate but related problems in dealing with the Separatist phenomenon, the problem of law and order and the political problem: The first related primarily to activity by terrorists, some of whom may be using the Separatist movement for their own ends – e.g., the establishment of a 'Cuban type' regime in Quebec. The problem posed by the Parti Québécois was not necessarily related to the problem of law and order but rather to the problem of national unity. It may therefore be necessary to deal with the two problems in different ways in order to avoid conflicts and the danger of being accused of using law and order as an anti-Separatist tool.

Mr. Turner pointed out that the federal role in law and order was fairly limited except in wartime, and was in fact tertiary in relation to political power and the use of force. Under the Criminal Code of Canada the primary responsibility for law and order lay with the Provincial Attorneys General except in cases of conspiracy. While the Federal Attorney General could institute proceedings in these cases it had only happened once in Canadian history. Action in the recent sedition cases in Quebec had been taken by the Quebec authorities. However, the nature of the problem was such that it was desirable that the Federal Government examine its role in peacetime and consider whether it should be expanded in order to give the Federal Attorney General more power to initiate action in offenses of this kind. His department was therefore considering the establishment of a Federal Jurisdiction Act.

The Secretary of State for External Affairs [deleted words]

The Secretary of State said there were two categories of phenomena dealt with in the Memorandum, the first being the unrest and malaise arising from the politicization of youth, and the second the phenomenon of Quebec Separatism. While these posed a dangerous combination, it was important to recognize that even without Separatism the problem of alienation would continue to exist in all parts of the country. It was Mr. Pelletier's view that where police action was clearly required it would be welcomed by the mass of the population of Quebec, including the Parti Québécois, who were playing a respectable role and attempting to eliminate violent persons from that Party. He would particularly like to know more of what resources the R.C.M.P. had in the Province of Quebec in terms of people trained to deal with the problems of Separatism. It was his own fear that the R.C.M.P. in Quebec were not closely identified with the milieu, and he felt that unless the federal contribution in this regard could be greatly improved it would be preferable to leave the problem to the local authorities.

The Solicitor General said he welcomed the Memorandum and the opportunity to discuss this important subject. He was concerned at the suggestion that the intelligence resources of the Armed Forces might be increased to deal with

Separatism, in that there might be a conflict in having the Forces deal with essentially civilian problems. He noted that the term 'Separatism' tended to be used loosely to cover the activities of those who desired a separate state through political conviction and those others who were using Separatism to achieve a state of chaos.

[deleted words]

Concerning Mr. Pelletier's comments, *Mr. McIlraith* said he found them disturbing, and pointed out that the R.C.M. Police provided a great deal more intelligence on the problem than did the other Police Forces concerned. Cooperation among the various Forces was good, but needed to be improved. As to information, it was Mr. McIlraith's view that there was already far more available than was being put to effective use, and he cited as an example information which had been provided to the Privy Council Office on a continuing basis concerning activities of certain members of [deleted words]

The Minister of National Defence said he disagreed with the Solicitor General on the question of using the Armed Forces to gather information about Separatism in Quebec. He felt that this activity could be usefully expanded and directed more specifically to this problem. As to the use of information, he noted that whatever was available had been so severely limited in circulation that Ministers were not fully aware of its implications. A review was being made of procedures for aid to civil power, and it was tentatively concluded that the greatest failure lay in a lack of knowledge of the procedures by the municipal officials concerned, particularly in relation to the recent strike of the Montreal City Police.

The Prime Minister said it was necessary to distinguish between the law and order problem, which included aid to the civil power, and the general problem of national unity and the question of Separatism in particular. A great deal of information concerning the first problem would be required in order to deal effectively with the second. It was for consideration whether the Cabinet should establish a separate bureau to deal with information on both problems.

The Prime Minister said it would be important to determine what attitude should be adopted toward the problem of Separatism as a whole. In the past, Communism had been considered such a menace to democratic structures that the police had been empowered to gather information on Communist activities in Canada. This being the case, and the Federal Government being dedicated to the maintenance of Canada as a nation.

Mr. Sharp agreed that this posed a special problem in that some Separatists would not consider it disloyal to be so while others might be prepared to use Separatism for their own undemocratic purposes. He thought Canadians generally would not be disturbed if they knew the Government were working against revolutionaries.

Mr. *Pelletier* said it was important not to lose sight of the fundamental distinction involved. Until belief in Separatism had been made a criminal activity, it would not be legitimate to have the police follow Separatists in order to preserve law and order.

Mr. *Turner* agreed and noted that there was a basic difference between a legitimate Separatist and a person committed to the violent overthrow of existing government. As to the need to coordinate information, he would be concerned if such coordination did not distinguish between information relating to Separatism and that relating to real subversion. There was nothing in the criminal law to prevent 'peaceful subversion.'

The Prime Minister said it would be necessary to fight Separatists, but perhaps not in the same way as revolutionaries would have to be fought.

The Secretary to the Cabinet suggested that consideration be given the degree to which there should be a parallel between Communism and Separatism. He noted that, although the Communist Party in Canada was a legal organization, it had been recognized for years that it was a potentially subversive force and protective governmental action had been taken as distinguished from protection against criminal acts. Mr. Robertson agreed with a suggestion that one difference between Communism and Separatism was that the former implied allegiance to another country, but suggested that the latter implied allegiance to a future separate nation of Quebec.

The Commissioner of the R.C.M.P. said that he would require clear direction from the government before embarking on the same investigative activities against Separatists as he now conducted against Communists, because of the extreme sensitivity of the problem. The R.C.M.P. could produce documents on Separatist organizations, despite the lack of government direction in this area, and suggested that the problem was not so much that of obtaining more information but of putting to use information already available. [words missing] that such information was readily available to the government. As to taking further action to gather information by clandestine means, this was of course possible, but he would feel obliged to point out the risks involved.

The Committee then turned to a consideration of the conclusions and recommendations of the Memorandum under discussion and made the following points concerning the conclusions:

(a) The problem should be approached on the two levels of security and law and order on the one hand, dealing with the criminal subversive and violent aspects, and on the other the broader problem of national unity or 'anti-Separatism,' recognizing that the tools for dealing with each may have to be different.

(b) there was general agreement that information and action should be effectively analysed and coordinated, and that consideration should be given the appropriate *method* of providing essential analysis and coordination.

(c) While it was clear that closer Federal–Provincial cooperation would be necessary, it was important that federal initiative and independence be retained both in the gathering and analysis of information and in the conduct of operations.

(d) That the risks involved in new federal initiatives be carefully balanced against the probable positive effects.

Concerning the recommendations set out in Section X of the Memorandum, the following points were made:

(a) The general principles set out in the Memorandum were somewhat imprecise and did not appear to be necessary.

(b) It would be of first importance for the Government to determine precisely the attitude which should be adopted towards Separatism as a phenomenon, and to determine whether that attitude should be publicly expressed in terms of a policy statement.

(c) The proposed 'central body' to coordinate and analyse information should be further studied in terms of method rather than organization, bearing in mind the need to separate the problem of law and order from that concerning national unity.

(d) Although the R.C.M. Police had recently prepared an updated report on the present state of Separatism in Quebec, it should be further revised to provide a basis on which positive counter-action might be taken.

(e) It was agreed that an immediate review be made of Canadian intelligence resources other than the R.C.M.P., and it was noted that the Intelligence Policy Committee would shortly be examining a memorandum to set forth intelligence policy and objectives of the government for submission to and consideration by the Cabinet Committee.

(f) Although some Ministers expressed doubt as to the reliability of the proposed Joint Security Operations Planning Staff in conjunction with the Government of Quebec and with the City of Montreal, there was general agreement that a coordinating unit at the police level was desirable and should be further examined, possibly in the context of aid to the civil power.

(g) Further study would be required of the various contingencies which would have to be anticipated, particularly at the political level.

(h) Means of taking effective counter-action would be considered in due course by the Cabinet Committee on Priorities and Planning on the basis of the memoranda to be prepared by Messrs Sharp and Turner on the priority problems of national unity and law and order.

The Committee agreed:

(a) that the Memorandum under consideration be revised in the light of the foregoing discussion with a view to placing it before the Cabinet in due course;

(b) that the recommendation entitled 'Law Enforcement and Counter-Subversion' be reworded as follows:

> It is recommended that the Minister of Justice, in consultation with other Ministers concerned, bring forward proposals as to appropriate means of achieving closer Federal–Provincial cooperation in the fields of law and order and aid to the civil power, with a view to ensuring that the various governments concerned are fully informed on the criminal and subversive aspects of Separatism, and so organized as to deal with them effectively on a joint basis.

(c) that the Intelligence Policy Committee be asked to examine the current intelligence programme in the context of the priority problems under discussion and to report to the Cabinet Committee thereon.

D.F. Wall,
Secretary

Privy Council Office

Meeting re Stated Aims of 1969 (16 March 1973)

My Letter of 21 February 1973

Mr. Gordon Robertson,
Secretary to the Cabinet,
Room 229 – East Block,
Ottawa, Ontario.

Dear Gordon,

I suggested to you that it might be very helpful to Mike Dare if the Prime Minister would be willing to have a brief word with the Commissioner, in Mike's presence, to reemphasize the importance which the government attaches to the development of the Security Service along the lines set out by the Prime Minister in a speech to the House of Commons on 26 June 1969.

2. As I mentioned to you, when we had lunch on 2 January, it has not been easy in practice to achieve the degree of autonomy for the Security Service envisaged in that statement. Progress has been made. For example, the Security Service now has complete autonomy in operational matters. However, there continue to be unnecessary restrictions on the ability of the Security Service to develop, 'new and more flexible policies in relation to recruiting, training and career planning,' to enable it to be, 'capable of dealing fairly and effectively with the new and complex problems which we undoubtedly face in the future.'

3. With the approval of the Commissioner, the Security Service entered into a contract several months ago with the Bureau of Management Consulting of the Department of Supply and Services to examine in detail our organization and our structure and to make recommendations for improvement. I expect a preliminary report by the end of March. Without doubt, the report will recom-

mend a number of changes, especially in matters of financial and manpower control, which will assist importantly the process of making the Security Service, 'increasingly separate in structure and civilian in nature.'

4. Against this background, I think a reminder by the Prime Minister of his continued personal interest in ensuring that the Security Service, 'will grow and develop as a distinct and identifiable element within the basic structure of the Force,' would be of great help to Mike Dare. It would, moreover, be timely since many of the more important recommendations of the Bureau of Management Consulting will require the Commissioner's approval. That the Prime Minister would wish to do this when a change in the direction of the Security Service is taking place would seem quite natural and appropriate.

5. I attach a photostat copy of a memorandum I am leaving for the Commissioner setting out our suggestions on the timing and other matters related to the changeover which you may find useful.

6. I also suggested that the Prime Minister might think there would be advantages in seeking to inform Mr. Stanfield and leaders of the other political parties of the change before it is made public. This might prevent the matter from becoming a political issue and being misinterpreted in various ways to the disadvantage of the government and of the Security Service.

Yours sincerely,

John Starnes
Director General
Security Service

My Memorandum for File of 20 March 1973

At the Prime Minister's request, the Solicitor General, Mr. Gordon Robertson, the Commissioner, Mr. Dare and I met with him at 9:45 A.M. on March 16th in his office in the Parliament Buildings.

2. The Prime Minister began by saying that following announcement of my departure and Mr. Dare's appointment, he had wished to have an opportunity to review with the Minister and the Commissioner the progress which had been made in giving effect to the government's wishes that the Security Service should; 'grow and develop as a distinct and identifiable element within the basic structure of the Force and become ... 'increasingly separate in structure and civilian in nature.' He recalled the statement which he had made on this score in the House of Commons in June of 1969 at the time that he had tabled the Report of the Royal Commission on Security. The changeover seemed to

provide a suitable opportunity to review what had been done and to affirm the government's views on the manner in which the Security Service should develop. He asked me if I would care to comment on the progress which had been made.

3. I began by saying that I felt much had been done to make the Security Service more separate in structure and civilian in nature. However, there remained much that still needed to be done. I felt the Commissioner would agree with me that in operational matters the Security Service was very nearly autonomous. There were two important areas, having to do with the management of human resources and finances, in which greater autonomy clearly was desirable. The Commissioner and I had discussed these matters on many occasions. I felt we had worked towards a solution of the various problems which were involved, although, perhaps, more slowly than I would have wished. Within this context, I recalled that with the Commissioner's approval, we had sought the services of management consultants to examine the structure and the organization of the Security Service. These studies, which began over nine months ago, were nearly completed. From my talks with those responsible I felt sure that if their principal recommendations received the support of the Minister, the Commissioner and my successor, their implementation would go a long way towards making the Security Service more 'separate in structure and civilian in nature.' I also mentioned that with the agreement of the Commissioner, another study on the use of computers in the Security Service had been begun nearly two years ago. Hopefully, this would be completed in the near future. The recommendations flowing from this study, if accepted, would have a very far-reaching effect upon the work of the Security Service, its future capabilities and its organization.

4. I went on to say it was my hope that when these studies were completed, and particularly the study being undertaken by the Bureau of Management Consulting, we would be in a better position to identify various jobs within the Security Service which perhaps could be more appropriately done by civilians hired from outside. At this juncture the Prime Minister asked me what was the proportion of civilians to regular members. I replied that it was roughly fifty per cent civilian and fifty per cent regular members. I made it clear, however, that by far the largest proportion of the civilian component of the Security Service was made up of relatively junior personnel. It was my hope that in future, a greater proportion of civilians could be found to fill senior appointments.

5. I was asked by both the Prime Minister and Mr. Gordon Robertson what were the problems which now stood in the way of recruiting suitable persons for such jobs from outside the Security Service. I said the principal obstacle was the manner in which the Security Service was structured and which pro-

vided a rather rigid framework. In addition, of course, there were various problems associated with attracting suitable people to this kind of work. We had some success in attracting such persons to the Security Service. I mentioned, for example, that [words missing] I was convinced, however, that much more could be done, and particularly if the organization was restructured in ways which would offer job satisfaction and adequate career opportunities to persons with suitable academic qualifications.

6. The Prime Minister asked me when the consultants' study would be completed. I replied that a preliminary but fairly full report was expected to be ready by the middle of April. Thus, I hoped it would be on Mr. Dare's desk shortly after he took office.

7. At this point, the Commissioner said he believed a great deal had been done to give effect to the government's wishes to create a more distinct and separate security service within the framework of the RCMP. He felt it important not to overlook the high degree of professional excellence which existed in the Security Service among its regular members. Indeed, the Security Service would not be able to function without this considerable body of expertise. He felt the government had been well served by the reports which the Security Service was producing. Such reports were the product of a highly professional investigational capability which existed across Canada. He felt that the RCMP Security Service had a high degree of professionalism which was recognized both within and outside Canada. Many of the regular members, who were in the Security Service, possessed university degrees. This, coupled with operational experience, made them invaluable. He felt sure that there could be improvements – any organization could be improved – and he wished to assure the Prime Minister that he would do everything possible to see that the government's wishes were carried out. Certainly, he would look at the recommendations made by the consultants, and any other similar studies which might give effect to the government's wishes.

8. The Prime Minister said that he had been well satisfied with the quality of the reports made by the Security Service since 1970. He felt it only fair to comment, however, that prior to that, there had perhaps been certain shortcomings.

9. The Prime Minister apparently then reading from one of the briefs in front of him, referred to the need to re-orient the work of the Security Service. He pointed out that threats which had been apparent ten years ago no longer existed, or, at least, not in the same form. In the eyes of Ministers, they had been supplanted by other and more pressing threats.

[Paragraphs 10 and 11 deleted]

12. Mr. Dare said he felt one of the problems facing the intelligence community

(he made clear he was not speaking about the Security Service and internal security problems), was that it was to some extent divorced from government operations as a whole. That is to say, those responsible for gathering intelligence about different external threats were doing so in a vacuum and without meaningful guide lines. Perhaps certain of the problems associated with this state of affairs could be overcome by regular briefings. Possibly, these could be given on some regular basis to members of the Cabinet Committee on Security and Intelligence.

13. Mr. Robertson recalled to the Prime Minister that the Canadian intelligence collection program had been discussed in the Cabinet Committee on Security and Intelligence last year. A decision had been taken at that time to review the matter in the light of recommendations made by Mr. Charles Ritchie. These studies had become bogged down for various reasons. It had not seemed practicable to ask Ministers to address themselves to these problems immediately following the Federal elections last Fall and unwise to carry out a survey of user requirements in quite the way which had been contemplated last Summer. Accordingly, a more informal approach to users of such intelligence had recently been decided upon and this was now being carried out. Mr. Robertson hoped a report could be presented to Ministers in a few months' time.

14. At some time in this conversation, the Prime Minister referred to the discussions which had taken place on the Cabinet Committee on Security and Intelligence on [deleted words]

15. The Prime Minister summed up this part of our conversation by saying that after the Minister, the Commissioner and Mr. Dare had studied the recommendations of the Bureau of Management Consulting, it might be well to arrange another such discussion, possibly in June, to review what additional steps could be taken to make the Security Service more autonomous. At one point, he seemed to be suggesting a discussion of those recommendations in the Cabinet Committee on Security and Intelligence. While I did not think it appropriate to say so at the time, I entertain doubts about the wisdom of a detailed discussion of the consultants' report in a Cabinet Committee. It seems to me a better procedure might be a further discussion with the Prime Minister, perhaps centered on the principal recommendations of the consultants, followed by some suitable references by the Prime Minister in the Cabinet Committee to the steps which have and are being taken to make the Security Service more 'separate and civilian.'

[Paragraph 16 deleted]

John Starnes
Director General
Security Service

'The FLQ and Quebec' (1970)

[22 October 1970]

1. This memorandum attempts to place the events of the past fortnight within a conceptual framework and to suggest different ways of viewing the problems posed by the activities of the FLQ, together with possible courses of action for dealing with some of them. Clearly, a number of the measures discussed in this memorandum, embracing as they do broad issues of public policy, lie well outside of the purview of law enforcement agencies as such and call for a sophisticated blend of the use of the executive and the administrative powers of government at different levels. It should be added perhaps that this memorandum has been written without benefit of the material on government dossiers and no doubt suffers thereby.

2. There seems to be no exact parallel between the situation in Quebec and the activities of the Front de Libération du Quebec (FLQ) and similar situations which have arisen elsewhere in recent years. Indeed, in many ways the situation we are faced with in Quebec appears to be unique. For example, the French experience in Algeria seems to offer us little help except perhaps insofar as the development by the French of short term techniques and tactics for dealing with terrorist activities which are not perhaps applicable in Canada. The situation facing the French in Algeria in the late 1950's was quite different from the situation facing the Canadian and Quebec governments in 1970. The Algerian Liberation movement was quite unlike the FLQ and the economic, political and sociological aspects of the situation in Algeria in the 1950's were quite different than those existing in Quebec in 1970. Moreover, the position of the French armed forces in Algeria has nothing in common with the use of the Canadian Armed Forces in Quebec. Among other things, it will be recalled that in May 1958 the French Army in Algeria was on the verge of drastic action

which clearly would have led to a military coup d'etat in France itself if deGaulle had not assumed power.

3. The FLQ had its beginnings in about 1962 as a clandestine revolutionary movement organized on the basis of more or less autonomous cells which act or appear to act independently. A separate French-speaking state in Quebec has remained a central theme of FLQ policy. Latterly, however, the essentially ultra-nationalistic aims of the FLQ appear to have undergone subtle and important modifications, perhaps reflecting the changing and diverse nature of its membership and the revolutionary inspiration which the movement has derived from elsewhere. The FLQ Manifesto read over Radio Canada on 15 October is a curious and a clever mixture of Marx, Che Guevara and Maoist slogans with heavy emphasis on the shortcomings and injustices of the capitalist system.

4. While it seems unlikely that the broad mass of people in Quebec will find much to attract them in the language of the FLQ manifesto, the fact remains that the movement has been able to remain alive and even to flourish because some part of the population of Quebec, either consciously or unconsciously, has supported at least some of the activities and apparent aims of the FLQ. No doubt there will be many among these erstwhile supporters who now will be repelled by the recent violent and savage acts of the FLQ. By the same token, alas, there will be some who now know they can condone violence and will not shrink from savage acts in future. However, it seems clear that among younger Quebecers, including those in the universities and the junior colleges, there is still support for the FLQ. To my mind, this support represents at least as serious a threat to stability in Quebec as the FLQ itself. Indeed, if there are parallels which can be drawn, perhaps recent events in Quebec can be more nearly equated with events in France in the Spring of 1968. Some of the grievances expressed in the manifesto nevertheless appear to have some basis in fact and their resolution is a pre-requisite to any attempts to wither the basis of support which the FLQ continues to receive in Quebec. Thus, dealing with the causes of disaffection among some elements of Quebec's youth, including the students, and the vigorous and immediate adoption of a wide range of social policies in Quebec probably are among the most practical ways of dealing with the long-term effects of the FLQ phenomenon. To this end the full range of the information media available to various levels of government should be used. At the Federal level full use should be made of Information Canada, the CBC and other information media to deal with the root causes of unrest among Quebec's youth, many of whom are confused, alienated and rootless. It should be said here that this condition is not peculiar to the youth of Quebec. It is a phenomenon found throughout Canada and in many other parts of the world.

What makes the attitude of youth in Quebec important and urgent is the evident attraction for many of them of the FLQ's activities and its philosophy
which they have equated to their own disaffection.

5. For the short term it seems clear, given the constitutional and jurisdictional
situation in Quebec, that a quickening and a widening of co-operation
between Federal, Provincial and Municipal authorities at all levels is most
important if the immediate threat posed by the FLQ is to be effectively contained and if longer term national interests are to be best served. Co-operation
has not always been effective or close, hampered as it has been at times by professional jealousies, jurisdictional differences, inadequate dialogue and lack of
mutual trust, i.e. the lack of confidence in the Montreal City Police brought
about by their strike action last year. The alternative, of course, is to attempt to
concentrate control of anti-FLQ measures entirely in Federal hands. I believe
this would be unwise on political grounds and quite impractical in other terms.
If this latter view is accepted then perhaps the most effective immediate measure to be taken would be the invocation at the highest level in all these governments, Federal, Provincial, and Municipal, of the need for closer co-
operation and coordination and to request a review of existing machinery to
ensure that this goal is being as effectively met as possible. At the same time
perhaps and independent of whatever action may be taken to achieve an
improved tri-partite co-operation, Federal capabilities in Quebec to cope with
the FLQ and similar threats to national unity should be built up. The mere
accretion of strength, however, will not of itself provide an answer since the
personnel required must be bilingual, and adequately trained, and the acquisition of new human and other sources, which might be expected to result from
an increase in the Federal government's law enforcement arm in Quebec, will
require time. Since the eventual break-up of the FLQ is not likely to be accomplished quickly or easily, the reallocation of existing resources and perhaps the
provision of new resources to this end seems justified and necessary if the Federal government wishes to improve its independent sources of information
about separatist/terrorist activities in Quebec.

6. The next immediate step in the police investigations will involve the interrogation of all those arrested – a formidable and time-consuming task – and the
evaluation and compilation of all the information thus gleaned. This may lead
to further arrests and to re-interrogations, a process in its totality which could
take several weeks. During this stage, no doubt, a number of those arrested
whose activities in the FLQ were peripheral may have to be released since
insufficient evidence may exist upon which to lay charges against them. It is
possible that some of these investigations may lead to the apprehension of
those responsible for the kidnappings and for Mr. Laporte's murder. It is

equally possible, however, that it will not and that many months of painstaking and detailed police work will have to take place before any leads are uncovered to the kidnappers and to those making up the hard core of the FLQ. This is a most difficult period for those taking decisions at all levels of government and for the different police authorities involved, and especially since responsibility for policy decisions and for operations must be shared between the Federal, Provincial and Municipal authorities. What seems essential is that no loss of confidence on either side, and between the executive and operational arms of government at different levels, be permitted to develop since it can only be to the advantage of the FLQ and to the detriment of the long-term interests of the country. More immediately, the arrests and the seizure of material should lead to a better understanding of the FLQ, its methods and more important the anatomy of its members. (Perhaps the recent findings of [missing words] in Montreal may be relevant.) Hopefully, many of those arrested can be successfully charged under the Public Order Regulations 1970 and thus removed from circulation.

7. Clearly, in the coming weeks it will be to the advantage of all the authorities concerned to keep the FLQ constantly off balance and all means to this end should be considered. Among such means is arrest and the threat of arrest, interception of FLQ communications, infiltration of FLQ cells by various means and the development of a sophisticated program of 'disinformation.'
[Paragraphs 8 and 9 deleted]

10. The truth is, of course, that the advantage, and particularly in a democratic society, appears to be with organizations like the FLQ at least in the short term. The following excerpt from Edward Luttwak's 'Coup d'Etat' seems to explain in succinct terms why this may be so:

Why have regimes in the twentieth century proved so fragile? It is, after all, paradoxical that this fragility has increased while the established procedures for security changes in government have on the whole become more flexible. The political scientist will reply that though the procedures have become more flexible, pressures for change have also become stronger, and that the rate of increase in flexibility has not kept up with the growth of social and economic pressures. Perhaps the ultimate source of destabilizing pressures has been the spectacular progress of scientific discovery and the resultant technological change.

11. There are more potential hostages and targets than there are policemen and soldiers to guard them day and night. Thus, long term solutions to the various problems do not lie only in measures aimed at achieving physical security. For the short term and until the immediate threat can be contained there

seems no doubt that extraordinary physical security precautions are necessary and effective. The trick, of course, is to judge for exactly how long these precautions should be continued and when they can safely be progressively withdrawn. [deleted words]

It would seem important to sever these links, and, where possible, to prevent the establishment of new ones. The most obvious way to do this is to restrict the admission to Canada of persons who, by their record of activities elsewhere, are likely to support the FLQ, and the withdrawal of passport facilities for Canadians who are known or suspected FLQ supporters and couriers. Clearly, this will require an immediate tightening up of existing immigration regulations and a far more exacting application of them. No doubt, the existence of the Public Order Regulations 1970 may assist this process.

13. Although a somewhat banal note on which to end such a memorandum, it occurs to me to suggest a further punitive measure against the FLQ which clearly could not be introduced while Mr. Cross' fate remains uncertain. I suggest consideration be given to enacting the necessary legislation to revoke the citizenship of all those already convicted of criminal offenses on behalf of the FLQ and a declaration of intent by the government to take similar action against those convicted of such offenses in future. I have in mind also the deterrent effect which such a declaration of intent might have. [deleted words] Apart from the symbolic value of withdrawing from those concerned the attributes of Canadian citizenship, an action which probably would strike a chord among a majority of Canadians, revoking of citizenship presumably would mean that such persons no longer could travel on a Canadian passport or enjoy the advantages abroad of being a Canadian. They would indeed be outlawed which seems a fitting punishment among others for those who seek to destroy Canada.

John Starnes
Director General
Security and Intelligence

Ottawa
22-10-70

CCPP Minutes on 'Law and Order' (1970)

The Cabinet Committee on Priorities and Planning
[Minutes, 24 November 1970]

A meeting of the Cabinet Committee on Priorities and Planning was held in Room 340-S, House of Commons, on Tuesday, November 24, 1971 [should read '1970'], at 10:00 a.m.

Present

The Prime Minister (Mr. Trudeau) in the Chair
The Minister of Public Works (Mr. Laing),
The President of the Treasury Board (Mr. Drury),
The Minister of Regional Economic Expansion (Mr. Marchand)
The Minister of Justice (Mr. Turner),
The Minister of Indian Affairs and Northern Development (Mr. Chrétien),
The Minister of National Defence (Mr. Macdonald),
The Minister of National Health and Welfare (Mr. Munro),
The Minister of Manpower and Immigration (Mr. Lang),
The Solicitor General (Mr. McIlraith).

Also Present

Mr. D.S. Maxwell
Mr. D. Christie (Department of Justice)
Mr. H.B. Robinson
Mr. A.D. Hunt
Mr. D.A. Davidson
Mr. A.S. Stephenson (Department of Indian Affairs and Northern Development)
Lt. Gen. M.R. Dare (Department of National Defence)

Mr. L. Couillard
Mr. E.P. Beasley (Department of Manpower and Immigration)
Commissioner J.R.R. Carriere
Mr. J.K. Starnes (Royal Canadian Mounted Police)
Mr. E. Côté (Department of the Solicitor General)
Mr. R.G. Robertson
Mr. D.F. Wall (Privy Council Office)
Mr. J. Davey (Prime Minister's Office).

Secretary

Mr. P.M. Pitfield (Privy Council Office)

Assistant Secretaries

Mr. M.E. Butler (Privy Council Office)
Mr. L.L. Trudel (Privy Council Office)

[deleted words]

Law and Order

The Minister of Justice introduced Cabinet Document 1323-70, Law and Order. *Mr. Turner* said it was a report of the interdepartmental committee established to examine the various issues involved in law and order and as such represented the views of officials. He did not support fully all of the views represented but said it was a good analysis of the immediate problems that existed. He noted the suggestion that the federal government retract its delegation of enforcement of the law for crimes of national significance. It raised the question of what additional legislation might be required to deal with emergency situations such as the F.L.Q. crisis. He stated that the primary responsibility in the current situation lay with the Province of Quebec. The attitudes of the provincial attorneys general had not been very favourable in his recent discussions with them on permanent legislation to deal with emergency situations. He said Parliament could not control now the exercise of these powers by the provinces. He saw two problems: one a federal-provincial problem; the other a constitutional and political problem. Under 'police operations' he said the problem that existed was one of effectiveness given the three levels of police forces involved: federal, provincial and municipal. The inherent contradiction in the R.C.M. Police, in trying to cope with both security and police matters would have to be considered carefully. He felt that sooner or later the operations of the security and intelligence branch would affect the image of the R.C.M. Police.

The Prime Minister asked the Committee to consider each section of the document, one at a time, keeping in mind the series of questions listed at the beginning and the series of short-run problems that had to be dealt with. He noted that the paper did not deal essentially with the priority problem 'Law and Order.'

The Deputy Minister of Justice said that it had been impossible within the time available to canvass adequately the subject matter of the priority problem 'Law and Order.' He stated that the interdepartmental committee felt that the strength of the federal police in Quebec, and probably in Ontario as well, was insufficient to deal with emergency situations. In other provinces the existing contracts allowed the R.C.M. Police to be in a better position. In Ontario and Quebec, the R.C.M. Police had to rely on the provincial police forces. He suggested that legislation had developed in its present form because of the different provincial arrangements for policing.

The Prime Minister spoke of the liberal tradition and the democratic framework in Canada. He noted some of the changes that were occurring but he felt that they did not lead to the conclusion that there was a need for more police, more powers, and security forces using hard and tough ways, to results. He said that before the national police force was extended there would be a requirement for basic changes in the liberal philosophy and ethics. He said that such a step would require the removal of considerable amount of uncertainty first. On the other hand, he agreed that some additional powers would be needed before the expiry of the current legislation on April 30, 1971.

The President of the Treasury Board referred to the trade-off which existed necessarily between law and order and individual freedom. The maximum individual freedom could only be tolerated within and consistent with an orderly and balanced societal framework. He asked that the Committee obtain all the facts before deciding on whether or not additional police powers were necessary.

The Minister of National Defence said that the trend was to assume that the legal apparatus was adequate and that if possible greater freedom of the individual should be tolerated. He said that any swift and abrupt change in direction would be opposed.

The Minister of Justice said that the law had to reflect more closely the mores of society. He felt that providing the government remained credible such changes were acceptable. He saw little difficulty in extending civil liberties while at the same time making the police more effective. He stressed the necessity of renewing the government's credibility.

Mr. Davey was of the opinion that the law and order problem in large cities was a political problem. He said that some of the dissident groups which had been identified, aimed at the systematic destruction of the forces of law and order for their own ends. What was occurring was taking place outside the normal framework, and only some of it within the legal framework. The existing system might have to be extended in order to prevent certain people from exploiting society. Certain people could not be dealt with by the courts and the police, but they could possibly be dealt with by the political system. In Quebec, the information lead one to think that the dissidents were trying to bring government to a halt by using the intermediary structures.

The Prime Minister said that a lot of these factors would have to be considered within a ways and means paper on the priority problem of 'Law and Order,' in order to understand more fully what was happening in society. He agreed it was a multi-dimensional problem and would have to be examined within a very broad framework. He asked that consideration be given to hiring outside resources to work on the priority problem if that appeared to be necessary. He added that similar problems and occurrences had prevailed in other countries and that Canada could benefit from their experience. He asked Ministers to read the document carefully *and particularly Mr. Starnes' paper* [perhaps 'The FLQ and Quebec' (Appendix H, above)] *before the next meeting of Priorities and Planning when the discussion would be continued.* He said that the Cabinet Committee on Security and Intelligence and the Security Panel would be examining some of the more immediate problems but that he would like Priorities and Planning to look at the long term priority problem.

The Committee agreed to continue discussion of Law and Order at the next meeting.

P.M. Pitfield,
Secretary.

The Cabinet Committee on Priorities and Planning
Minutes
[1 December 1970]

A meeting of the Cabinet Committee on Priorities and Planning was held in Room 340-S, House of Commons on Tuesday, December 1st, 1970, at 10:00 a.m.

Present

The Prime Minister (Mr. Trudeau) in the Chair
The President of the Queen's Privy Council for Canada (Mr. MacEachen)
The President of the Treasury Board (Mr. Drury)
The Minister of Finance (Mr. Benson)
The Minister of Transport (Mr. Jamieson)
The Minister of Industry, Trade and Commerce (Mr. Pépin)
The Minister of Regional Economic Expansion (Mr. Marchand)
The Minister of Justice (Mr. Turner)
The Minister without Portfolio (Mr. Andras)

Also Present

Mr.. R.G. Robertson (Privy Council Office)
Mr. Lalonde (The Prime Minister's Office)
Mr. S. Reisman (Department of Finance)
Mr. L.E. Couillard (Department of Manpower and Immigration)
Commissioner W.L. Higgitt (Royal Canadian Mounted Police)
Mr. D. Christie (Department of Justice)
Mr. E.P. Beasley (Department of Manpower and Immigration)
Mr. D. Maxwell (Department of Justice)
Mr. E. Côté (Solicitor General's Department)
General M. Dare (Department of National Defence)
Deputy Commissioner J.R. Carrière (Royal Canadian Mounted Police)
Mr. J. Starnes (Royal Canadian Mounted Police)
Mr. J. Davey (Prime Minister's Office)
Mr. D. Wall (Privy Council Office)

Secretary

Mr. P.M. Pitfield (Privy Council Office)

Assistant Secretaries

Mr. M.E. Butler (Privy Council Office)
Mr. L.L. Trudel (Privy Council Office)

Contents

Law and Order
(Previous reference November 24th)

The Minister of Justice continued the discussion on the Law and Order paper, Cabinet Document 1323-70. He said that the paper identified the more immediate problems of police enforcement, but that only after considerable research into the social climate, could he hope to table the long term ramifications resulting from the problem. There was a need for more research staff and other resources in his department to find out just how law and order forces would have to operate in future. In this regard the establishment and development of the National Law Reform Commission would be helpful but he cautioned against hoping for too much for the first couple of years.

In the meantime, the problem was to find more immediate and effective ways of dealing with violence, particularly violence associated with political movements.

He suggested that the committee deal with the document according to the following main headings:
(a) Administration of Justice;
(b) Police Operations;
(c) University Campuses;
(d) Additional Emergency Powers;
(e) Diplomatic and Consular Promises;
(f) Immigration.

He said that the current debate in the House on the Public Order (Temporary Measures) Act showed how difficult the introduction of new legislation in this field would be. In his opinion, the government had lost some of its credit with the Canadian people and that as a result civil rights were becoming very topical. He said that the orchestration of the continuing reforms in the legal, social and economic areas should be finely timed in order to restore the public posture of the government as reform-minded. He mentioned the Bail Reform Bill, Electronic Eavesdropping, the Abolition of Corporal Punishment, Intermittent Sentences and Vagrancy reforms as examples. He reminded the committee that there were gaps in procedures and in the law and that these could be improved upon without waiting for the research necessary for long term order under the law. He reiterated the need for additional resources for his department but he said that he would commission the work immediately and report back to the committee.

He explained that the studies he saw as necessary would attempt to pinpoint the factors underlying alienation between the individual and the state; unemployment; education for jobs that did not exist; possibilities of short-cuts to reform and the role of the media; all of the above within the long term context of order under law.

The Prime Minister agreed that the long term social factors were the key. He noted however, that these studies cut across the work of the Secretary of State for External Affairs on 'National Unity,' the Special Operations Centre under Mr. Robertson and Mr. Lalonde and the work of the Deputy Solicitor General. He felt that the best approach would be a Ways and Means Paper on how to study the longer term aspects of the priority problem Law and Order. He said the Cabinet Committee on Priorities and Planning could ensure that there were no overlaps in the work and studies involved in developing a strategy for 'Freedom Within The Law' the revised title of the priority problem 'Law and Order.' He said that this hypothesis would not necessarily weaken the Criminal Law but might even strengthen it.

The Minister of Justice said that a lot of work had already been done through the consideration of the Ouimet Report particularly on correctional practices and sentencing. He thought that a lot of factors were beyond the control of any government. It was difficult to predict people's attitudes in areas such as pornography and marijuana. The problem of enforcing the law became most important. He further argued that in cases such as abortion, public opinion seemed to be divided 50/50 whereas the Liberal Party had come out 4:1 in favour of abortion. This resulted in greater expectations of government action which, when not met, resulted in frustration and further alienation.

The Minister of Transport said that the studies should find out what people really wanted as opposed to those articulators who would have the government move in their particular way. The national mood and not the intentions of one small group should determine the governmental thrust.

The Prime Minister spoke of the rapidly changing values of Canadian society. He agreed that one group of people were often ahead of public opinion while others seemed to lag behind. The government had to decide where the consensus lay while recognizing that some of the problems were difficult to solve if they were in fact solvable.

The Minister of Justice said that it was the duty of the government to lead but that in so doing it should be neither too far ahead nor too far behind the public mood. The attitudinal and social revolutions must be kept constantly under review to ensure the relevancy, credibility and enforceability of the law. Frustration and alienation must be kept at minimum.

The President of the Treasury Board said there was a basic conflict between the personal and articulated freedom of the individual as opposed to the needs of society. The latter more often than not was used as an argument for the status quo. He maintained that the resolution of this conflict lay in the trade-off that was possible and plausible. The initiatives of the government were in general to amend the Criminal Law to permit greater individual freedom.

The Minister of Justice said that the presumption of innocence equalized the impact of the law on everyone and that it was most important to use the law and enforcement powers reasonably. He cited the Bail Reform Bill as an example, adding that there was rationalization and discretion used by the police every day. He said that personal and individual options were being widened so that moral options were left to the individual whereas legal options were left to the courts and to the police. He said there were more articulated demands for change that reflected a particular life style. The Department of Justice was studying them fully and was attempting to ensure equality of impact of the law. He thought the media was very active in pressuring for changes in the Criminal Code which would reflect new life styles of particular groups and not necessarily those of the silent majority.

The Deputy Minister of Justice said that the development of criminal law enforcement in Canada might require re-examination, [deleted words] The provinces were carrying a very heavy financial burden. Perhaps it would be worthwhile examining the establishment of a separate federal court system and police force to ease this financial burden. He suggested that initially discussions could be opened with the two central provinces, Ontario and Quebec, with a view to relieving some or all of this burden. Such an adjustment if feasible and acceptable might lead to improvements in the enforcement of the Criminal Code. He said that all of the Criminal Code or alternatively, only certain sections could be studied.

The Prime Minister did not see how law enforcement could be divided. He said the best way to have the Criminal Code respected might be to have it administered by the local authorities.

The President of the Treasury Board said that a case for relieving the financial burden of the provinces would have to be clearly established. The efficiency of law enforcement should be the criterion rather than the financial burden of the provinces. He said the federal government was likely to be more concerned with certain groups such as syndicates and organized crime. National activities and crimes of significance should be met by national (federal) police forces whereas local issues should be dealt with by local police forces. He noted that where campuses were concerned it might be difficult to be categorical.

The Minister of Justice stated that the will to act and to accept responsibility were critical factors in law enforcement when considering issues of national significance. In his opinion, the circumstances were all important. He felt that a minority government whether federal or provincial might not be as responsive as a majority one.

The Prime Minister stated that it was relatively easy in other provinces to identify dissidents such as Maoists [deleted words]

Commissioner Higgitt said that 97% of the R.C.M. Police in the province of Quebec were bilingual. He said that the formula for deciding on the number of R.C.M. Police in Quebec needed to be adjusted to the problems that had developed. He said that in Quebec it was not as easy to isolate the factors involved such as urban size and incidence of crime. He said there was a combination of regular R.C.M. Police and S. & I. personnel on duty because of both the FLQ and the criminal elements.

The Prime Minister noted that for all practical purposes and also for political reasons the administration of justice in Quebec is left to the Province. The enforcement, however, depended on the crime involved.

The Deputy Minister of Justice said that the increase in the number of R.C.M. Police in Ontario and Quebec was not due to an increase in their normal responsibilities but to do the work associated with the current crisis.

The Commissioner of the R.C.M. Police said that more S. & I. personnel usually led to greater discovery, more information and subsequent legal action for criminal activity such as with bombs.

The Prime Minister asked that a specific paper on the Security & Intelligence resources be referred to the Cabinet Committee on Security and Intelligence and that the S. & I. Committee decide on the question and inform the Treasury Board.

The Minister of Industry, Trade and Commerce said that the following alternatives should be delineated:
(a) [deleted words]
(b) A clear division of jurisdictional responsibility by offences for law enforcement;
(c) The status quo, with greater emphasis on crimes of national significance;
(d) The contract formula;
(e) [deleted words]

The Deputy Solicitor General said that the R.C.M. Police had a handicap in dealing manually with information. He said the electronic data processing equipment would not be fully operational until 1972. He noted that there was a good deal of information to go into the computers which should result in a significant difference in law enforcement.

The Commissioner of the R.C.M. Police added that the force was training personnel from other police forces and that a more broadly-based expertise was being developed.

The Minister of Justice said it was incumbent on the government to draw lessons from the FLQ incident. [missing words] On the question of the inherent contradiction in police operations, the *Prime Minister* said that certain activities of the Security and Intelligence service might not result in prosecution for security reasons. The Cabinet Committee on Security and Intelligence was the more appropriate place to look at the whole question of the integration of information and intelligence, Dr. Isbister's Report on it, and the other questions on security and intelligence raised in the document. He added that an overview of the current FLQ situation and the status of security and intelligence could be examined, and a decision made on a briefing for Cabinet. *He noted that the image of the R.C.M. Police could be misrepresented if the security and intelligence forces were caught breaking the law in order to obtain information. This situation had existed for some time in the R.C.M. Police and he asked that the whole question be referred to the Cabinet Committee on Security and Intelligence for consideration.*

On the question of additional emergency powers, *the Minister of Justice* said that amendments to the Criminal Code were being examined to meet emergency situations such as the October crisis. He said that it would be necessary to ensure the right climate of public opinion before introducing amendments of this nature. He thought that it was important that proposals of this nature came forward through parliamentary consensus rather than from the government in a bill. [deleted words] The opposition would want to have a hard look at any new permanent legislation dealing with emergency situations in place of the Public Order (Temporary Measures) Act. He would bring back a paper for consideration by Cabinet outlining what was likely to be required in the way of new legislation, when it might be introduced into the House with the pros and cons of different methods and how public opinion would likely react.

The Prime Minister stated that it was important to make sure that the police forces were sufficiently numerous to deal with the likely situations and that they be backed up by adequate intelligence and information services. He said it was necessary, however, for the government to do its utmost to ensure that it would not be necessary in six months time to reintroduce the War Measures Act should the forces of law and order not be able to cope. He asked that a bill be prepared by January, 1971, and considered by Cabinet Committee so that the government would be prepared for any development and not have to rely solely on the War Measures Act.

On the subject of immigration, *the President of the Treasury Board* said that not only immigrants should be considered but also visitors and aliens. *The Deputy Minister of Manpower and Immigration* said that a paper on Immigration policy was being prepared for Cabinet consideration and that it should be ready within the next month. He said that this paper attempted to close most of the loopholes in the Immigration Act which had been used by non-immigrants. He thought the latter paper, or companion piece, could be published in due course. In addition to immigration policy, the document would review the numerous interfaces of law and order and immigration.

On the use of the Armed Forces for security and policy [*sic*] operations, *General Dare* said that the Judge Advocate General in the Department of National Defence was reviewing the regulations dealing with aid to the civil power and that additionally, the Department had prepared a paper on the protection of vital points such as power and communications installations. *Mr. Robertson* added that a paper was coming forward from the Emergency Measures Organization on vital points. *Mr. Davey* said that it was critical that the mechanism for dealing with these new situations be alerted and ready. He said that the police would not be in a position to do so for a couple of years and that in the interim, plans must cater for any likely emergency. Such emergencies must be realistically assessed.

The Prime Minister concluded the discussion by noting that there was a need for these studies on law and order to be developed. He said that a new ways and means paper, on all of the causes and factors involved, could lead to the development of a comprehensive approach to crime, violence and alienation.

The Committee agreed that:

(a) the Minister of Justice should prepare for Cabinet consideration a ways and means paper on the longer term aspects of law and order including the development of a government strategy for freedom under the law. This would require research in depth into the atmosphere in which the law was administered, including the causes of frustration and alienation which created a fertile atmosphere for agitation, lawlessness and anarchy;

(b) the Minister of Justice, in preparing the ways and means paper, should take note of the work being done by the Secretary of State for External Affairs on National Unity, by the Deputy Solicitor General on the background and strategy of the FLQ, and by Mr. Davey with the Special Operations Centre;

(c) the longer term aspects of the proposal on Administration of Justice (Police

Organization) should be considered in the proposed law and order study; and the closing of existing gaps, including:

(i) the short term aspects of Administration of Justice (Police Organization);

(ii) Police Operations (Inherent Contradiction);

(iii) University Campuses; and

(iv) Diplomatic and Consular Premises,

should be referred to the Security Panel and the Cabinet Committee on Security and Intelligence;

(d) the Minister of Justice be asked to draft legislation, as soon as possible, to provide continuing but limited authority for the taking of necessary emergency action to control lawlessness or violence threatening the peace or public order; and that during December he should discuss with the Prime Minister the procedure for consideration of this draft legislation early in February by Cabinet Committee;

(e) the Minister of Manpower and Immigration should bring forward a paper, as soon as possible, dealing with the law and order aspects of Immigration, including the control of non-immigrants, and that there should be thorough interdepartmental consultation within the next three weeks.

P.M. Pitfield,
Secretary.

Notes

Italic numbers refer to pages in the text; where references would otherwise not be clear, the last few words of the sentence or phrase to which they refer are given first, also in italic.

Preface

x   Charles Ritchie, *The Siren Years: A Canadian Diplomat Abroad, 1937–1945* (Toronto: Macmillan of Canada, 1974), Preface.

x   N.K. (Kevin) O'Neill, 'History of CBNRC' [Communications Branch, National Research Council], 3 vols., typescript (1987).

Chapter 1: Joining Up

11   F.H. Hinsley, *British Intelligence in the Second World War* (Cambridge: Cambridge University Press, 1993).

11   John Starnes, *Latonya* (New York: Vantage, 1994).

Chapter 2: Secret Intelligence Work

20   M.R.D. Foot, *SOE: An Outline History of the Special Operations Executive, 1940–46* (London: British Broadcasting Corporation, 1984).

20   Roy MacLaren, *Canadians behind Enemy Lines, 1939–1945* (Vancouver: University of British Columbia Press, 1981), 27–36.

20   Felix Walter's 'Cloak and Dagger' was a highly classified document prepared for the chairman of the Chiefs of Staff in 1945. Now declassified, it is held in the archives of the Department of National Defence.

Chapter 4: On Foot in the Blackout

36   Peter Wright, *Spy Catcher: The Candid Autobiography of a Senior Intelligence Officer* (New York: Viking, 1987).

45   N.K. O'Neill, 'History of CBNRC,' 3 vols., typescript (1987).
46   Yuri Modin, with Jean-Charles Deniau and Agnieszka Ziarek, *My Five Cambridge Friends*, trans. Anthony Roberts, intro. David Leitch (London: Headline, 1994).

Chapter 5: Chargé d'Affaires

54   John Hadwen, 'John Holmes: Thou Shouldst Be Living at This Hour,' *bout de papier* 13, no. 2 (1996).
57   Elton Trueblood, *The Predicament of Modern Man*, 6th ed. (New York: Harper & Brothers, 1944).
59   Leopold Schwarzschild, *Primer of the Coming World* (New York: A.A. Knopf, 1944); Robert Gilbert, Baron Vansittart, *The Bones of Contention* (London: Hutchinson, 1945); William Henry Beveridge, *The Price of Peace* (London: Pilot Press, 1945).

Chapter 6: Robertson, Pearson, St Laurent

68   Dean Beeby and William Kaplan, eds., *Moscow Despatches: Inside Cold War Russia* (Toronto: James Lorimer and Company, 1987).
68   ... *beyond question and beyond praise*': *Montreal Gazette*, 14 May 1924.
69   ... *may take out of it*': F.N. McCrea, MP, House of Commons, 8 June 1925, Hansard, 3987.
72   ... *move Robertson out of Ottawa*: J.W. Pickersgill, *Seeing Canada Whole: A Memoir* (Toronto: Fitzhenry and Whiteside, 1994), 291.
74   ... *'Foreign Service Wives Manual*': See John Hilliker and Donald Barry, *Canada's Department of External Affairs*, vol. 2, *Coming of Age, 1946–1968* (Montreal: McGill-Queen's University Press, 1995).
74   Lawrence Durrell, *Esprit de Corps: Sketches from Diplomatic Life* (London: Faber and Faber, 1957).
78   ... *Tube Alloys Project in December 1943*: See Christopher M. Andrew and Oleg Gordievsky, *KGB: The Inside Story of Its Foreign Operations from Lenin to Gorbachev* (London: Hodder & Stoughton, 1990).
81   ... *decode these telegrams*': For more information on Pearson in the War Office, see N.K. O'Neill, 'History of CBNRC,' 3 vols., typescript (1987).

Chapter 7: New York and Frisco, Bonn and Paris

84   ... *to him for assistance:* Lester B. Pearson, *Mike: The Memoirs of the Rt. Hon. Lester B. Pearson*, vol. 1 (Toronto: University of Toronto Press, 1972).

89   Charles Ritchie, *Diplomatic Passport: More Undiplomatic Diairies, 1946–1962* (Toronto: Macmillan of Canada, 1981).

91   ... *the Russians had penetrated*: Oleg Kalugin with Fen Montaigne, *The First Directorate: My 32 Years in Intelligence and Espionage against the West* (New York: St Martin's Press, 1994).

Chapter 8: A Rotten, Stinking, Depressing Job

92   ... *reporting directly to Norman Robertson*: See J.L. Granatstein, *A Man of Influence: Norman A. Robertson and Canadian Statecraft, 1929–1968* (Ottawa: Deneau Publishers, 1981).

97   ... *one particular espionage case*: For different accounts see John Sawatsky, *Men in the Shadows: The RCMP Security Service* (Toronto: Doubleday Canada, 1980), 140–2, and John Barron, *KGB* (New York: Reader's Digest Press, 1974), 12.

104   John Starnes, Review of Tom Bower, *The Perfect English Spy: Sir Dick White and the Secret War, 1935–1990* (London: Heinemann, 1995), in *bout de papier* 12, no. 4 (1995).

105   ... *intelligence from photo-reconnaissance flights*: Fascinating accounts of these efforts by the United States are provided by Dino A. Brugioni in 'Science in Pictures: The Art and Science of Imagery Interpretation,' *Scientific American* (March 1996), and Stuart F. Brown in 'America's First Eyes in Space,' *Popular Science* (Feb. 1996).

Chapter 9: Intense Midday Heat

112   Lawrence Durrell, *Alexandria Quartet* (London: Faber and Faber, 1957–60); Olivia Manning, *The Levant Trilogy* (Harmondsworth: Penguin, 1983); Naguib Mahfouz, *Cairo Trilogy* (New York: Doubleday, 1992); Artemis Cooper, *Cairo in the War, 1939–1945* (London: Hamish Hamilton, 1989).

Chapter 10: Winds of Change

127   ... *initiatives launched by Trudeau and Ivan Head*: Geoffrey Murray, Review of Ivan L. Head and Pierre Elliott Trudeau, *The Canadian Way: Shaping Canada's Foreign Policy, 1968–1984* (Toronto: McClelland and Stewart, c. 1995), in *bout de papier* 13, no. 2 (1996).

Chapter 11: Compromise Candidate

135   ... *work of the Mackenzie Commission:* The commission was appointed by an order-in-council on 16 November 1966; the report was released 23 September 1968.

138   Professor Nikitin: See Christopher M. Andrew and Oleg Gordievsky, *KGB: The Inside Story of Its Foreign Operations from Lenin to Gorbachev* (London: Hodder & Stoughton, 1990), 238–9.

141   Peter Wright, *Spy Catcher: The Candid Autobiography of a Senior Intelligence Officer* (New York: Viking, 1987), 307.

142   John Starnes, Review of Tom Mangold, *Cold Warrior: James Jesus Angleton, the CIA's Master Spy Hunter* (New York: Simon & Schuster, 1991), in *bout de papier* 9, no. 4 (1992).

142   Harry Allen Overstreet and Bonaro Overstreet, *The FBI in Our Open Society* (New York: W.W. Norton and Co., 1969).

Chapter 12: Tough Cases

154   ... Dinner in Moscow ... with Andropov: Christopher M. Andrew and Oleg Gordievsky, *KGB: The Inside Story of Its Foreign Operations from Lenin to Gorbachev* (London: Hodder & Stoughton, 1990), 368–9.

155   ... I have expressed some views on the matter: *Ottawa Citizen*, 2 July 1992, Op-Ed Page, and *Globe and Mail*, 18 Sept. 1995, Commentary.

Chapter 13: October 1970

160   ... circulated by word of mouth: See Reg Whitaker, 'Apprehended Insurrection? RCMP Intelligence and the October Crisis,' *Queen's Quarterly* 100, no. 2 (summer 1993).

160   ... persons who should be arrested: John Starnes, 'The Careful Commissioner,' *Ottawa Citizen*, 29 Jan. 1992, Op-Ed Page.

Chapter 14: McDonald, Keable, CSIS

165   Inquiries Act: 'Royal Commissions,' in *The Canadian Encyclopedia Plus*, CD-ROM (Toronto: McClelland and Stewart, 1995).

166   ... 'a foreign intelligence service': McDonald Commission, *Freedom and Security under the Law*, Second Report (Ottawa: The Commission, 1981), chap. 7c, 'Should Canada Have a Foreign Intelligence Service?'

169   .. extensively reported in the ... press: For example, Paul Jackson's article in the *Ottawa Journal*, 4 Feb. 1982.

171   ... from an article in the Globe and Mail: Graham Fraser, 'Abuses Had Trudeau's Consent,' *Globe and Mail*, 14 May 1997.

173   .. of the Starnes–McIlraith conflict': McDonald Commission, Third

Report (Ottawa: The Commission, August 1981), 37–54 (re Starnes), and quotes from two commissioners (73–8) and from McDonald (78–80).

174   ... *commission documents classified top secret*: Commission of Inquiry, OB sec. A 21, 22, 23, pp. 17042–4.

Chapter 15: Spy Novelist

177   ... *national security aspects of immigration policy*: John Starnes and Manuel Chetcuti, 'National Security Aspects of Canadian Immigration Policy,' Sept. 1975, released in 1997 under the Access to Information Act.
177   J.L. Granatstein, *A Man of Influence: Norman A. Robertson and Canadian Statecraft, 1929–1968* (Ottawa: Deneau Publishers, 1981).
179   ... 'Why I Write Spy Fiction': In Wesley K. Wark, ed., *Spy Fiction, Spy Films and Real Intelligence* (London: Frank Cass, 1991), 204.
185   John Bryden, *Best-Kept Secret: Canadian Secret Intelligence in the Second World War* (Toronto: Lester Publishing, 1993).

Appendix A

189   *ISTD:* F.H. Hinsley with E.E. Thomas, C.F.G. Ransom, and R.C. Knight, *British Intelligence in the Second World War* (Cambridge: Cambridge University Press, 1979), vol. 1: 161, 292.
190   '*Camp X*': David Stafford, *Camp X* (Toronto: Lester & Orpen Dennys, 1986).

Index